ART OF PENOBSCOT BAY

CARL LITTLE AND DAVID LITTLE

ART OF PENOBSCOT BAY
CARL LITTLE AND DAVID LITTLE

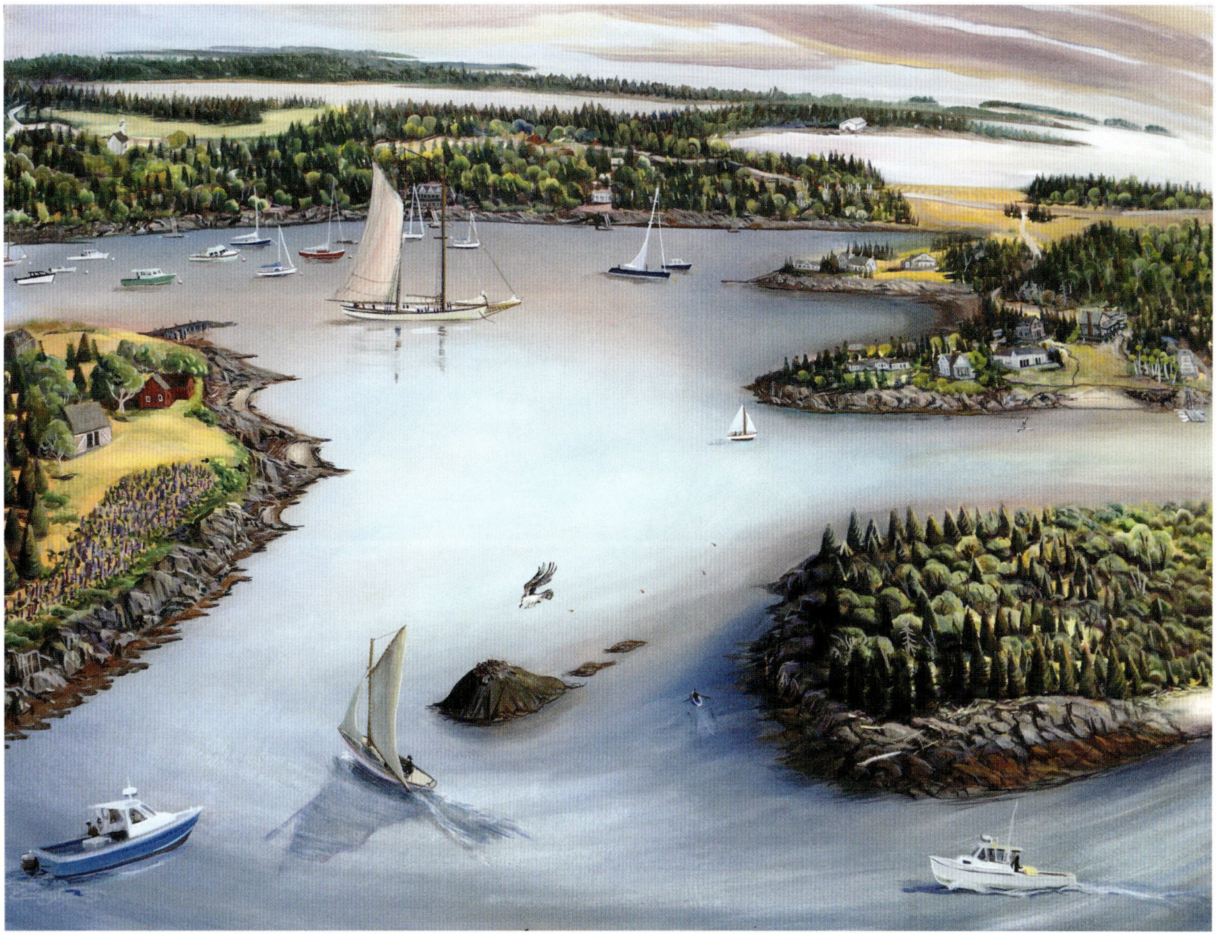

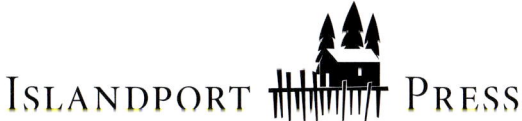

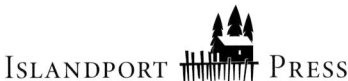

Islandport Press
P.O. Box 10
247 Portland Street
Yarmouth, Maine 04096
www.islandportpress.com
info@islandportpress.com

First Islandport Edition, December 2023

Copyright © 2023 by Carl Little and David Little.

All rights reserved. No part of this book may be reproduced in any manner without the express written consent of Islandport Press, except in the case of brief excerpts in critical reviews and articles.

Print ISBN: 978-1-952143-50-2
Library of Congress Control Number: 2022933580

Dean L. Lunt | Editor-in-Chief, Publisher
Shannon M. Butler | Vice President
Emily A. Lunt | Book Design
Dylan R. Andrews | Book Design
Emily Boyer | Cover Design
Printed in the USA.

To Mikki.

—David Little

To Peggy and my children, Emily and James, and their children, Maria, Serita, James, and Anika.

—Carl Little

To our siblings and their children and grandkids, and to our many friends.
We are blessed by their company and grateful for their love and support.

—David and Carl Little

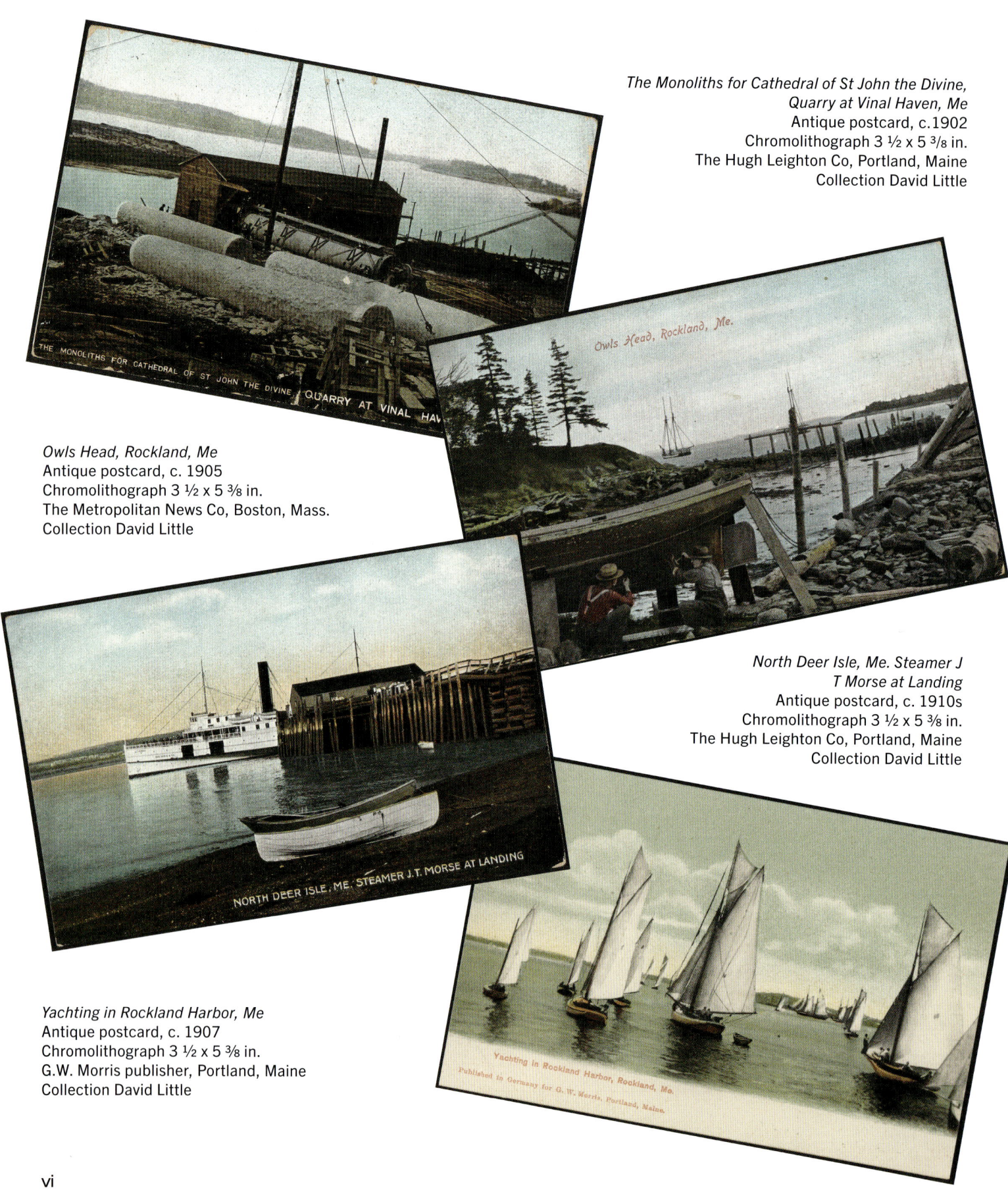

The Monoliths for Cathedral of St John the Divine, Quarry at Vinal Haven, Me
Antique postcard, c.1902
Chromolithograph 3 ½ x 5 ⅜ in.
The Hugh Leighton Co, Portland, Maine
Collection David Little

Owls Head, Rockland, Me
Antique postcard, c. 1905
Chromolithograph 3 ½ x 5 ⅜ in.
The Metropolitan News Co, Boston, Mass.
Collection David Little

North Deer Isle, Me. Steamer J T Morse at Landing
Antique postcard, c. 1910s
Chromolithograph 3 ½ x 5 ⅜ in.
The Hugh Leighton Co, Portland, Maine
Collection David Little

Yachting in Rockland Harbor, Me
Antique postcard, c. 1907
Chromolithograph 3 ½ x 5 ⅜ in.
G.W. Morris publisher, Portland, Maine
Collection David Little

Preface

Now I see why I live here.

Now I see why I live here. Penobscot Bay still looks today, much as it does in Alvan Fisher's *Camden Hills and Harbor* (ca. 1852), in George Bellows's *Freeman Young's Place* (1916), and in Willard Metcalf's *Ebbing Tide—Version 2* (1907). I can't quite tell if the red boatsheds of Rockport Marine are the same red buildings (perhaps boatsheds then, too) in Max Kuehne's *Rockport Harbor, Maine* (1919), but the view from offshore looks the same today. Leon Kroll's *Lowering Day, Camden* (1916) lacks only the Camden Deli perched atop the white waterfalls tumbling then as now into the harbor.

I love the warp and weft of this place, its look and texture. I love venturing upon its waters in large sailboats and small kayaks, scrambling over its islands, visiting human-scaled villages. The paintings in this book all say "home" to me.

Penobscot Bay is to Maine what Maine is to the rest of the United States—a singularity tucked inside a geographical anomaly, the deepest indentation in a famously jagged coastline. Around 3,500 squiggly miles of shoreline lie within the overall 230-mile length of Maine's Atlantic coast; one thousand miles of that are contained by the thirty-five-by-twenty miles of Penobscot Bay. This is a world of granite and tree-girt islands—several hundred or several thousand, depending on who's counting—bordered by two long flanks of the mainland coast. "This bay is the goal of many cruising men and . . . the best cruising ground on the coast," proclaimed the authoritative *A Cruising Guide to the New England Coast* in 1937. That opinion has held true through decades of later editions.

Penobscot Bay, preeminent among all its neighbors, has a distinct identity. When people think of Maine, particularly regarding paintings they have seen, they are probably seeing in their imagination Penobscot Bay. It is here that many of Maine's artists have come to paint. There's a primeval quality on view here: those huge granite rocks everybody paints, the detritus of glacial moraine, the dense unscarred pelt of fir trees—all appears unchanged for eons. Only the windmills rising above Vinalhaven Island in Anneli Skaar's *Three Turbines* (2018) would not be recognized by earlier voyagers and visitors who found sustenance in the waters of Penobscot Bay.

"This place has gotten me by the nape of the neck," John Marin wrote to his New York City dealer Alfred Stieglitz on September 11, 1926. "Once I get here, I forget other places, which is a failing I have that I am perfectly aware of."

I know how he felt. Every time I come home to Maine, fleeing the tumult of contemporary America or Europe, the Piscataqua River Bridge that carries me from New Hampshire into Maine acts as a portal that transports me into another world. Since the 1980s, Maine has done away with roadside billboards—people come here looking for the state's natural wonders, not the litter of advertising. But there is a sign, just as you come off the bridge, that displays a simple proud maxim: "Maine: The Way Life Should Be." For many, for the artists who have come here, it could read: "The Way Life Should Look."

Every August, vacation-bound traffic may crawl through the tolls on Interstate 95 and along Route 1 through downtown Camden, but on a bike in North Haven, Islesboro, Cape Rosier, or Deer Isle, or from the deck of a boat anywhere on Penobscot Bay, the views painted by Fitz Henry Lane, John Marin, Fairfield Porter, N.C, Andrew, and Jamie Wyeth, and such contemporary artists as John Neville, Siri Beckman, still hold true. There is a quality of light, shadow, and primal tug of tide and time that binds all these painters and their work through the ages, so much so that within this volume all these paintings—whatever their style, date, or view— coexist happily. William Zorach's *Boat in the Early Morning, Stonington (1926)*, full of the fractal shapes of sails, boatsheds, shards of light from a troubled sky, might have been painted by the French Cubist Georges Braque, yet it complements Susan Webster's modern *Deer Isle*. The two paintings are different facets of the same gemstone. Probably because the artists, the rusticators, the vacationers who have come here, do the same things.

"In the daytime," recalled Webster, "we harvested mussels, walked trails, explored beaches, and napped on the deck and porch. At night we cooked, ate by candlelight, played board games, read by the gaslight lamps, and slept with windows open to the lulling sound of the ocean's constant movement. Time stood still."

Man's only apparent embellishment upon nature here—save for the wind turbines—is largely restricted to the spare Shaker-plain rectangles and triangles of the sheds and houses that artists have loved and painted as much as the interplay of sea and rock and tree: sometimes an austere clapboard building fills most of a canvas, with a glimpse of the water, a dock, a lobster boat, in the background—Greg Dunham's *Eaton's Boatyard;* or the foreground of rooftops in Loretta Krupinski's *Matinicus Rock Light*. Sometimes, as in Judy Taylor's *Bucksport from the Penobscot Narrows Bridge*, the buildings are dotted like sugar cubes on a distant shore. But absent this scattered decoration, the timeless quality of the scenes on view here, so prized by Maine's artists and vacation visitors, has existed for millennia.

Buildings aside, Penobscot Bay would have appeared much the same in the early seventeenth century, when great numbers of European vessels engaged in the fishery and the fur trades, wrote a French chronicler, André Thevet. By the late eighteenth century, the native population had been decimated by disease brought by the Europeans, and much of the mainland coast bordering Penobscot Bay was cleared for farming, and by the felling of the tall pines, whole forests of them, marked where they stood before the Revolution as the English king's property to make masts for his naval fleets.

But this chopping, clearing, "improvement" of the landscape, which certainly would have been evident all around the bay, was short-lived. By the late nineteenth century, most of the farms were abandoned, their people gone to work in the mills, the quarries, the shipbuilding and seafaring trades, and forests grew over the land again, with the stone walls that had once bordered cleared fields now running through the woods, and it appeared once more as it had when Europeans first saw it.

But absent this scattered decoration, the timeless quality of the scenes on view here, so prized by Maine's artists and vacation visitors, has existed for millennia.

In 1974, Jon Wilson, a college dropout, founded *Wooden Boat* magazine to celebrate the beauty and construction of wooden boats at a time when fiberglass was threatening to reduce such craft to obsolete antiques. He started with a telephone nailed to a tree in North Brooksville. He soon moved to offices in Brooklin on the western shore of Penobscot Bay.

The magazine took off, far beyond Wilson's expectation, and the subsequent resurgence in wooden boatbuilding was an electric jolt felt all over Maine waters. Old and slumbering boatyards woke up like Rip Van Winkle. Early American sailing craft, restored and new, are now seen all around the bay, giving it the appearance of an earlier maritime age come to life. But this is not a recreation, like the Mystic Seaport Museum, or history preserved in aspic. Nineteenth-century windjammer coasting schooners, sailing out of Camden, Rockport, and Rockland, cruise the bay with passengers, for a few hours or a week, mainstays of the vibrant tourist industry.

Joel White's Brooklin Boatyard, next door to *Wooden Boat* Magazine, was in the vanguard of this new age of wooden boats. Joel designed and built efficient yachts pioneering modern techniques that combined thin veneers of wood molded into boaty shapes with epoxy glue; some looked old and classical, some were long hydrodynamically engineered racing machines, but all were beautiful. Joel was so revered in boat circles around Penobscot Bay that his father, writer E.B. White, was locally better known as "Joel's dad."

Wooden boats with tall sails, restored classics, windjammer schooners, and modern racing yachts are seen all over Penobscot Bay. The view of them from the shore is no different than in Jonas Lie's paintings of the 1920s, *Yachting on the Maine Coast* and *Romantic Sunset, Maine.* Lobster boats, despite measures taken to protect the remaining right whales from fishing gear, are as ubiquitous as ever, their design unchanged from the first motorized lobster boats of a hundred years ago.

Boatyards and harbors appear now as they do in George S. Wasson's *Wharves at Castine (1908)*; or in the background of Edward Hopper's *Schooner's Hull (1926)*, which shows in the foreground a decaying fishing schooner—that boat would be repaired and sailing in today's Maine. Those same buildings are now all renovated and efficiently functioning, with double-glazed windows. Some are still boatyards, others just as likely shops, restaurants, art galleries, yacht brokers, or the offices of high-tech entrepreneurial ventures communicating with the world by invisible WiFi.

The artists in this book, who largely came "from away," as Mainers would put it, found compelling subjects in the working, sometimes sagging, waterfronts, small villages, and harbors, in the old boats, in the virgin rocky, tree-lined shores. They captured what might easily have been a disappearing world. But all that is still here to see, apparently little changed.

The scenes are no longer dilapidated, but today's Penobscot Bay is remarkable for its unspoiled appearance. There are no vast malls anywhere near the coast, nor the ghastly cruise-ship-stacked condo developments of Florida or the Mediterranean Rivieras, the fate of so many alluring, once-beautiful seaside destinations. Somehow, through a combination of the wealth that has always sought out the iconic beauty and old-world charm of the Maine coast, and the resurgent suitability of this place to the concerns of the modern world, what you see in the paintings in this book is what you will still find here. Not in narrow bracketed views, blocking out unsightly modern constructions, but everywhere you look in Penobscot Bay.

—Peter Nichols
October 2023

Peter Nichols is the author of the bestselling books *The Rocks, A Voyage for Madmen,* and *Evolution's Captain,* and four other books of fiction, memoir, and nonfiction. He has also worked in advertising, as a screenwriter, and sailed alone in a small boat across the Atlantic. He lives on Penobscot Bay.

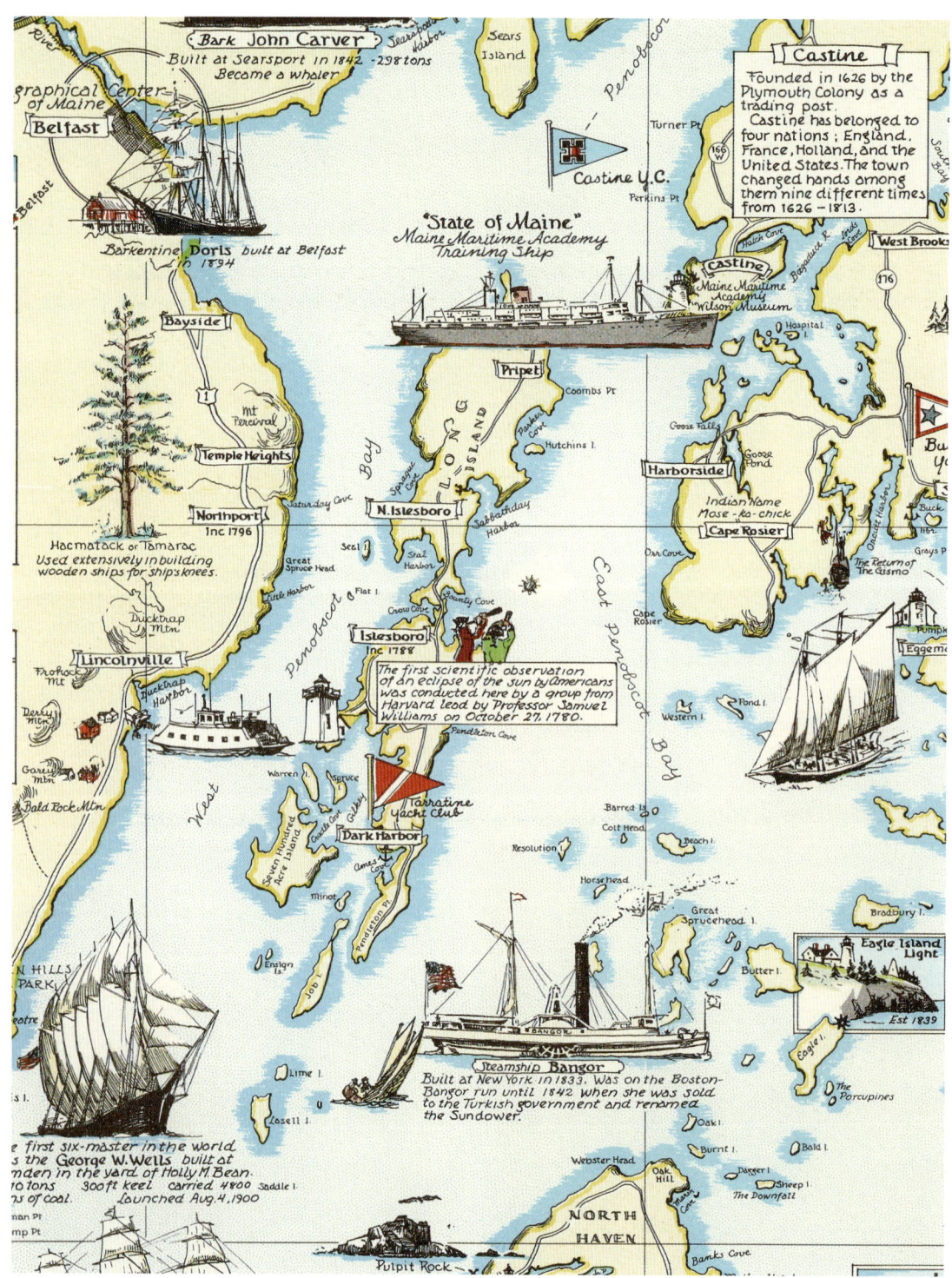

Ruth Rhoads Lepper
A Map of the Maine Coast from Rockland, thru Schoodic, to Corea (detail), 1970
Color lithograph, 20 x 48 in.
Osher Map Library and Smith Center for Cartographic Education
Photo by David Neikerk

Prologue

Casting off.

As we embarked on writing *Art of Penobscot Bay*, one of our first steps was to determine what, exactly, *is* Penobscot Bay. While its length and breadth are fittingly somewhat fluid, for the sake of accuracy we needed to get a grip on its dimensions.

We're not the first to seek clarification. "Where does Penobscot Bay begin?" asks writer Gorham Munson in his book *Penobscot, Downeast Paradise* (1959). He starts with Matinicus Island at latitude 44°0'51"N and longitude 68°0'53"W and then draws an imaginary line just below the 44th parallel to designate where the Gulf of Maine becomes Penobscot Bay.

The authors of *Penobscot: The Forest, River and Bay* recognize the difficulty of defining the exact boundaries. "This is a more straightforward exercise at the head and flanks of the bay than on its seaward margin," they explain, "where the bay merges imperceptibly with the waters of the Gulf of Maine."

Leave it to Philip Conkling and company at the Island Institute to embrace the expanse in its entirety. "Penobscot Bay is Maine's largest bay," they write in the landmark *Islands in Time*, "measuring twenty miles across from Whitehead to Isle au Haut, and trending thirty miles north to the mouth of the equally grand river of the same name." The bay, they note, encompasses almost one thousand miles of shoreline, and encircles 624 islands and ledges. And they brag: "Penobscot Bay is . . . the second largest embayment on the Atlantic coast of the United States, after Chesapeake Bay."

"Embayment" is a perfect word to describe this body of water, "an indentation of a shoreline larger than a cove but smaller than a gulf," as one dictionary defines it.

A multitude of indentations create Penobscot Bay as illustrated by the two maps included here. **Bob Rose's** map from *A Cruising Guide to the Maine Coast* provides a simplified overview of the major towns, cities, and islands—an easy-to-orient-yourself rendering of the bay. By contrast, **Molly Brown's** depiction—a monoprint with watercolor added—has an as-seen-from-space feeling, the land and water scattered like pieces of a jigsaw puzzle.

For something more pictorial, consider a detail from **Ruth Rhoads Lepper's** 1970 "Map of the Maine Coast from Rockland thru Schoodic, to Corea." The mapmaker offers vignettes related to the region, many of them linked to seafaring history. There's the Maine Maritime Academy's training ship *State of Maine* and the steamship *Bangor*, but also the marker on Islesboro for the site of the "first scientific observation of an eclipse of the sun by Americans" in 1780.

The long-lived Lepper (1905–2011) developed her love of mapmaking as a draftsman for the U.S. Navy during World War I. She later spent time aboard the Maine Seacoast Mission's *Sunbeam*, "God's tugboat," as it brought services to residents of far-flung islands. "Maps are precise, time-consuming projects," she wrote, "but if your work gives you pleasure, what the heck."

What makes Penobscot Bay so attractive to so many artists? With its unpredictable weather, the bay has awesome visual drama, days of clearest light and densest fog, sudden squalls, and pristine sunsets. Because of its many islands and the backdrop of distant hills, the bay also has a multitude of natural vantage points from where artists can set up to work.

For our own map, when it came to envisioning this book, we set out to follow artists, from history and those painting now, in their visual explorations of the myriad inlets, islands, coves, and peninsulas—the "nooks and corners" along Penobscot Bay that Samuel Adams Drake wrote about in 1875. Penobscot Bay

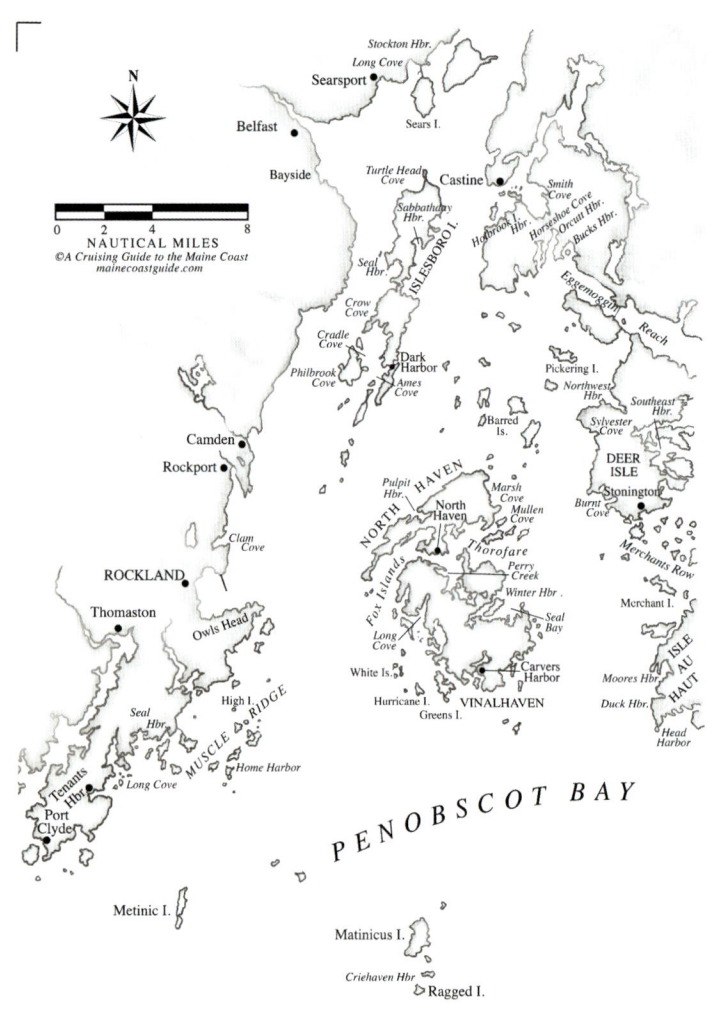

Map of Penobscot Bay (modified)
© *A Cruising Guide to the Maine Coast*
www.mainecoastguide.com
Courtesy of Curtis Rindlaub

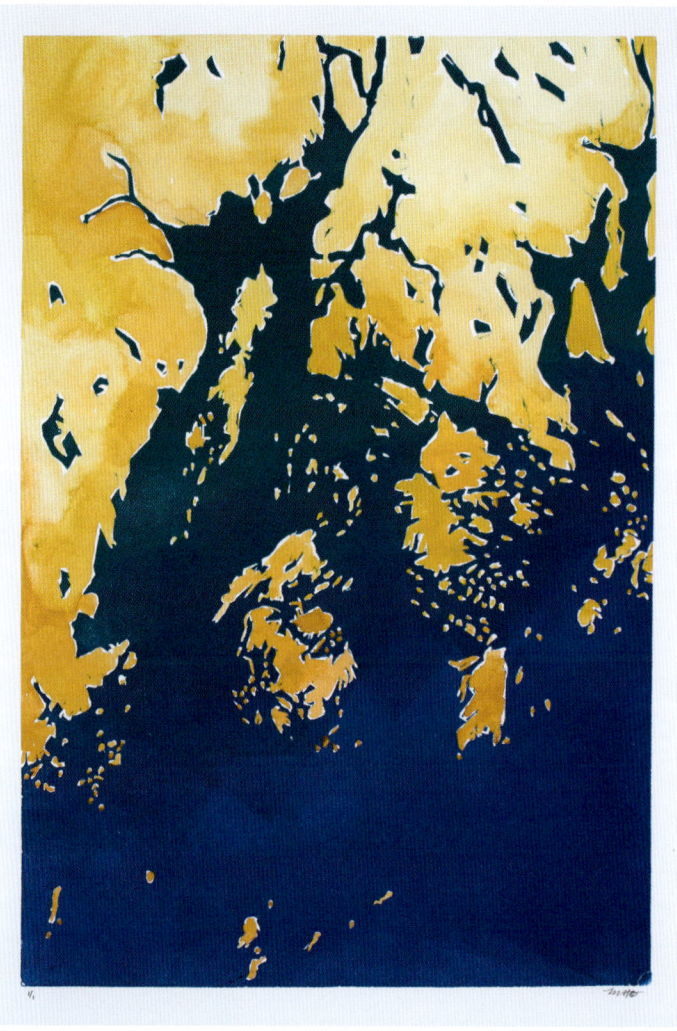

Molly Holmberg Brown
Penobscot Bay, 2019
Monoprint with watercolor 18 x 12 in.
Collection of the artist

in its vastness, far north and east of the Hudson River Valley, became part of the early unexplored American wilderness, the coastal waters and shore part of the new nation's identity. The paintings in this book are part of this legacy.

Inspired by Penobscot Bay's physical beauty, maritime history, and role in American art, together we dive into nature through the periods of diverse visual interpretation and style, from romantic realism through impressionism to abstraction, searching for a narrative and context that fires the imagination.

While the historical section of the book is laid out chronologically, the contemporary sections will instead take the reader on a geographical tour.

To the landscape painter, Penobscot Bay and its surroundings offer an endless number of superb motifs. In gathering images, we quickly found the most popular subject was the view of a distant island. Anyone who has looked out over the water at a far-off isle knows the appeal and poetry of such a scene. The attraction may be related to built-in memories of an ancient need to explore and escape—and to the joy of sighting land and eventual arrival. It is no accident that the same views return in different paintings through the decades. The lives of human beings are short compared to the glacial renderings and rock formations found in nature.

And just as the artists of yesteryear, you may find yourself today, driving along Route 1 and come to one of those stretches where the view opens up to reveal a sparkling expanse. You could find yourself on the ferry to North Haven, marveling at the archipelago that surrounds you. You might be spending the night on a mooring enjoying the dark skies. Standing on the Stonington waterfront you might gaze in amazement at the armada of lobster boats floating in the harbor. And after climbing Mount Megunticook in the Camden Hills at dawn, you might experience what poet Edna St. Vincent Millay felt as a young girl:

And nobody awake
In all the world but you!—
Who lie on a high cliff until your elbows ache,
To see the sun come up over Penobscot Bay.

We sought to represent as many places as possible, but found that while some locales like Rockland, Stonington, Camden, and Vinalhaven are rich in images, others have seemingly yet to find their painter champion. Who will be the first to paint Nettle Island in the Muscle Ridge archipelago, Saturday Cove in Northport, or Sabbathday Harbor in Islesboro?

The prize, if you will, for a single place's inspiration might go to Great Spruce Head Island at the center of the bay. From the photographs of Eliot Porter and the paintings of his brother Fairfield to the bounty of art created there over the past several decades by a host of visiting artists, the island keeps rousing the creative spirit.

To this day, word of mouth and the lure of landscape continue to draw artists with a range of experience and reputation from just about everywhere.

"Who says," **Eliot Porter** asked in his book *Summer Island*, "that to dream away an afternoon with a foam-streaked bay spread out before your half-shut eyes and a wind stroking your face is not as purifying as gathering a small basket of bullet-hard berries for cranberry jelly?"

We reveled in the place names, some Native American in origin and some based on an industry or an individual or a configuration of land or incident of natural history. Hurricane Island, Cape Rosier, Eggemoggin Reach—each place has its history and its art.

Art of Penobscot Bay highlights various shoreline activities while showcasing pure offshore landscapes. The bay's waterfronts are busy with all manner of marine activities, from boats

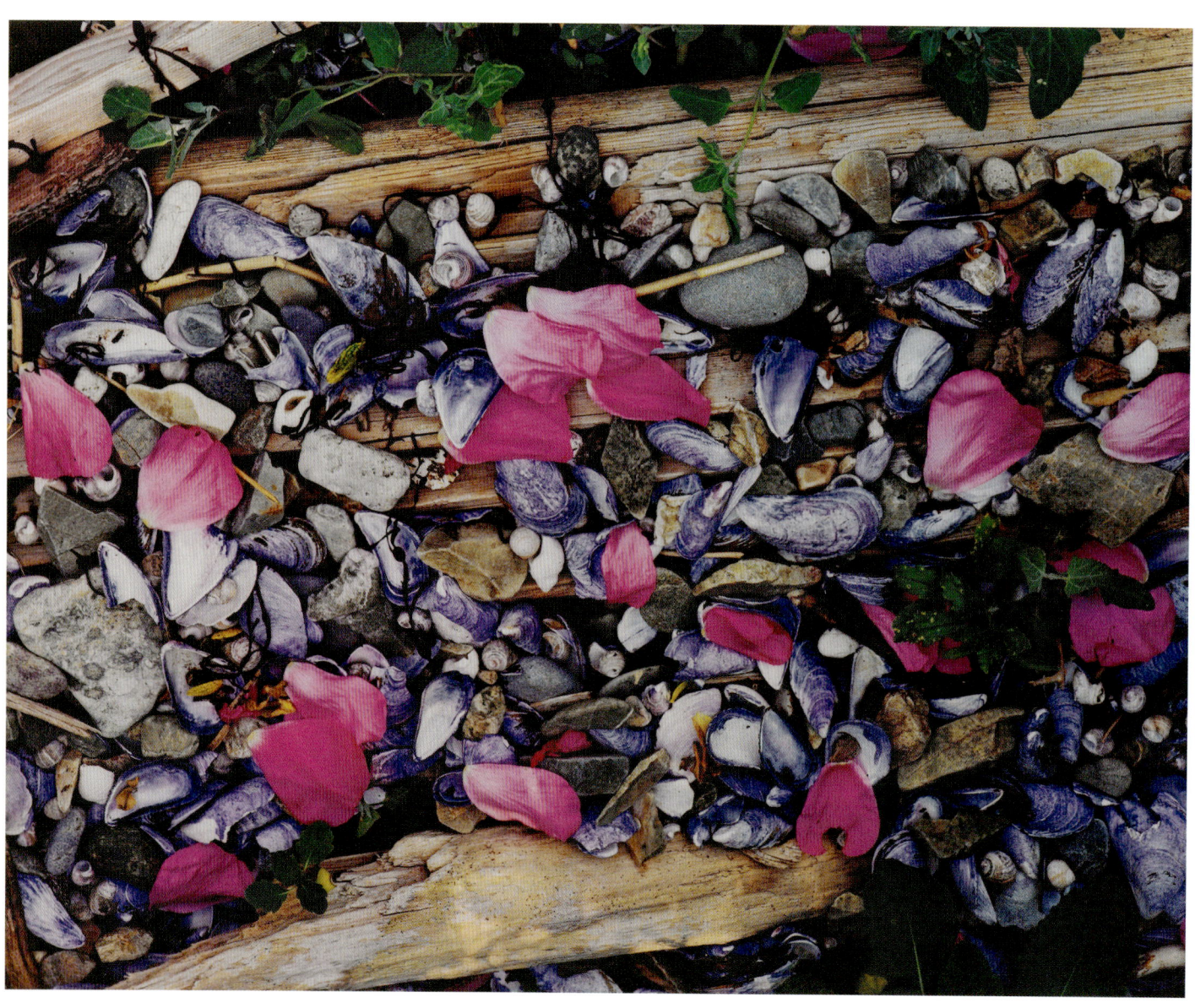

Eliot Porter
Rose Petals on Beach, Great Spruce Head Island, Maine, July 1, 1971
Dye imbibition print, 8 1/8 x 10 3/16 in.
Bequest of the artist
©1990 Amon Carter Museum of American Art

being repaired to cargo ships being unloaded. As a group of vintage postcards shows, the bay has been a place of industry and pleasure [see page vi].

Once we understood the bay's reach, we made some difficult decisions. For example, you won't find Monhegan Island here—most maps locate it just over the line in neighboring Muscongus Bay. Truth be told, we were relieved by this geographical fact. A much larger book would have been required to incorporate the plenteous art that single island has prompted.

At the same time, we made some exceptions, so to speak. Thus, you will find paintings of Eggemoggin Reach in the mix. While not strictly part of Penobscot Bay, that exquisite length of water, the sailor's paradise, is directly connected to it at either end. Likewise, Bucksport might be considered slightly beyond our purview, but we couldn't resist **Judy Taylor's** view of the town as seen from atop the Penobscot Narrows Bridge.

Thanks to the Island Institute, the first advocacy group for the state's vast archipelago, we have a much greater knowledge and appreciation of the bay and its ecology. For all its grandeur and sparkle, the bay faces many challenges. Climate change is warming its waters, threatening its fisheries. As David Platt writes in *Penobscot: The Forest, River, and Bay*, "The success or failure of a fishery can affect the economic health of the entire region, changing even the lives of people who live far from salt water and don't think of themselves as 'coastal' residents."

In his history of Penobscot Bay islands published in 1997, Charles McLane noted geologists estimated that the Gulf of

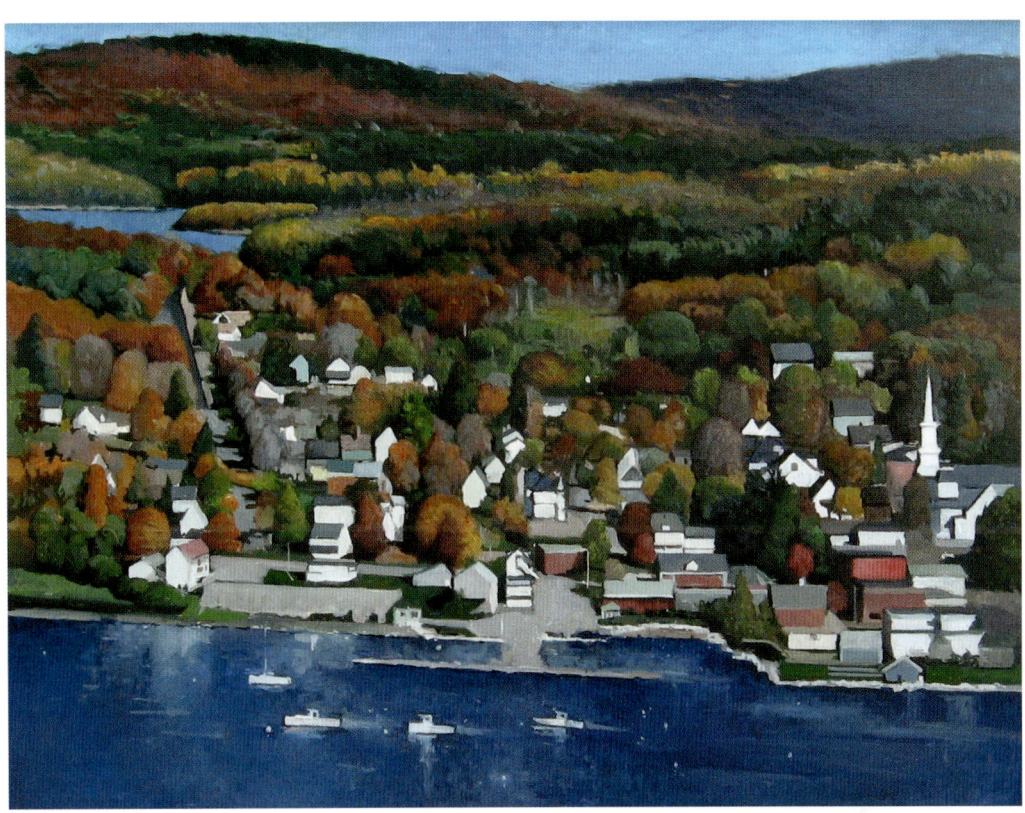

Judy Taylor
Bucksport from the Penobscot Narrows Bridge, 2012
Oil on linen, 36 x 48 in.
Private collection

Maine rose twenty feet in the last five thousand years, which meant, he wrote, "that most of today's coastal islands were once part of the main or of the larger offshore islands." The bay is sure to shift even more as temperatures rise.

At the same time, changing technologies are transforming the bay's maritime activities as are local, regional, and global demands for products. Where coal used to be a common import, now wind turbine components are part of the cargo. **Anneli Skaar's** painting of the turbines on Vinalhaven highlight that conversion.

When we consider the images of Penobscot Bay made over the last seventy or so years, no real "schools" take shape to

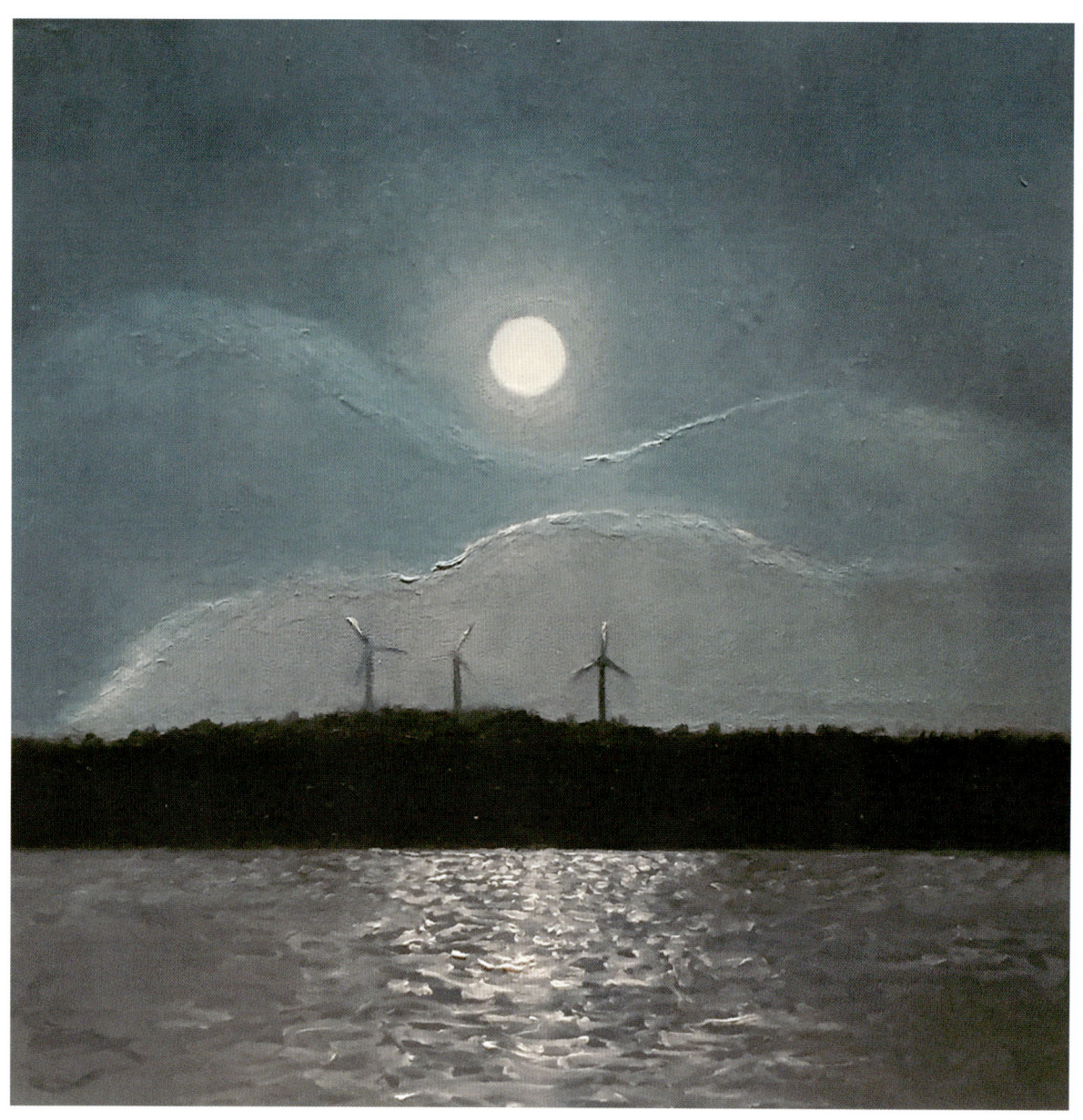

Anneli Skaar
Three Turbines, 2018
Oil on wood panel, 8 x 8 in.

categorize the work. One of the earliest pieces in this section, Alex Katz's *Clamdiggers at Ducktrap* (1956), might appear to have some relation to his famous Pop Art paintings, but it's more about his individual response to a landscape he had just begun exploring, having first come to Maine via the Skowhegan School of Painting and Sculpture in 1949.

Katz was part of an impressive cohort of painters that included Lois Dodd and Yvonne Jacquette who traveled to the mid-coast in the 1950s to escape summer in the city. They found fairly inexpensive real estate and subject matter that inspired them to expand their landscape painting repertoire.

To this day, word of mouth and the lure of landscape continue to draw artists with a range of experience and reputation from just about everywhere. At the same time, some painters have chosen to stay and thereby been exposed to, and inspired by, the beauty of Maine in winter.

We cast a wide net for the paintings, seeking a broad range of subject matter. To be sure, there are lighthouses, sailboats, and islands, but also rockweed, a floating house, and a parade. There are working waterfronts, but also people playing chess.

The paintings that follow represent a wide-ranging diversity of vision and aesthetics. They were chosen for their remarkable representation of place—and, more importantly, perhaps, because the chosen artists are devoted to their parts of Maine and are, in our opinion, among the most important painters on the scene today.

Because the art history of this era is still taking shape, we chose to present this section in a geographic rather than chronological manner, starting with Matinicus Island, following the bay's western coast to Castine—visiting islands along the way—and ending on its eastern fringe, at Stonington and Isle au Haut. We tried to find images of as many spots as possible, to provide a true sense of the breadth of landscape found on and around Penobscot Bay.

Today, Penobscot Bay in all its resilient glory continues to attract and inspire a multitude of artists. As we write these words, someone is setting up an easel overlooking Camden Harbor or has his or her eyes fixed on a stretch of coastline or that distant island. The waters flash, the fog obscures, snow lends light to a midwinter view. These painters share the glory with all of us.

We invite you to expand your visual horizons and enjoy these visions of Penobscot Bay—beauty, breadth, and beyond.

Enjoy the journey.

—Carl and David Little
December 2023

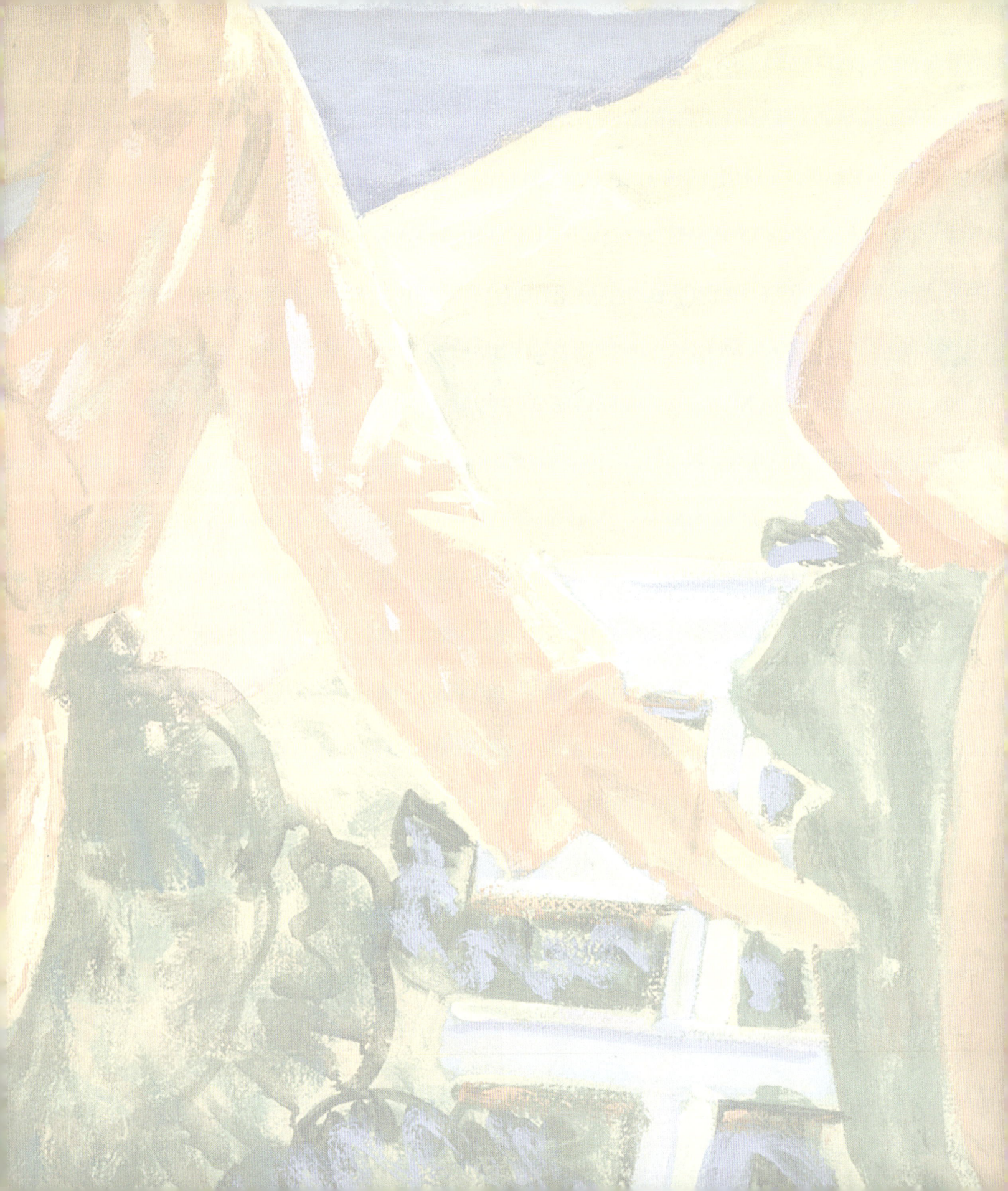

Yesterday

The 19th & 20th Centuries

Penobscot Bay is the outlet of a more than 8,600-square-mile watershed that has been stewarded by the Penobscot Nation for generations. The bay area served as an important gathering place where the Penobscot have come together with their Wabanaki relations and allies, the Abenaki, Maliseet, Mi'kmaq, and Passamaquoddy, for millennia.

In his history of the islands of Penobscot Bay, Charles McLane cites archaeologist Bruce Bourque's thesis that for five thousand years or more Wabanaki fished the coasts of Maine.

In their book *Asticou's Domain*, anthropologists Bunny McBride and Harold Prins relate how Penobscot families set up temporary homes on White Island and Black Island at the eastern end of Eggemoggin Reach. Their conical wigwams could be seen in Deer Isle fields in the 1920s. A genre scene of a woman with papoose

R. McFarlane
Landscape with Indian and Papoose, 1855
Oil on canvas, 19 ¼ x 26 in.
Photograph courtesy of Sotheby's, Inc. © 2022

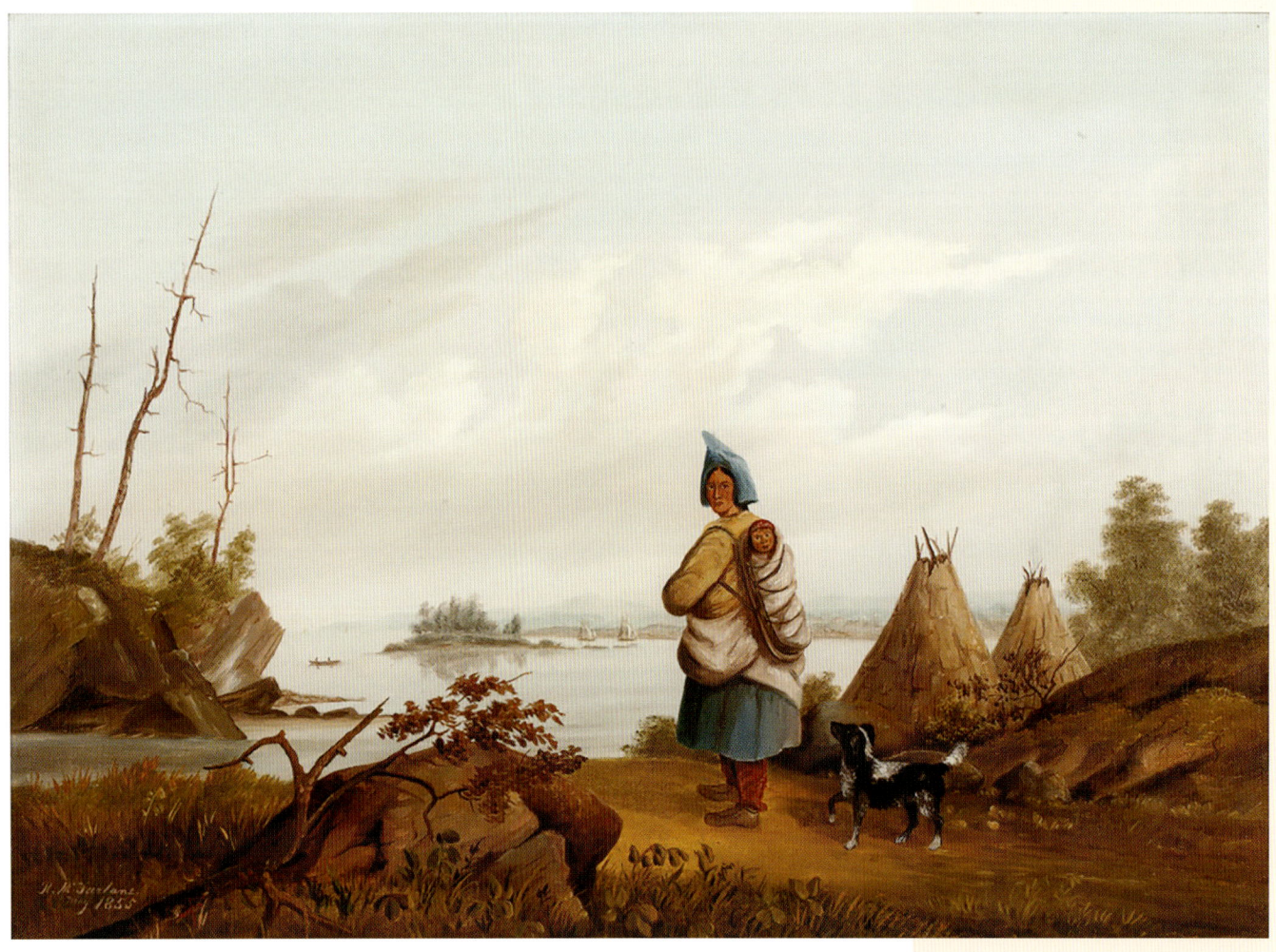

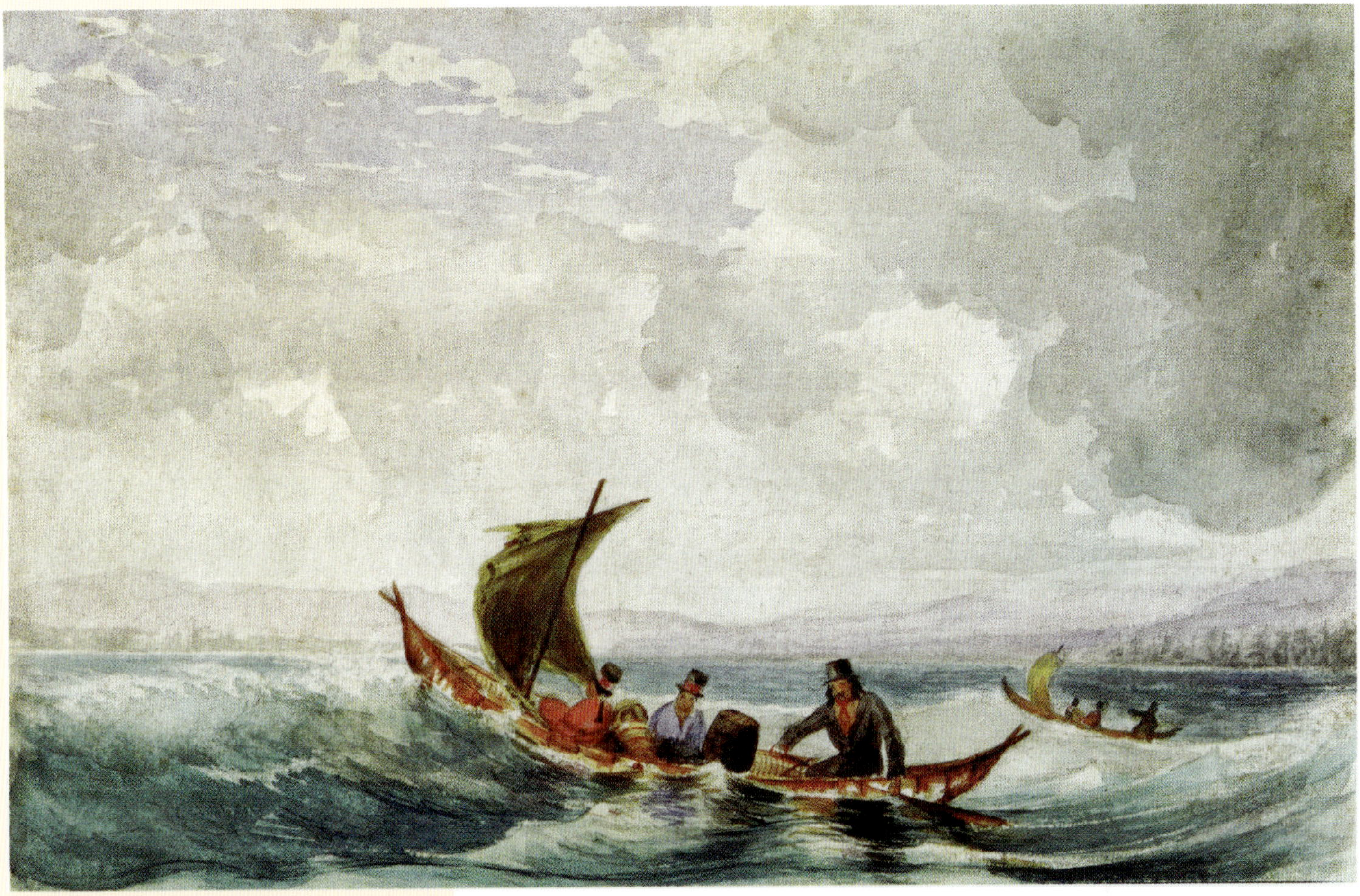

Yesterday

William Robert Herries
Passamaquoddy Sailing Canoe in New Brunswick, c. 1836-37
Courtesy of the National Archives, Canada, c–102861

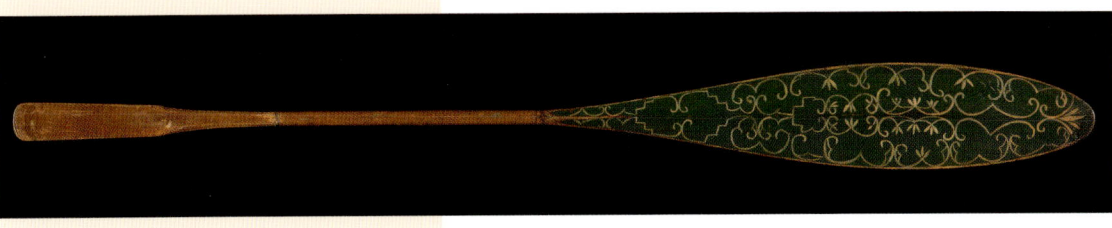

Eastern Abenaki Canoe Paddle, n.d.
Wood, pigment, paint, and brass,
71 x 7 x 2 in.
Gift of Heirs of David Kimball, 1899
Image © President and Fellows of Harvard College
Peabody Museum of Archeology and Ethnology 99–12–10/53655

by **R. McFarlane** from the mid–1800s evoke these visits, albeit with a mix of what McBride and Prins might call "knowledge and naïveté." The figures in the painting are thought to be Mi'kmaqs of Algonquin descent from the Canadian Maritimes.

According to McLane, "When the first Europeans reached the shores of Maine in the sixteenth and seventeenth centuries they were struck by the sophistication of Indian fishing gear," including the keyhole-shaped weirs used to trap herring. They may have also taken note of their expertise in navigation and their manufacture of sea-going craft like the Passamaquoddy sailing canoe in a painting by **William Robert Herries** (1818–1845).

Like the ornate eyes often painted on birch canoes, the decorative double-curve motif on an Eastern Abenaki paddle suggested a power symbol of protection to help manage challenging conditions at sea.

3

James Eric Francis Sr., director of cultural and historic preservation for the Penobscot Nation, carries on this artistic tradition in his paintings. In 2021, Francis was one of three Indigenous artists commissioned by the U.S. Fish and Wildlife Service Museum and Archives to create art for its permanent collection. His contribution, *Atlantic Salmon,* was inspired by the removal of dams from the Penobscot River watershed, the addition of fish passages, and the subsequent return of sea-run fish. "For me," Francis says, "letting nature be how nature is supposed to be is the ultimate place to go."

James Eric Francis, Sr.
Atlantic Salmon, 2021
Acrylic paint on canvas
Collection U.S. Fish and Wildlife Service Museum, West Virginia

The painting serves, in Francis's words, "to welcome home the salmon," with each dot representing one fish. The fishing spear, or *enikakw* in the Penobscot language, "is the cultural connection" between his tribe and the salmon. At the same time, his remarkable painting connects the bay to the rivers and tributaries upstream.

The legacy of the artistic traditions and skills of the Wabanakis living in the Maritime Peninsula, making utilitarian and decorative objects, and fine art paintings is very much alive today. The collections of the Abbe Museum in Bar Harbor help visitors understand the spiritual connection between art and nature and their respect for plants and animals as part of the natural order.

Yesterday

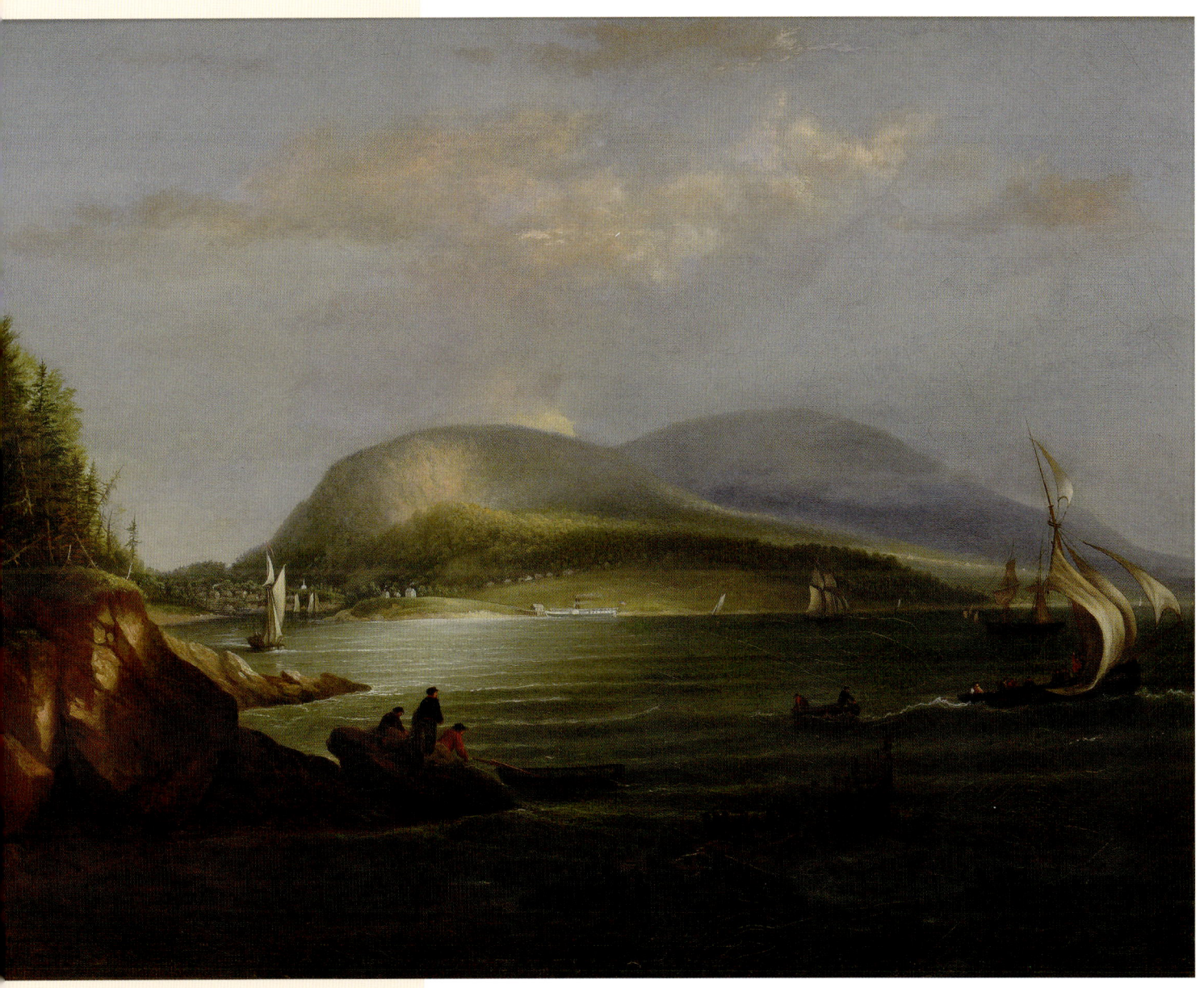

Alvan Fisher
Camden Hills and Harbor, c. 1852
Oil on canvas, 27 1/8 x 35 7/8 in.
Gift of Philip and Frances Hofer
The Farnsworth Art Museum

Many of the first artists to explore Penobscot Bay came by boat, their paintings often providing a seaboard perspective of the coast. A dramatically lit view of the Camden hills and harbor by Boston-based painter **Alvan Fisher** (1792–1863) captures their graceful contours.

"As one of the earliest art tourists," writes art historian Fred Adelson, "[Fisher] helped to introduce [Penobscot Bay's] shoreline, islands, and lighthouses as imagery." Other painters in the romantic tradition of the Hudson River School would soon venture down east to limn the Maine coast and thereby play a role in attracting the so-called "rusticators" to the glories of Penobscot Bay.

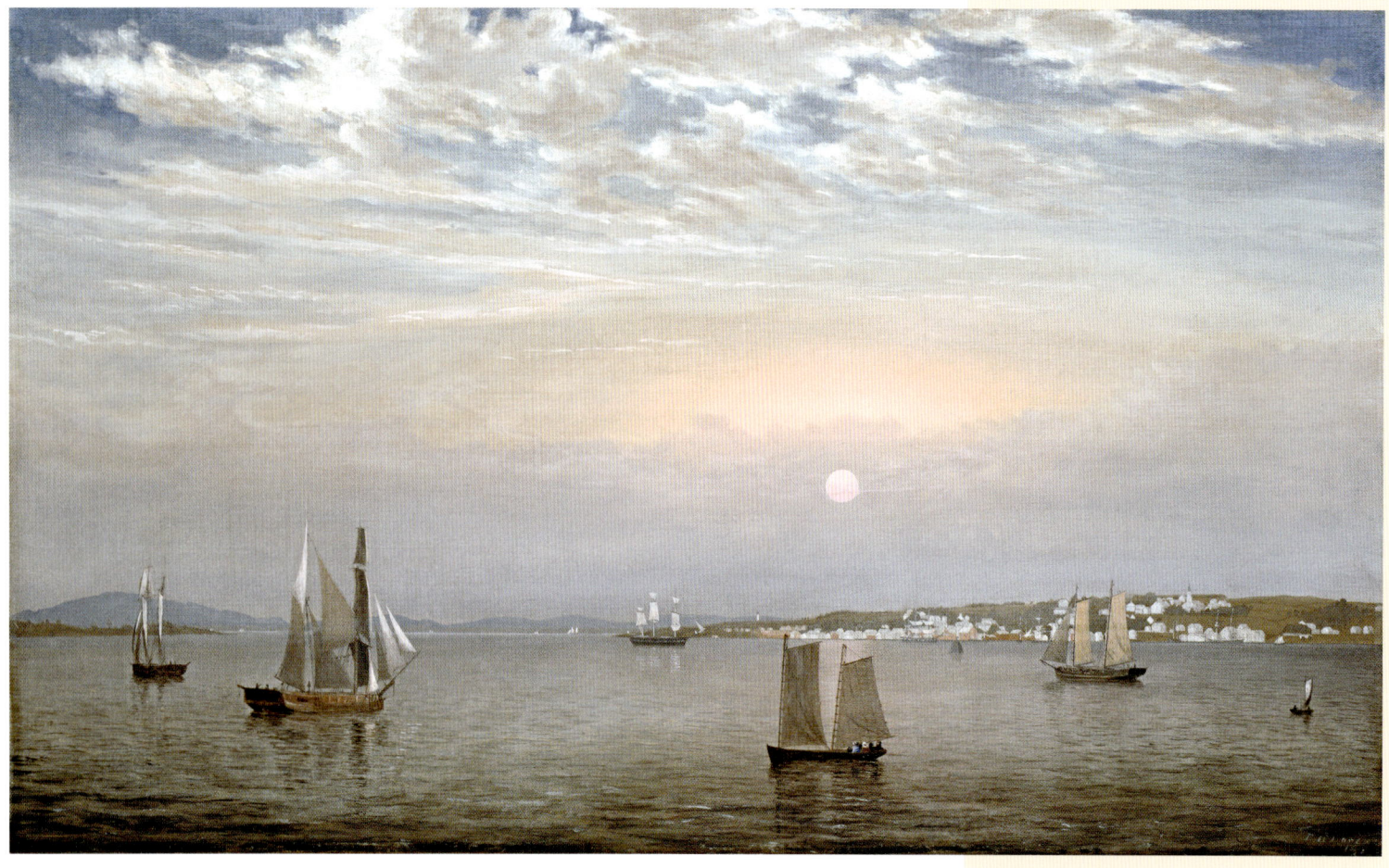

Fitz Henry Lane
Castine Harbor and Town, 1851
Oil on canvas, 20 x 33 ¼ in.
Putnam Foundation
Timken Museum of Art, San Diego

Writer Gorham Munson explains the Camden Hills have a special place in Maine coast iconography and drew the admiration of European and American explorer-travelers. "They begin near Rockland," he writes, "and step up and march northward: the 'great mountains' [English explorer James] Rosier sighted [1605], 'the high mountains of Penobscot against whose feet doth beat the sea' that impressed Captain John Smith [1614], 'the Camden Hills' that 'attracted my eyes' of which [Henry David] Thoreau [1853] wrote in his journals."

Fitz Henry Lane (1804–1865), who like many of his peers started out in printmaking, followed Fisher's lead, making trips by ship north and east from his home in Gloucester, Mass., drawn by the prospect of fresh landscape subjects and, later, by commissions. He made lithographs and painted many views of Castine where his friend and patron Joseph L. Stevens, Jr. (1823–1908) had a seasonal home. Looking back in a letter written in 1903, Stevens claimed to have known just

Yesterday

about every painting Lane made. Furthermore, Stevens said he sometimes served as Lane's "chooser of spots and bearer of materials when he sketched in the home neighborhood."

Lane's *Castine Harbor and Town* (1851) provides an across-the-water view of the town from a promontory under fair skies, with a variety of vessels tugged by a light wind. The glow of the sky and the tranquil waters exemplify what would come to be called "luminism" by art historians in the 1950s.

By contrast, Lane's view of Owls Head Light at the entrance of Rockland Harbor shows a turbulent sea, with choppy waves and rocking boats. The painter's attention to the details of marine architecture and placement of vessels and his subtle use of color values place his site-specific seascapes at the pinnacle of nineteenth-century American maritime art.

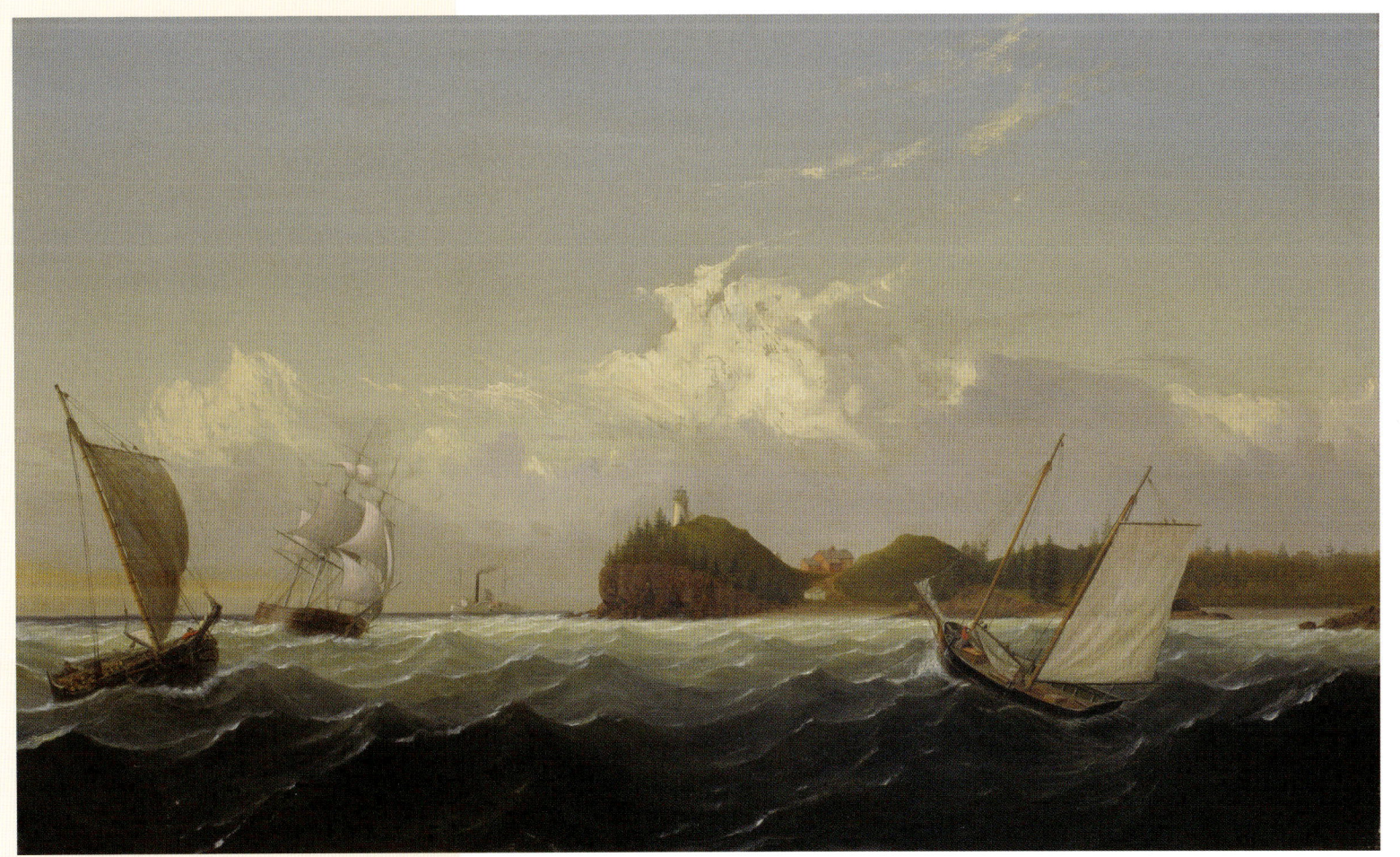

Fitz Henry Lane
Owls Head Light, Rockland, Maine
c.1856
Oil on canvas, 20 1/8 x 33 1/8 in.
Bequest of Mrs. Elizabeth B. Noyce
The Farnsworth Art Museum

Art of Penobscot Bay

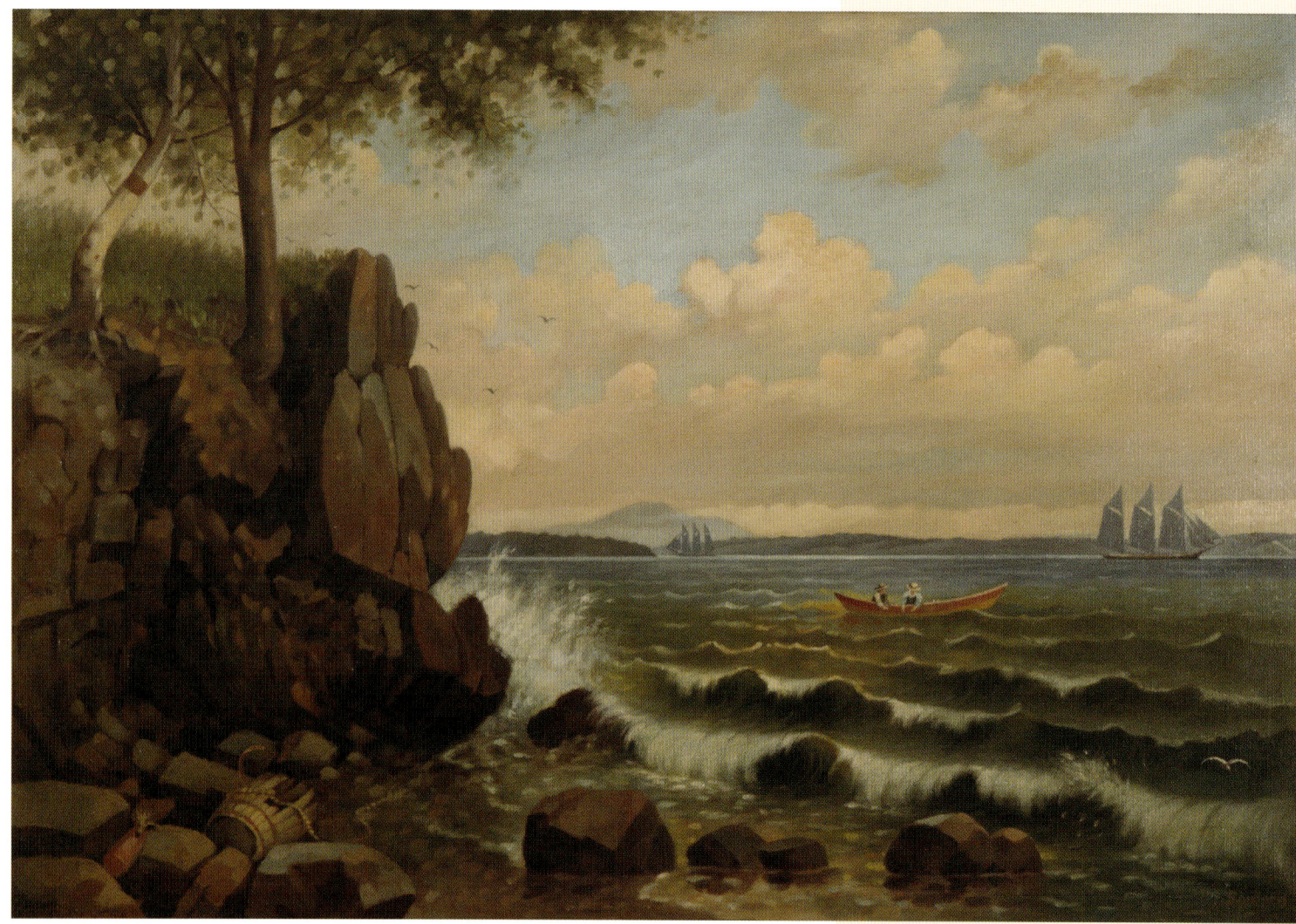

Similar whitecaps appear in **Percy Sanborn's** view of Penobscot Bay from Moose Point in Searsport. The self-taught Sanborn (1849–1929), who was born in Waldo, specialized in ship portraits but was also proficient in still life and animal subjects. His Penobscot Bay prospect features two three-masted schooners crossing the bay in opposite directions. In the foreground fishermen handline from a dory while Blue Hill hovers in the distance. Once a farm owned by the Carver family, Moose Point became a state park in 1963.

Percy A. Sanborn
Moose Point and Penobscot Bay,
c. 1880
Oil on canvas, 24 ¾ x 34 ⅞ in.
Courtesy Penobscot Marine Museum
PMM Image ID 1999.18

Yesterday

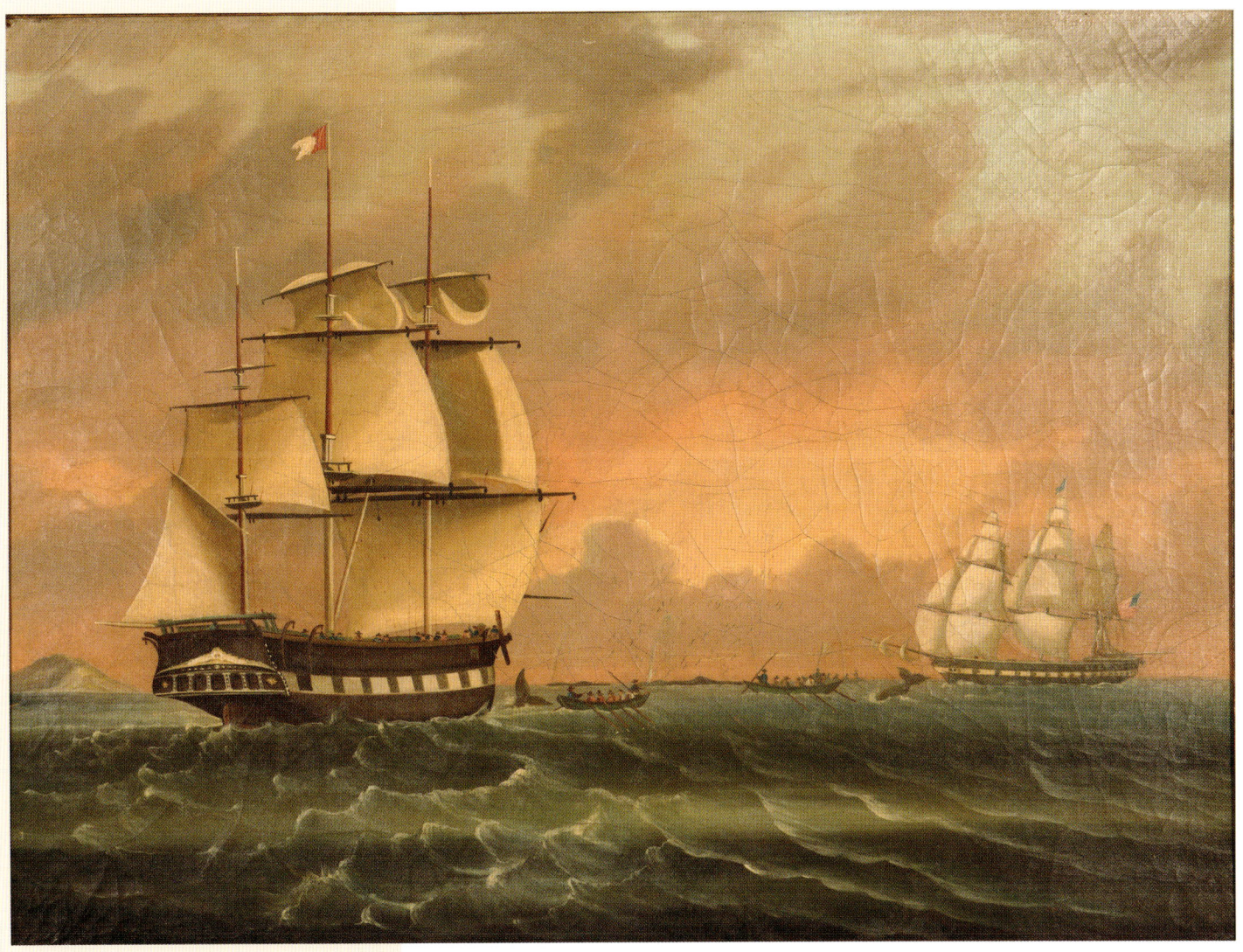

Thomas Chambers
Bark John Carver, c. 1850
Oil on canvas, 18 ⅛ x 24 ½ in.
Courtesy Penobscot Marine Museum
PMM Image ID 1962.44

John Carver was a master boatbuilder—and a prolific one. According to the Penobscot Marine Museum, his Searsport shipyard built twenty-five schooners, six brigs, five barks, and three ships between 1824 and 1864. One of those vessels carried his name: the bark *John Carver*, built in 1841. In a painting by the English-born **Thomas Chambers** (1808–1869), the ship pursues whales.

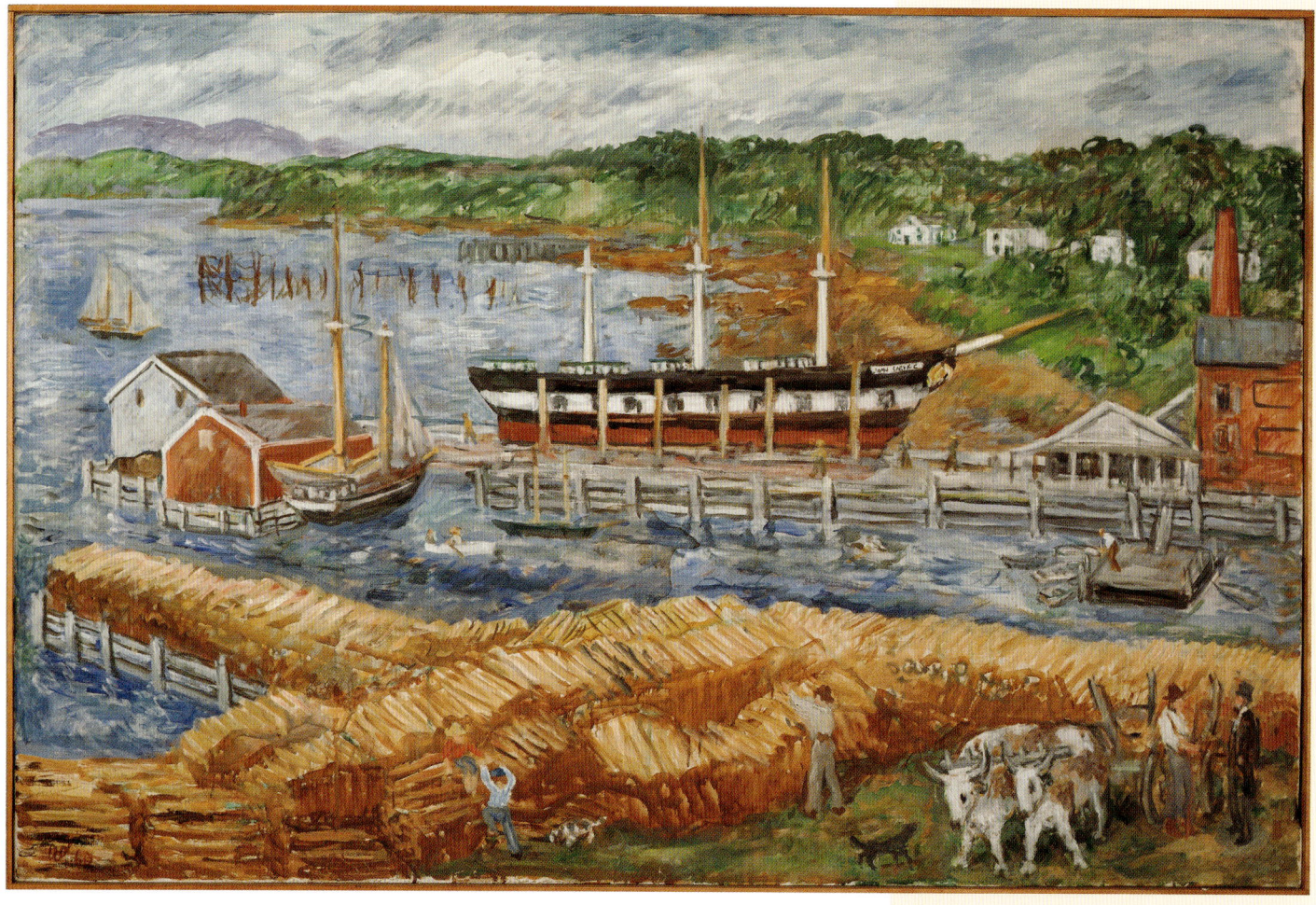

More than a century later, the painter **Waldo Peirce** (1884–1970) imagined what Carver's shipyard might have looked like with the namesake ship on the ways. Peirce's painting includes details related to shipbuilding, including stacks of barrel staves and various structures, among them, the steam shed and the oakum and blacksmith's shops.

Ship portraits were for the most part commissioned as visual records of investments by the vessels' captains, owners, and investors. These stakeholders felt pride in the beauty of their ships and wanted, almost exclusively, handsome broadside views with sails set at or close to the day of launching; these keepsakes would bring good luck to the voyage and safe return. These paintings were part of a similar tradition of portraits of families and homesteads. They would be superseded by landscape and

Waldo Peirce
Carver Yard with the John Carver on the Ways, 1960
Oil on canvas, 35 ¾ x 55 ¾ in.
Courtesy Penobscot Marine Museum
PMM Image ID 1961.3.1

Yesterday

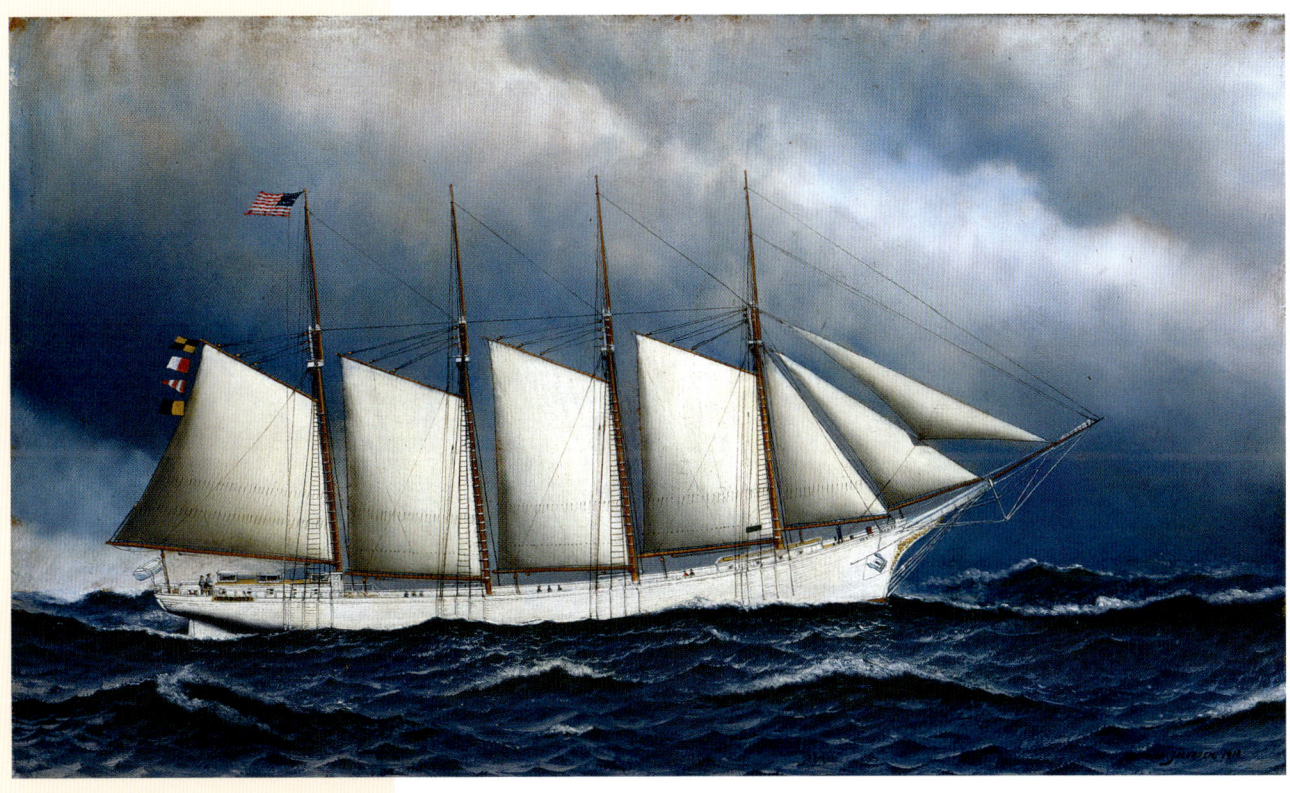

Antonio Jacobsen
Schooner Nancy Hanks, 1918
Oil on millboard, 14 ¾ x 24 ½ in.
Courtesy Penobscot Marine Museum
PMM Image ID 1962.14.1

seascape subjects, the popular appeal of which might lead, depending on the artist's reputation, to lucrative commissions.

The Danish-born painter **Antonio Jacobsen** (1850–1921) gained fame for the accuracy of his ship portraits. In his hands, the 1,162-ton four-masted schooner *Nancy Hanks*, named for Abraham Lincoln's mother, makes for a fine display of white hull and full sails set upon the deep. Built in Thomaston's Dunn & Elliott shipyard and owned by Searsport captains, including members of the Carver family, the ship carried coal, lumber, salt, and lime as far as Cape Town.

Art of Penobscot Bay

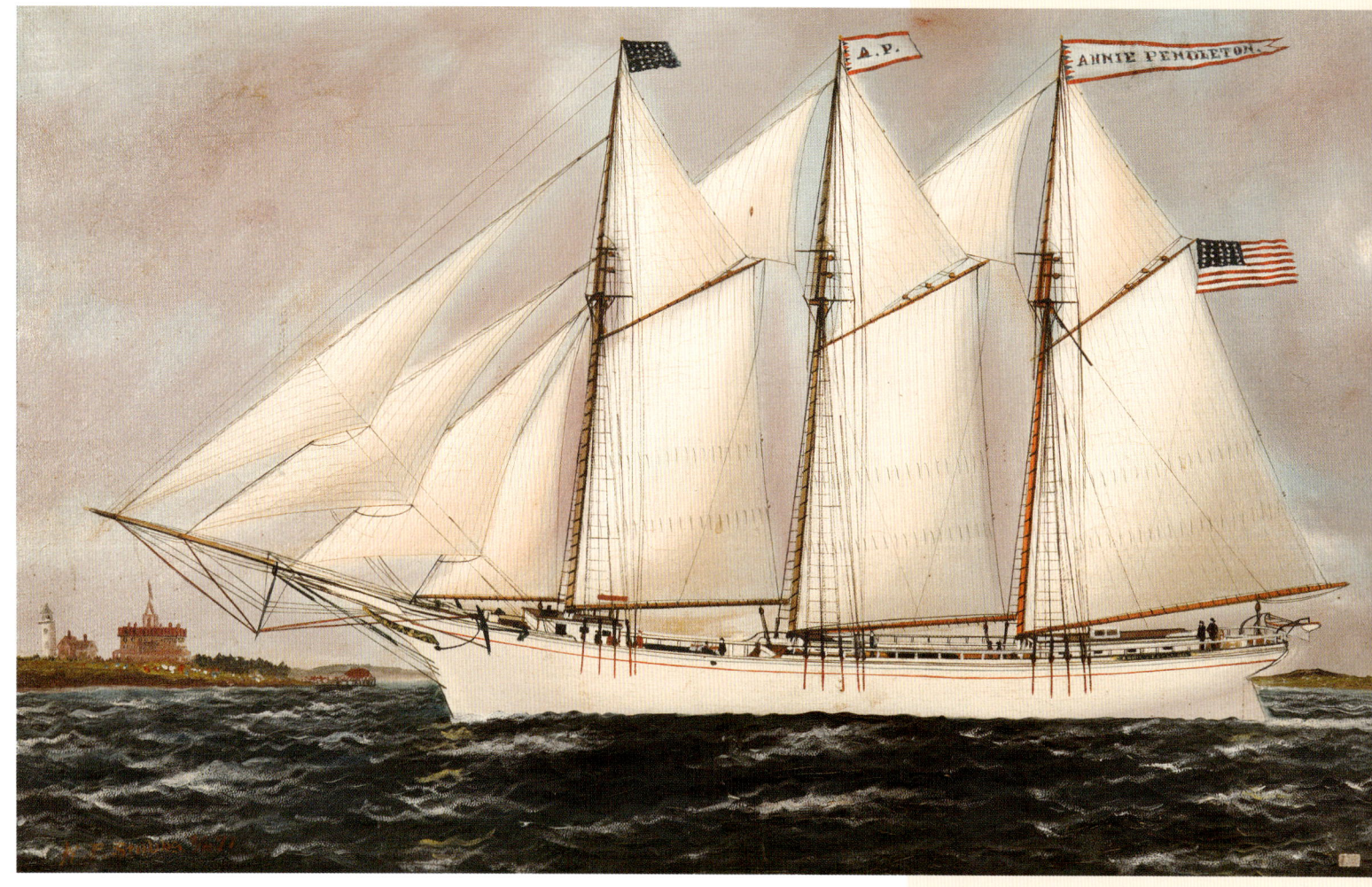

William Pierce Stubbs
Schooner Eliza J. Pendleton, 1891
Oil on canvas, 22 ⅛ x 36 ⅛ in.
Courtesy Penobscot Marine Museum
PMM Image ID 172

As the Bucksport-born son of a shipmaster, **William Pierce Stubbs** (1842–1909) knew his subjects well. His painting of the *Eliza J. Pendleton* not only documents the Belfast-built schooner, but also offers area history: The Fort Point Hotel in Stockton Springs (seen to the right of the lighthouse) burned down seven years after Stubbs made the painting. The artist also misnamed the ship the *Annie J. Pendleton*.

The paintings of **George Savary Wasson** (1855–1932) testify to the artist's firsthand knowledge of boats and their environment. Descended from shipbuilders who were active in Penobscot Bay after the American Revolution, Wasson had the history in his blood. As a boy he spent summers in Brooksville with his grandfather, "Squire" David Wasson, absorbing the seacoast milieu.

"No one can paint a vessel well who does not know the part of her that is under water," folklorist Fannie Eckstorm (1865–1946) wrote, in admiring Wasson's canvases. She said from the time he became a marine painter, Wasson was never without a boat of his own (they often served as floating studios). Wasson's last sloop, *Wave Crest*, which is now in the collection of the Penobscot Marine Museum, was

Yesterday

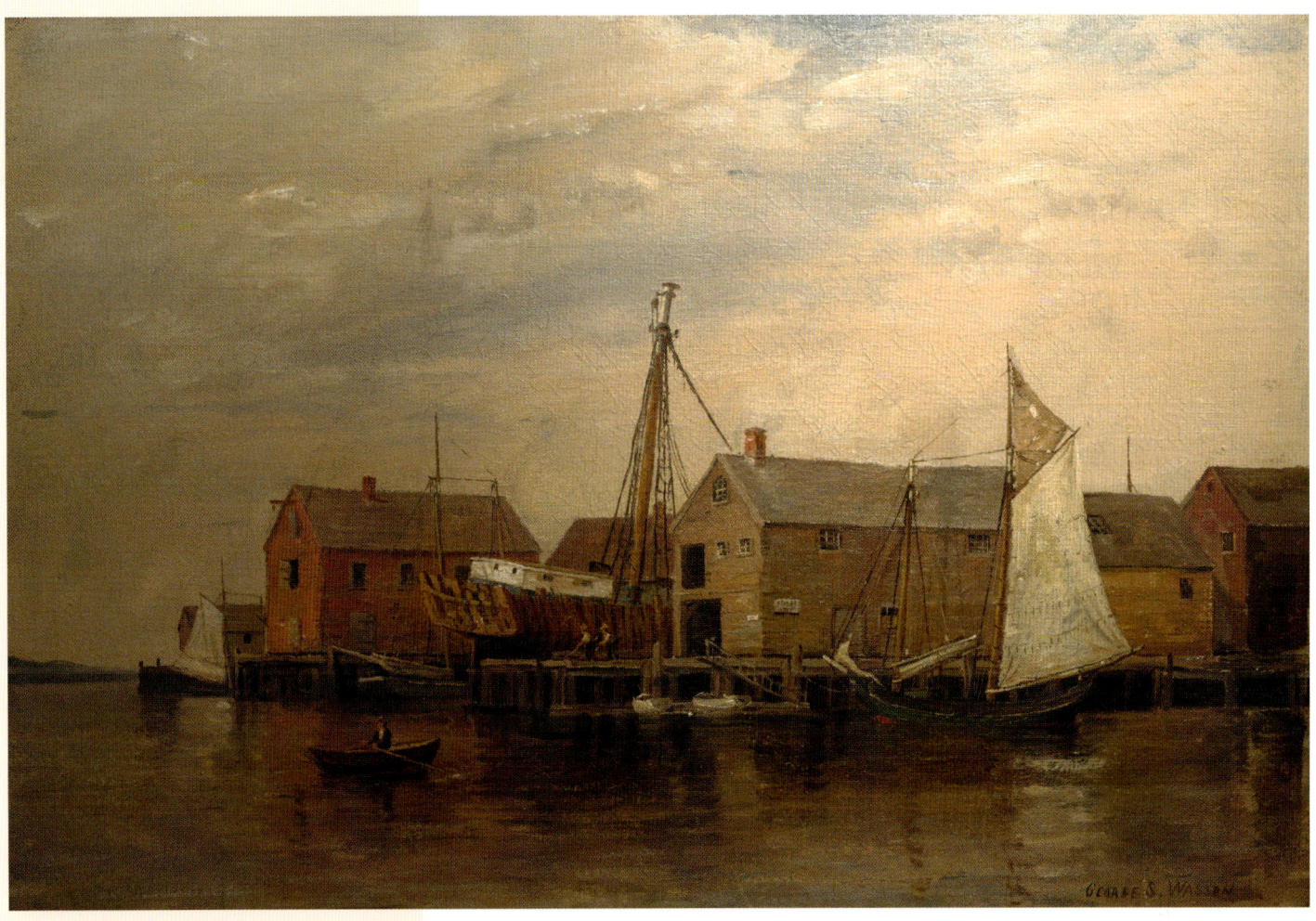

George Savary Wasson
Wharves at Castine, c. 1908
Oil on canvas, 18 x 26 ¼ in.
Courtesy Penobscot Marine Museum
PMM Image ID 2010.19.1

anchored in Castine. In his later years, the artist would row out to sleep aboard it in the summer, leaving his wife, who didn't like being on the water, in a boarding house or hotel.

Wasson's view of Castine's wharves captures the waterfront activities, including the replanking of a schooner. The pinky schooner anchored in the harbor speaks to the painter's passion for vessels of a bygone era, which he wrote about in his final book, *Sailing Days on the Penobscot* (1932).

None other than Mark Twain considered chapter eight of Wasson's story collection *Cap'n Simeon's Store* (1903), one of the funniest pieces of prose he ever read. In the chapter in question, "Rusticators at the Cove," the title character declares visiting painters "the biggest cranks o' the whole kerboodle" because they chose to depict ramshackle houses, seaworn sailors, and other unsightly subjects.

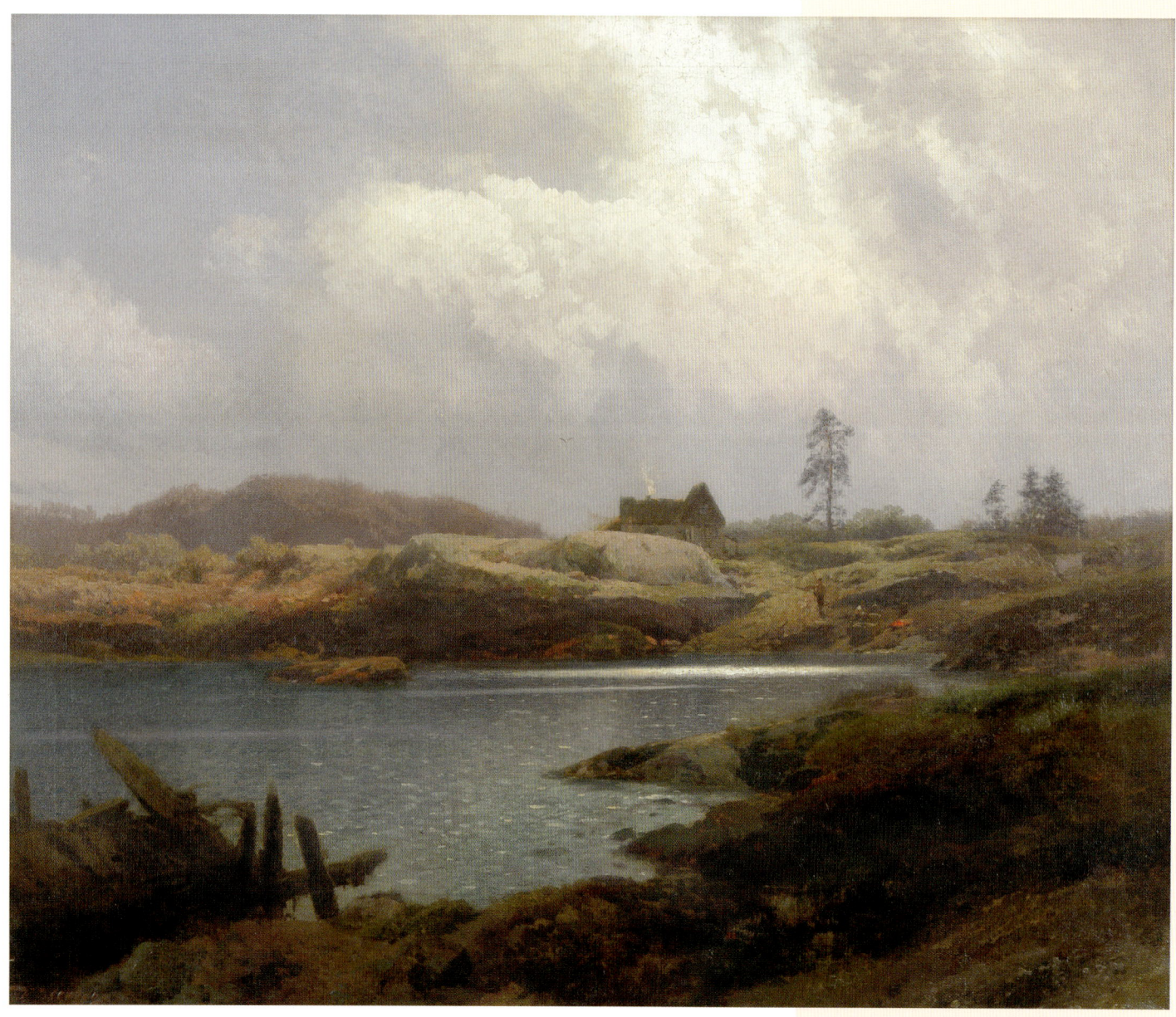

Hermann Ottomar Herzog (1831–1932) was one of those visiting painters—a rusticator but no crank. In his lifetime, the Philadelphia-based artist, who was born in Bremen, Germany, made a point of going to places off the beaten path, including Norway, Yosemite, and Downeast Maine.

The only sign of life in Herzog's atmospheric late 1800s view of a desolate stretch of coast at Stonington is a small house with a bit of smoke coming from the chimney.

Hermann Ottomar Herzog
Coast at Stonington, Maine, c. 1890
Oil on canvas, 30 1/16 x 36 in.
Gift from MBNA America
The Farnsworth Art Museum, 2000.4

Yesterday

Charles Copeland
Criehaven, c. 1910
Watercolor on paper,
22 1/16 x 34 1/2 in.
Gift of Mrs. W.B.D. Gray and Mrs. James Creighton
The Farnsworth Art Museum,
73.1883

Filling the sky with turbulent clouds and accenting the water with slivers of sunlight, he rendered the quiet grandeur and beauty of nature much in the tradition of the Hudson River School.

Like Wasson, **Charles Copeland** (1858–1945) had literary connections through his illustrations for popular magazines, such as *Youth's Companion* and *Harper's,* and books of the time, many related to life in the woods. He also illustrated *Robinson Crusoe*. Born in Thomaston, he was also known for marine paintings and seascapes. His early 1900s watercolor of a wave-swept, seaweed-draped rock off remote Criehaven, also known as Ragged Island, testifies to his brilliant handling of the notoriously unruly medium.

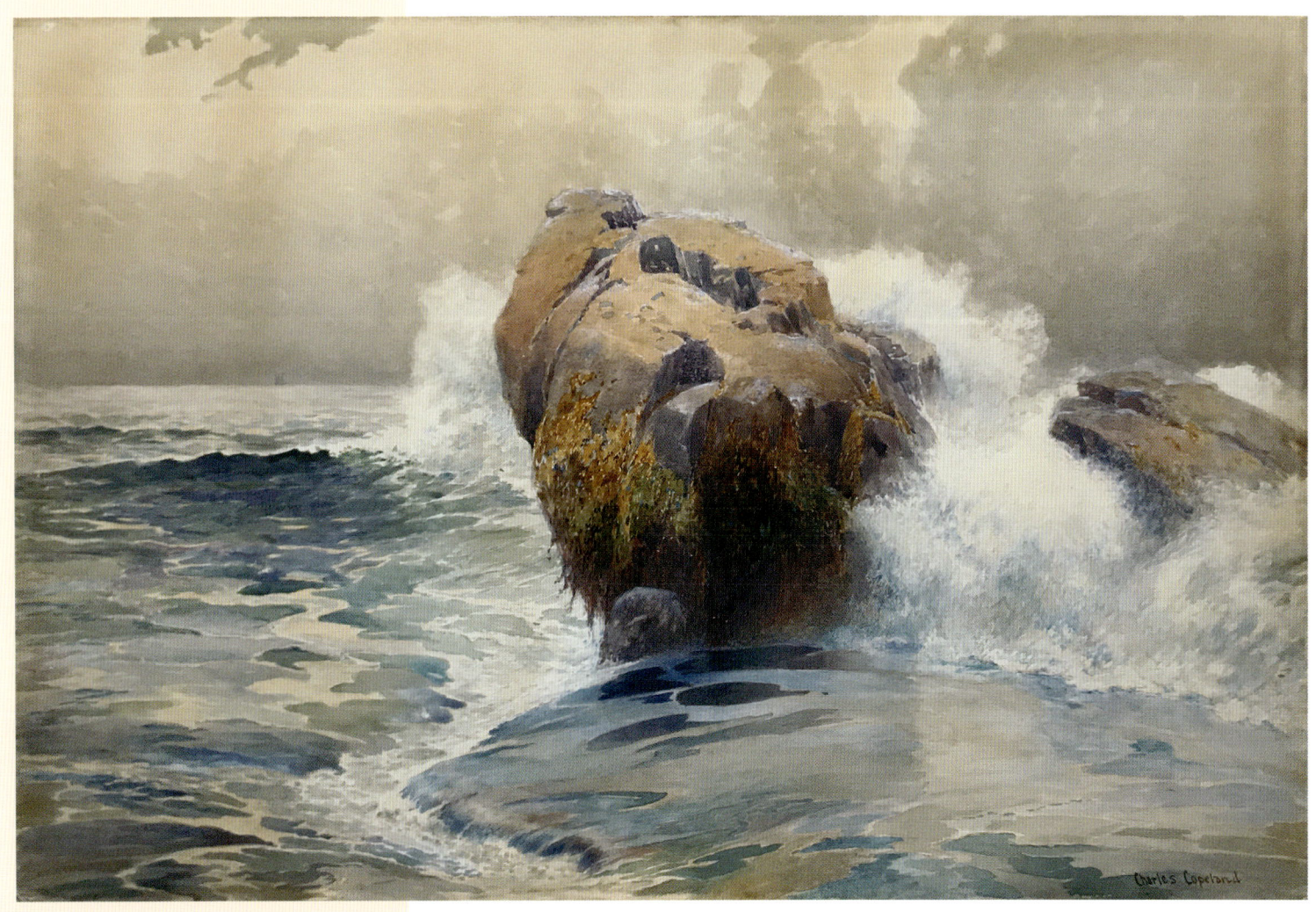

About six years later and a few miles away as the gull flies, **George Bellows** (1882–1925) took brush to plywood to paint Freeman Young's farm on Matinicus Island. He was drawn to Maine by his famed teacher Robert Henri (1865–1929), who was considered one of the founders of the Ashcan School. Bellows painted with bold, saturated colors that captured the workings of this small island farm. He wielded a swift and sure brush, fulfilling his teacher's definition of the true artist as one who, in viewing the landscape, "renders it upon his canvas as a living thing."

Author William Inness Homer noted that Henri stimulated "the development of the most advanced, non-academic art [realism] of the 1890s and 1900s." The Ashcan School, along with The Ten, a New-York–based, self-conceived academy of American Impressionism, challenged the policies and heavy-handed authority of the National Academy of Design and the Society of American Artists.

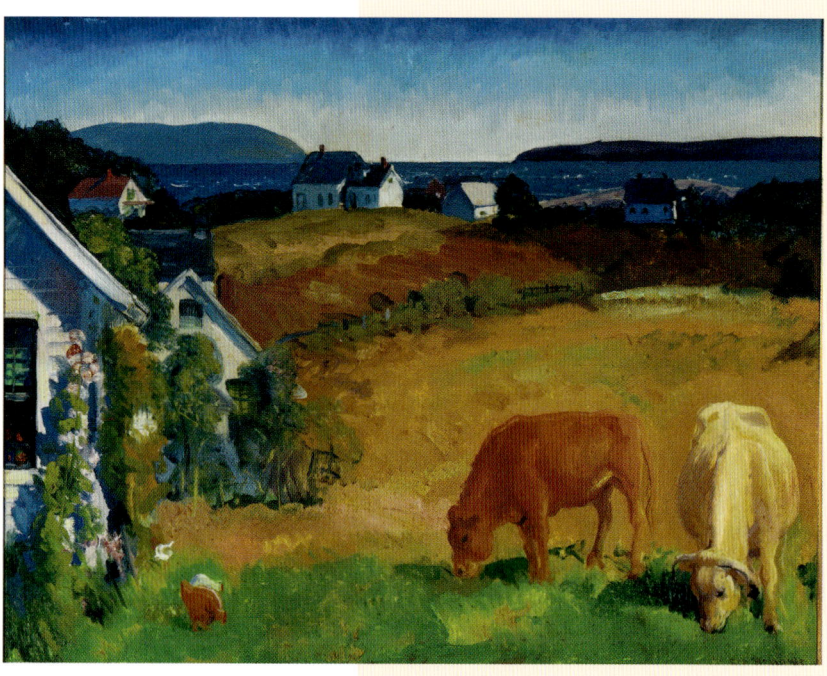

George Bellows
Freeman Young's Place, Matinicus Island, Maine, 1916
Oil on plywood, 22 x 28 in.
Bequest of Evelyn G. Muller
The Hyde Collection, 2020.1
Glens Falls, New York
Photo by mclaughlinphotography.com

Bellows stated in 1917, "It seems to me that an artist must be a spectator of life; a reverential, enthusiastic, emotional spectator." His fellow Henri disciple **George Luks** (1867–1933) might have had those words in mind when he painted *Poverty Hump,* a small weather-beaten outpost in the Muscle Ridge Shoals off South Thomaston.

In the painting, two men have arrived on the island, perhaps to supply a fishing station. The brushstrokes are deployed with brilliant force and vitality. The scene is dramatic, in setting and color scheme, even as it records an episode of Maine coast life. The artist's training in illustration and newspaper work helped him to sketch from life. Like Bellows and Henri, Luks managed to make the move from urban to rural realist.

Luks's reaction to the Maine coast expresses the kind of enthusiasm found in the letters and writings of Henri, Bellows, and other artists upon their introduction to this northern realm. In an interview with a reporter from the *Portland Evening Express* in 1922, the painter waxed lyrical about his surroundings:

"Talk about the chalk cliffs of [Cornwall], talk about the 'wonderful scenery' anywhere in Europe, Maine has it over them. Here you have that wonderful gray that is found only in such a climate as that of Maine and your rocks and shores

Yesterday

are so rugged and bold, they make other rocks and shores seem pretty and puny in comparison; and your characters, there are real American types here, types that you find nowhere else . . ."

George Luks
Poverty Hump, Maine, c. 1922
Oil on canvas, 25 x 30 in.
Gift of Macon and Joan Brock
Chrysler Museum of Art,
Norfolk, Virginia

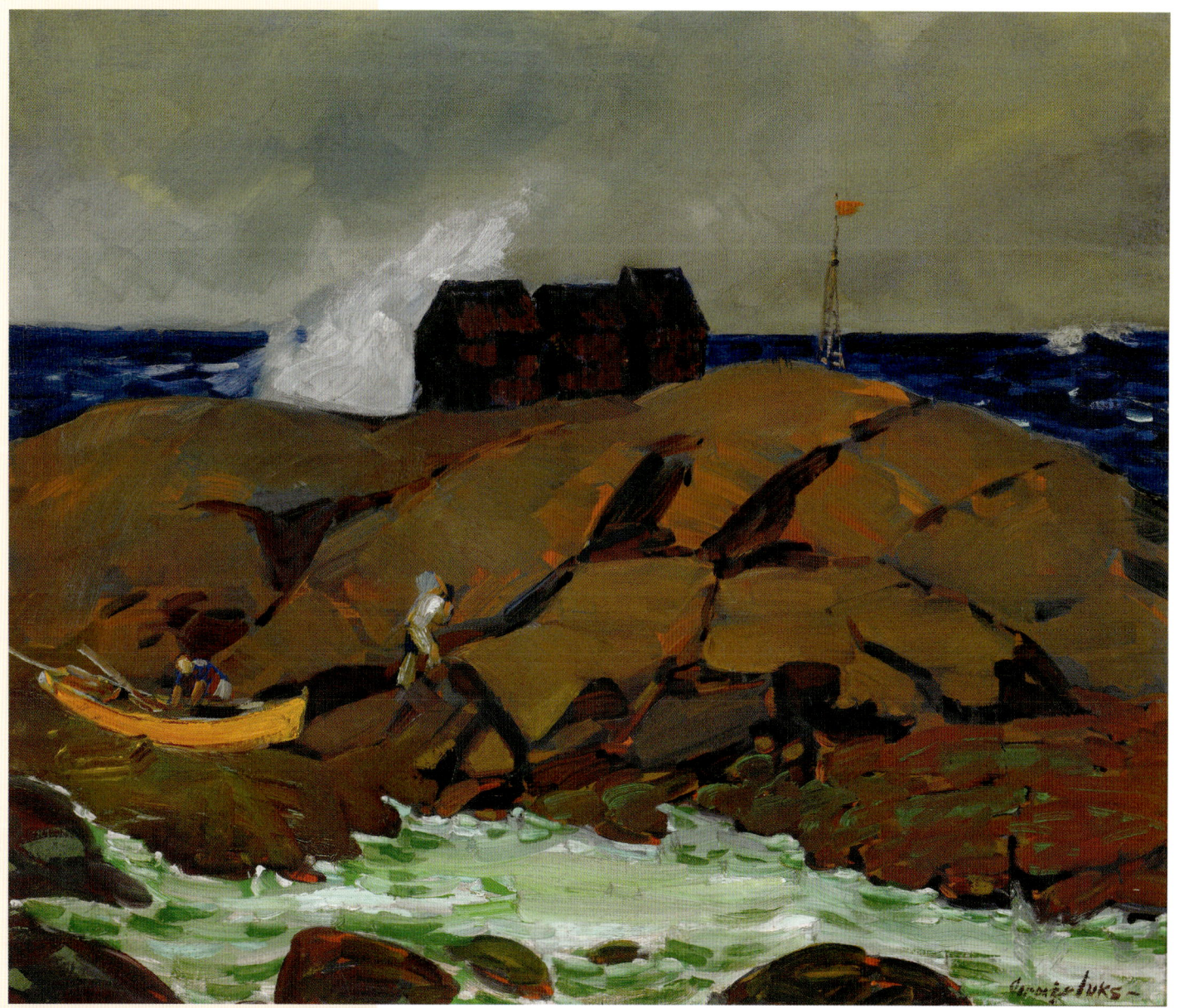

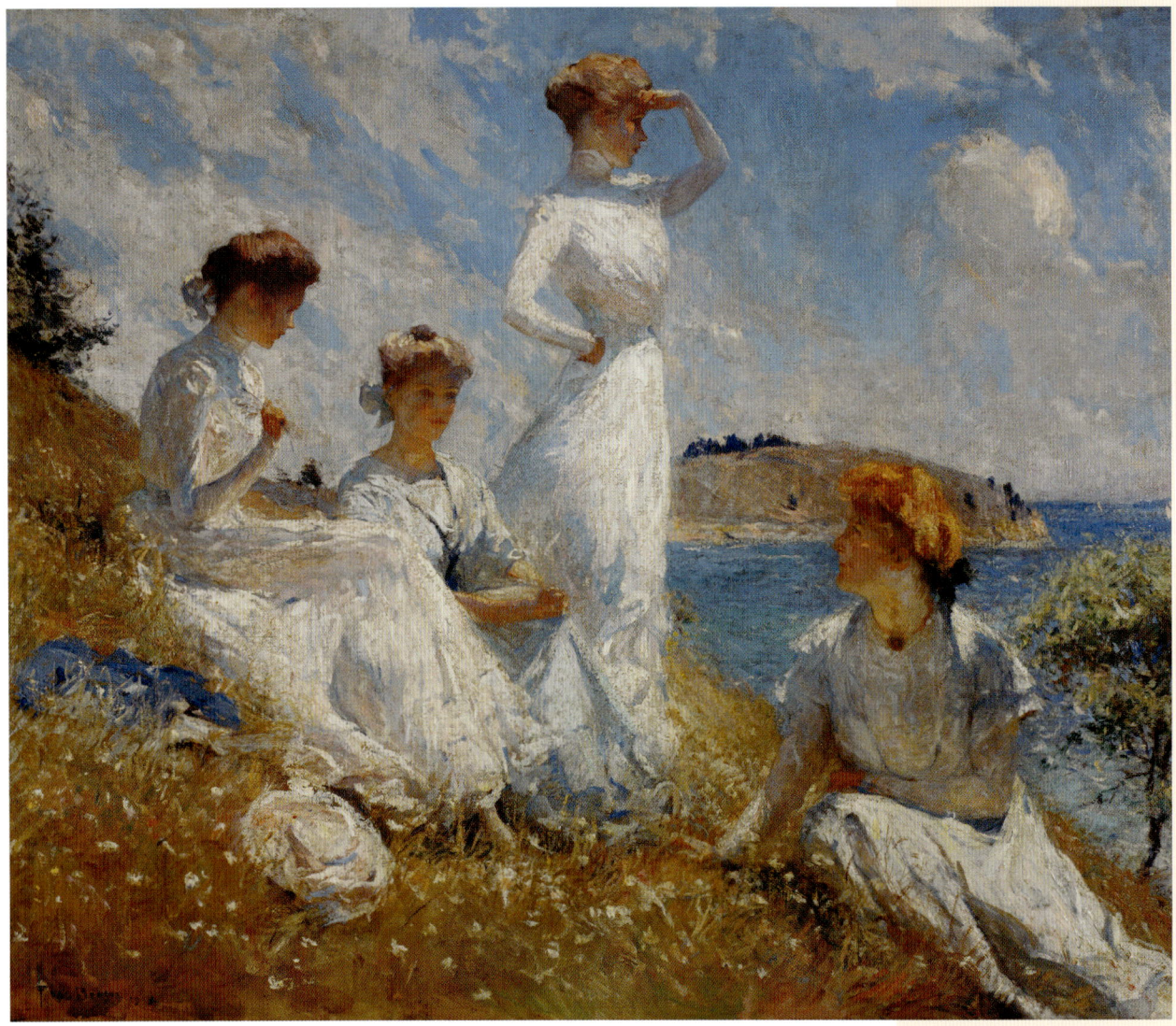

A quite different American type appears in the idyllic *Summer* (1909), by the eminent Boston painter **Frank W. Benson** (1862–1951). In this quintessential American impressionist plein-air picture, a group of young women in white dresses enjoy a sunlit afternoon on Lookout Hill on North Haven Island. In response to Benson's sun-drenched paintings, a critic of the time wrote, "I am convinced there is a little jar marked 'Sunshine' into which he dips his brush when he paints his pictures of the summer."

Benson was influenced and encouraged in his experimentation of plein air figure painting by members of The Ten. They may have seen the large 1886 exhibition of French impressionist works that included paintings by Renoir and Monet of figures out-of-doors. Benson once said, "I simply follow the light, where it comes from, where it goes." His close attention to placing highlights and shadows on clothing, faces, and hair made the figures pop.

Frank Weston Benson
Summer, 1909
Oil on canvas, 36 ⅛ x 44 ½ in.
Bequest of Isaac C. Bates
Museum of Art, Rhode Island School of Design

Frank Weston Benson
Osprey and Fish, 1924
Oil on canvas, 60 x 45 in.
Private collection
Photo by Osher Map Library, Portland

Yesterday

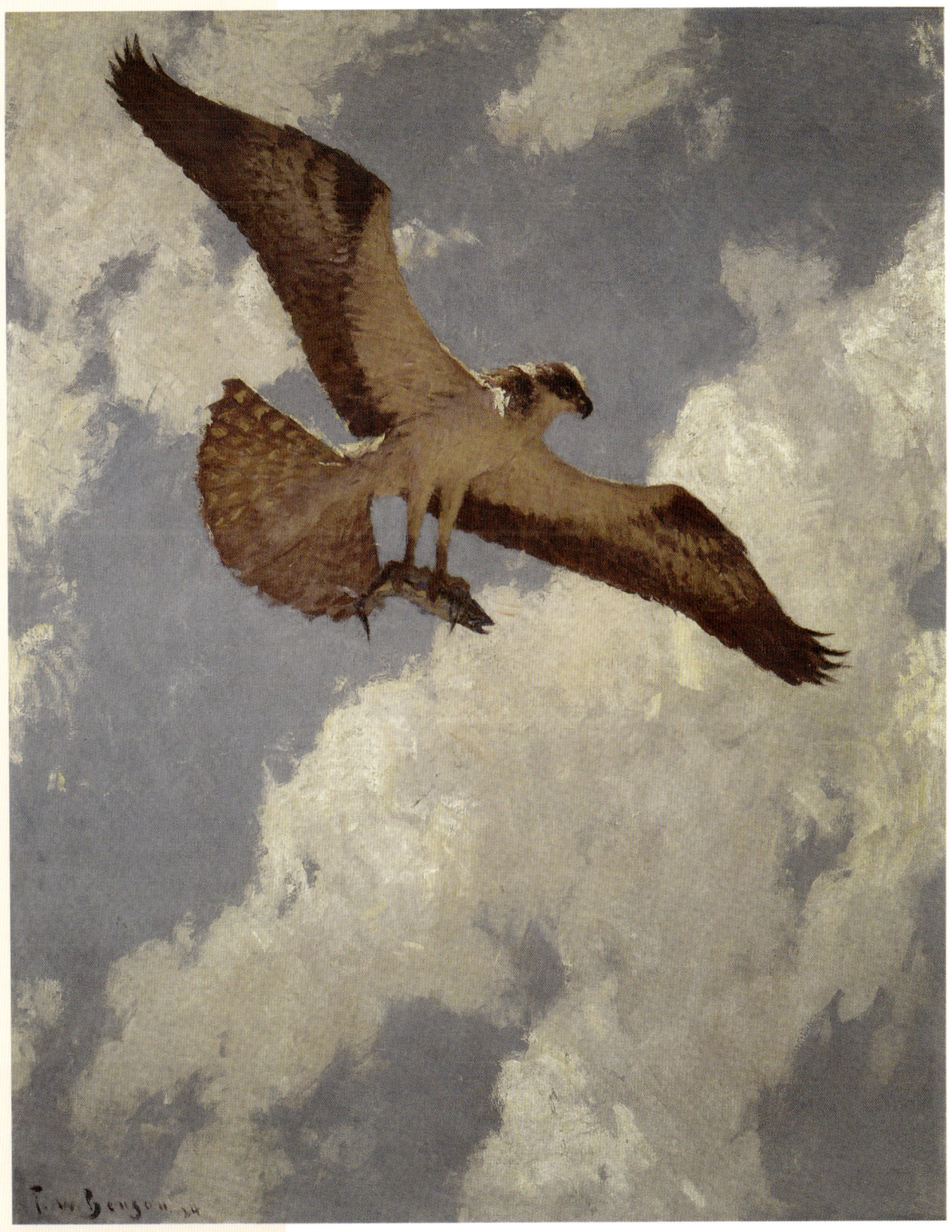

According to Peabody Essex Museum curator Dean Lahikainen, the painter turned to nature and "birds replaced the women and children as his objects of interest" when his images of a "pretty, genteel life" drew criticism for being portraits of the wealthy and privileged. The painter's dramatic rendering of an osprey in mid-air gripping a fish demonstrates his genius at rendering wildlife. Benson's use of photography as reference material for his paintings helped him develop variations for these popular subjects.

Benson purchased Wooster Farm on North Haven in 1906 after renting the place for several summers. He often invited fellow artists to join him in the middle of Penobscot Bay for some painting time. On a visit in 1907, fellow impressionist **Willard Metcalf** (1862–1951) painted *Ebbing Tide, Version 2*, a view of the thoroughfare that separates the islands of North Haven and Vinalhaven, in a style that recalls his colleague Childe Hassam's earlier Isles of Shoals paintings. Metcalf inscribed the light-filled painting to Benson "en souvenir"—as a special memento for his friend in thanks for his time on the island.

Another visitor, painter **Beatrice Whitney Van Ness** (1888–1981), studied with Benson at the Boston Museum School. She taught there as well and said, "I do not regret the time spent in teaching. Just as Mr. Benson said it would be: although I may have helped others, I learned the most!" Like her teacher, she embraced painting outdoors and bought an island home she called Hidden House, set above the beach in Bartlett's Harbor.

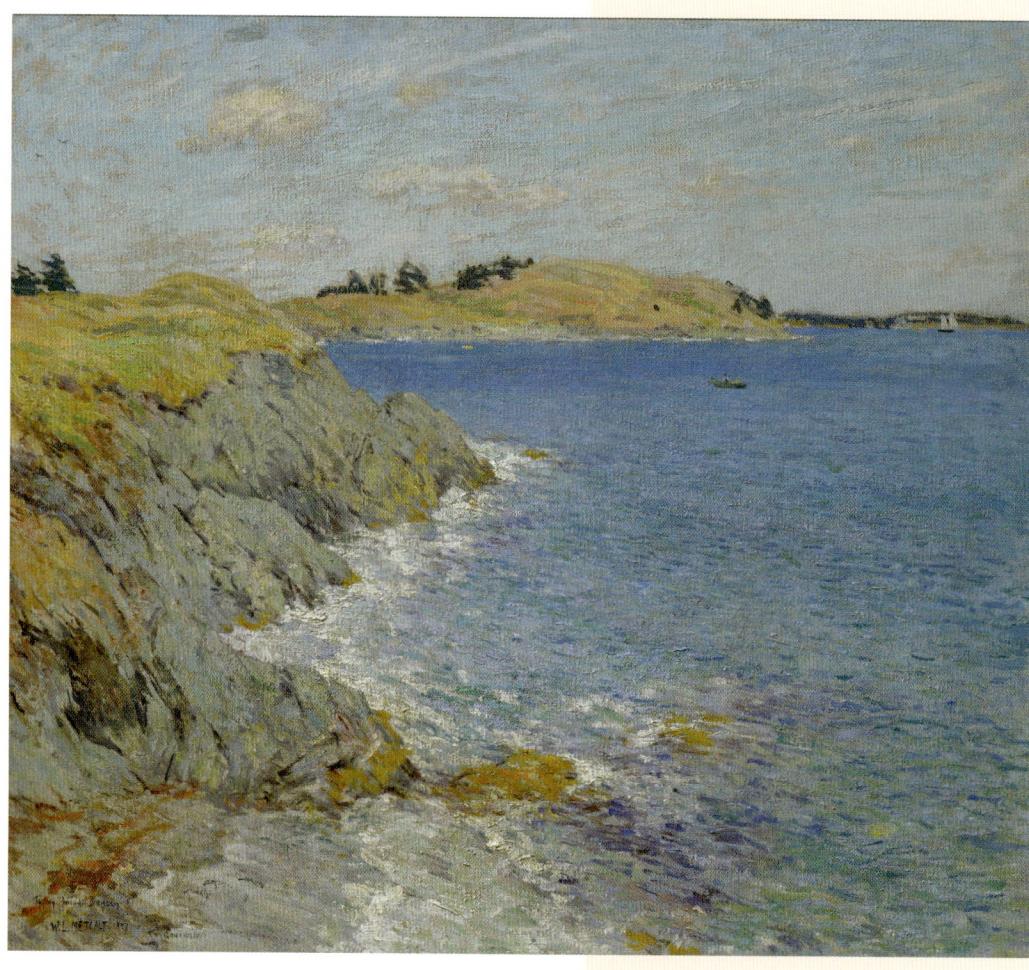

Willard Metcalf
Ebbing Tide, Version 2, 1907
Oil on canvas, 26 x 29 in.
Gift of the Estate of Sylvia Benson Lawson
The Farnsworth Art Museum, 1982.7

Yesterday

Beatrice Whitney Van Ness
Summer Sunlight, c. 1936
Oil on canvas, 40 ¼ x 50 ½ in.
Courtesy of the National Museum of Women in the Arts, Washington, D.C.
© Beatrice Whitney Van Ness
Photo by Lee Stalsworth

Also, like Benson, Van Ness turned to family and friends for models. Her painting *Summer Sunlight* (1936) features a daughter, a nephew, and a neighbor. The colors, shapes, and striped shirt bring Henri Matisse's French Riviera canvases to mind.

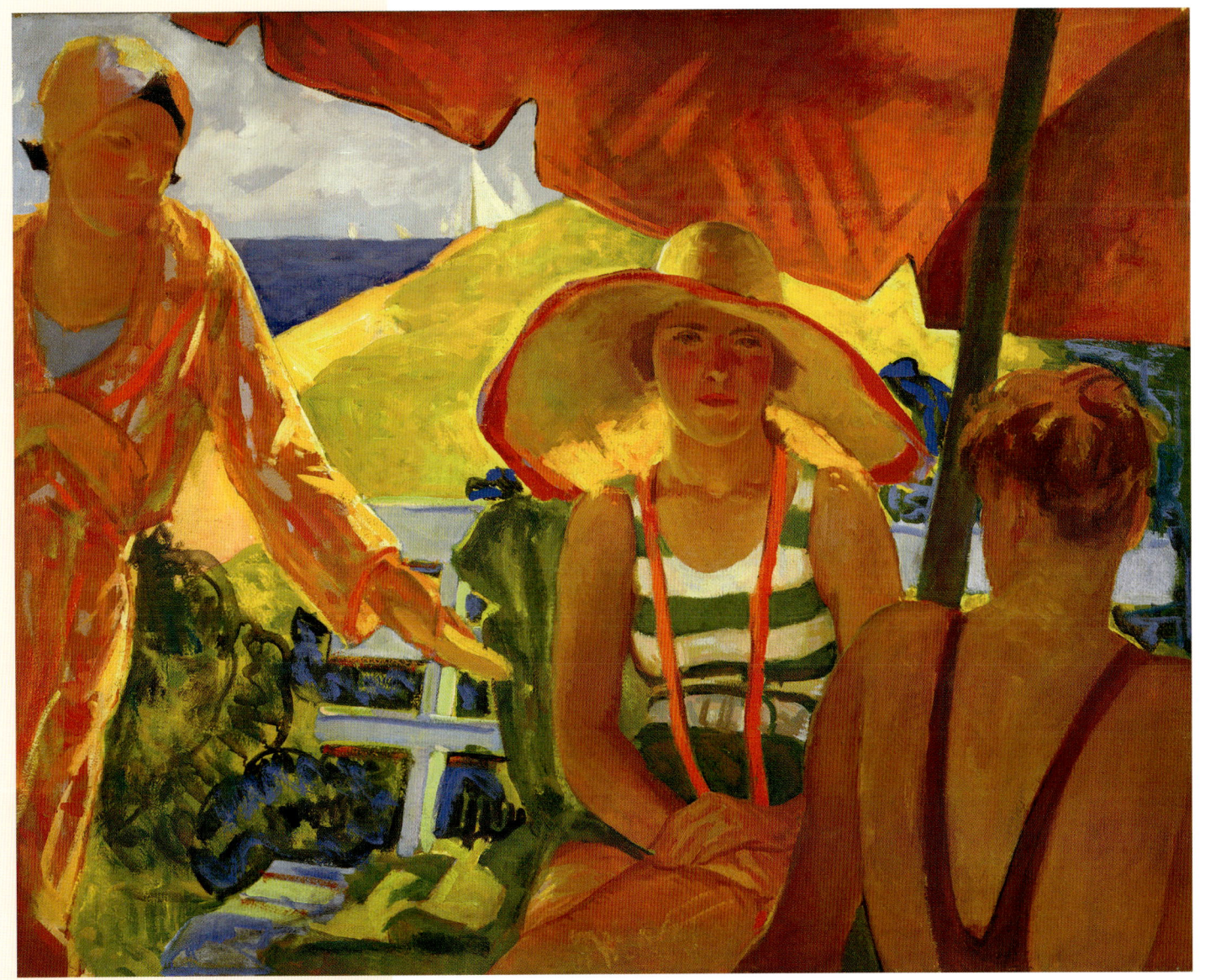

Art of Penobscot Bay

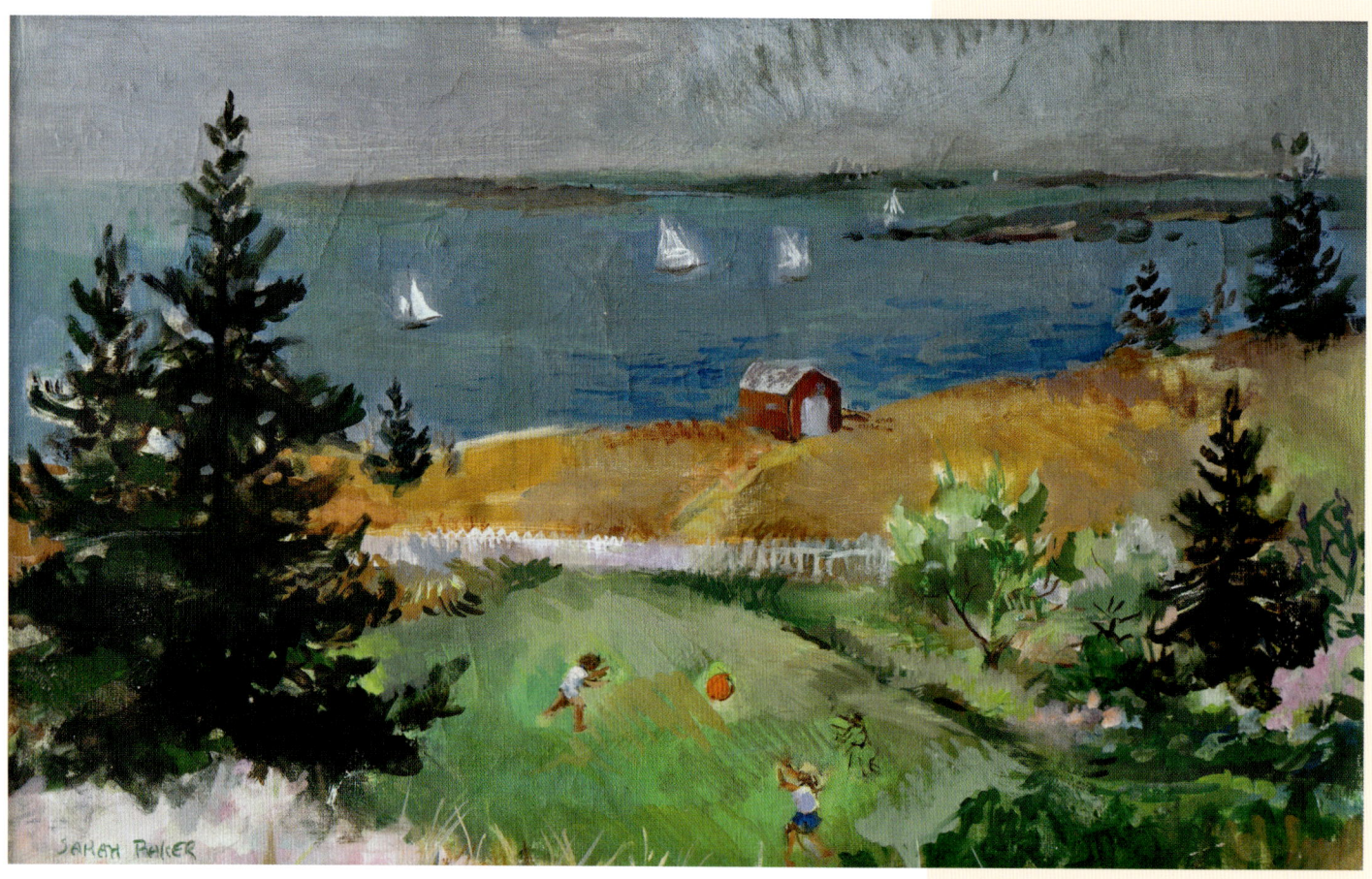

Years later, **Sarah Baker** (1899–1983) painted a scene of children playing on the lawn of the Benson farmhouse, with Vinalhaven and the White Islands in the distance. For more than twenty years the Memphis-born, European-trained painter spent summers in her studio on Southern Harbor creating impressionist views of North Haven. Her distinguished career in education included teaching several young islanders, including Eric and David Hopkins, how to paint.

Sarah Baker
June in Maine, 1964
Oil on canvas, 17 ¼ x 28 ¼ in.

Yesterday

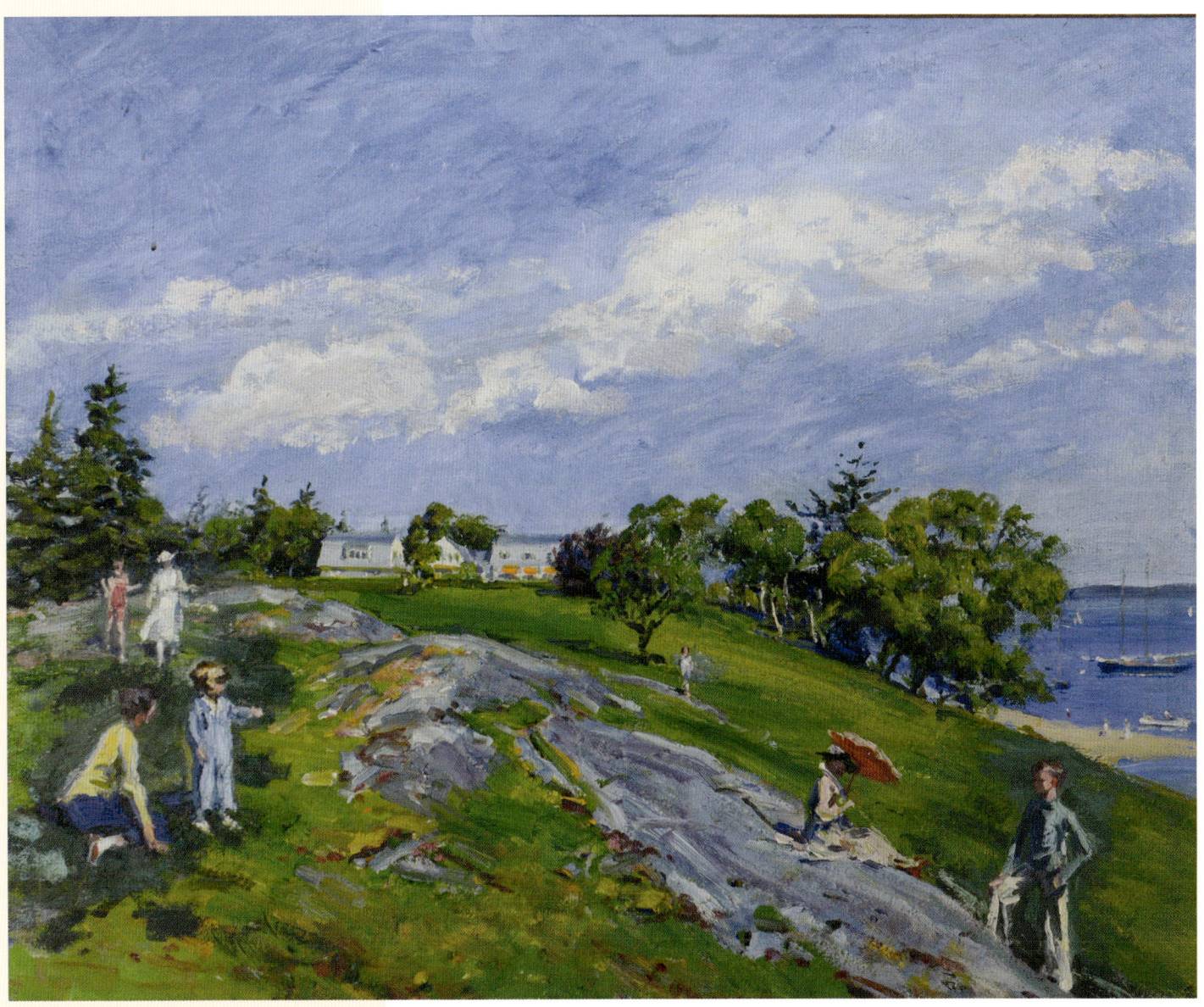

Charles Dana Gibson
A Family Outing on Gibson Point,
c. 1930s
Oil on canvas, 36 x 46 in.
Photo by Abe Goodale

On Seven Hundred Acre Island off Islesboro, the famed illustrator **Charles Dana Gibson** (1867–1944), creator of the iconic "Gibson Girl," set up his easel to paint scenes of summer life in the 1930s after he had mostly retired from illustration. In a lively view of the south side of Gibson Point, family members enjoy a sun-filled day on Penobscot Bay.

Art of Penobscot Bay

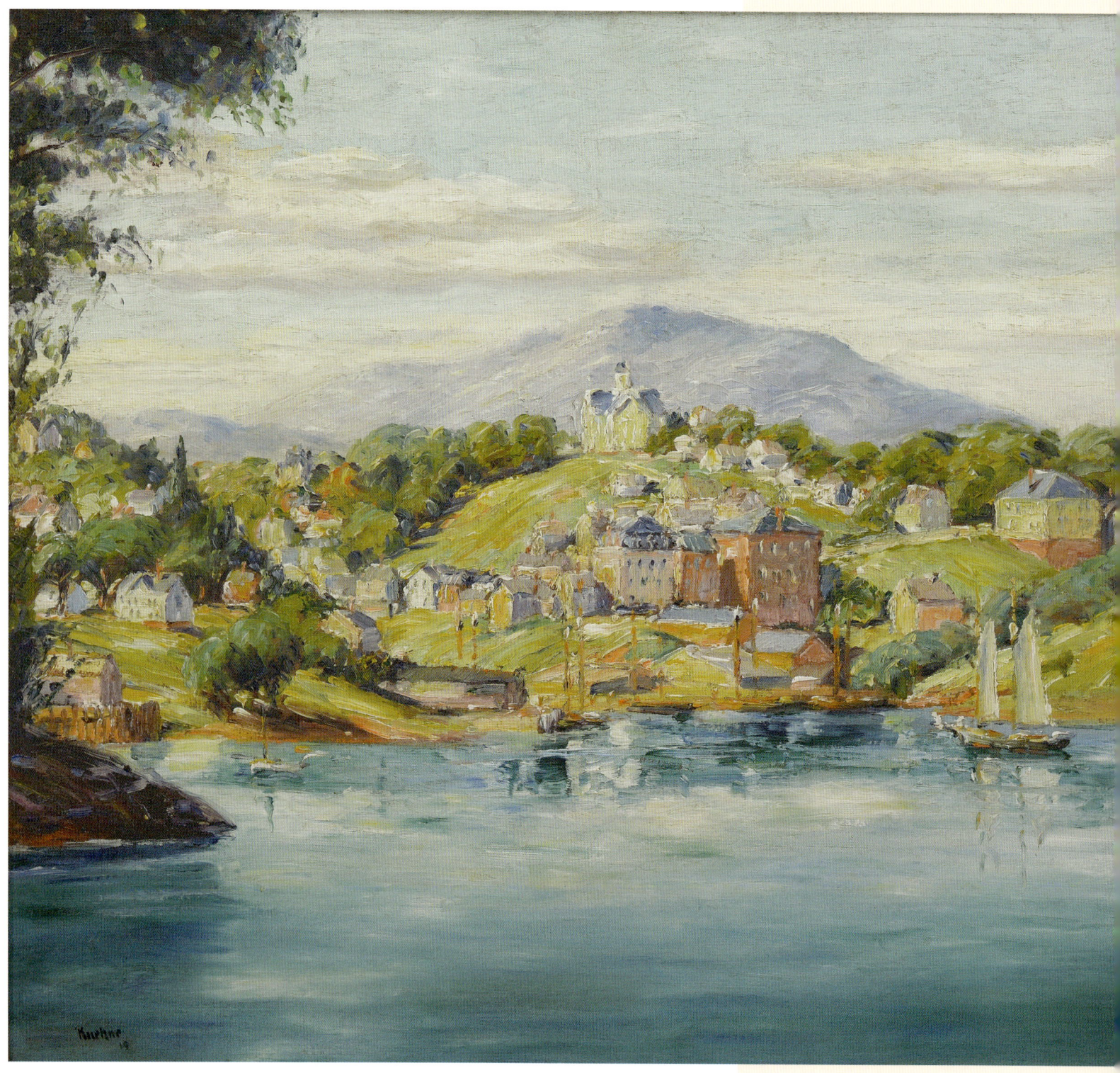

Yesterday

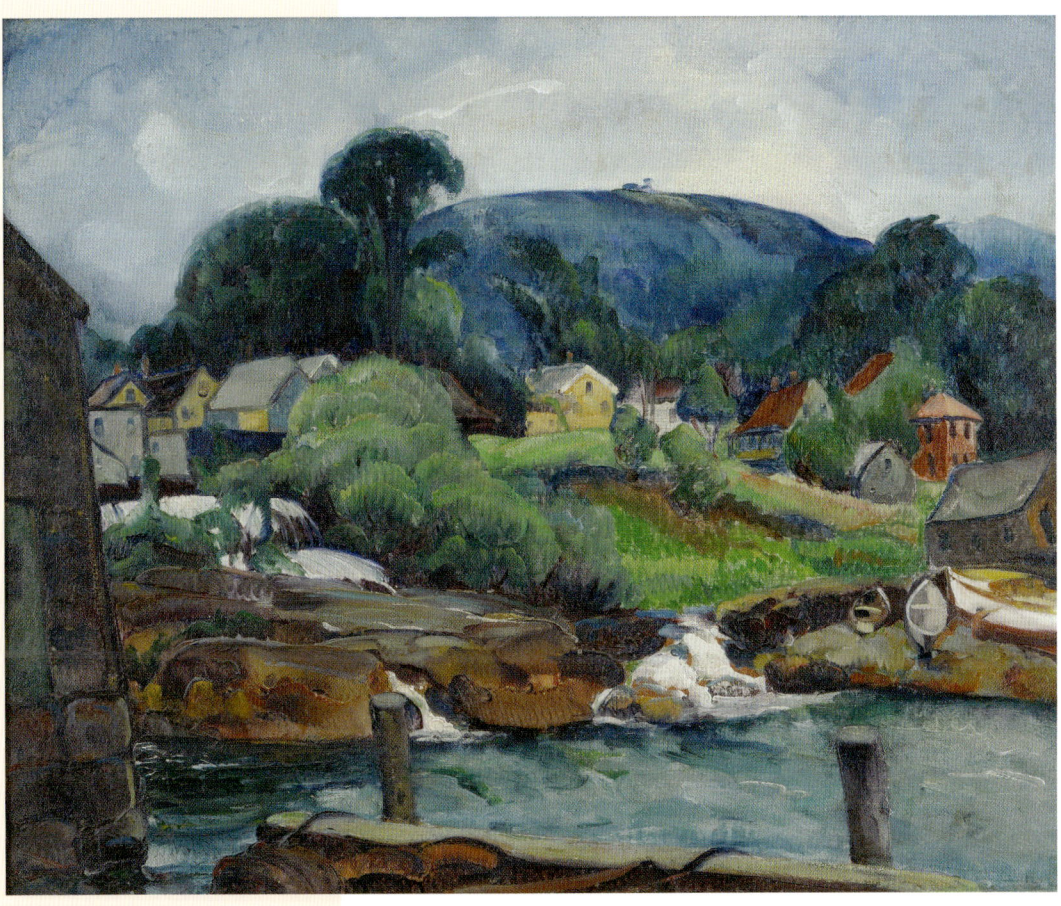

Leon Kroll
Lowering Day, Camden, 1916
Oil on canvas, 26 ¼ x 32 ⅛ in.
Bequest of Mrs. Elizabeth B. Noyce
The Farnsworth Art Museum

Max Kuehne
Rockport Harbor, Maine, 1919
Oil on canvas, 31 x 36 ⅛ in.
Bequest of Mrs. Elizabeth B. Noyce
The Farnsworth Art Museum

Back on the mainland, artists also painted realistic and impressionistic views of coastal towns, drawn to the arrangement of houses and other structures perched on the sloping seaside landscape.

The German-born **Max Kuehne** (1880–1968), who studied with William Merritt Chase, Robert Henri, and others in New York, provided a warm, semi-impressionist rendering of Rockport, a quiet harbor town nestled between Rockland and Camden. The brick Union Hall adds a red accent in the middle ground, the Methodist Church stands tall atop a hill, and Ragged Mountain looms beyond. His brush technique is immediate and fluid.

In contrast, **Leon Kroll** (1884–1974) chose to depict neighboring Camden on an overcast day, a lowering sky threatening rain, with the old mill stream, also known as Camden Falls, cascading into the harbor and the Summit House, which was torn down in 1920, just visible atop Mount Battie. The painting reflects the influence of the French Post-Impressionist Paul Cézanne whose work Kroll discovered while studying in Paris between 1908 and 1910. His close friend George Bellows was also painting in Camden the summer of 1916.

Art of Penobscot Bay

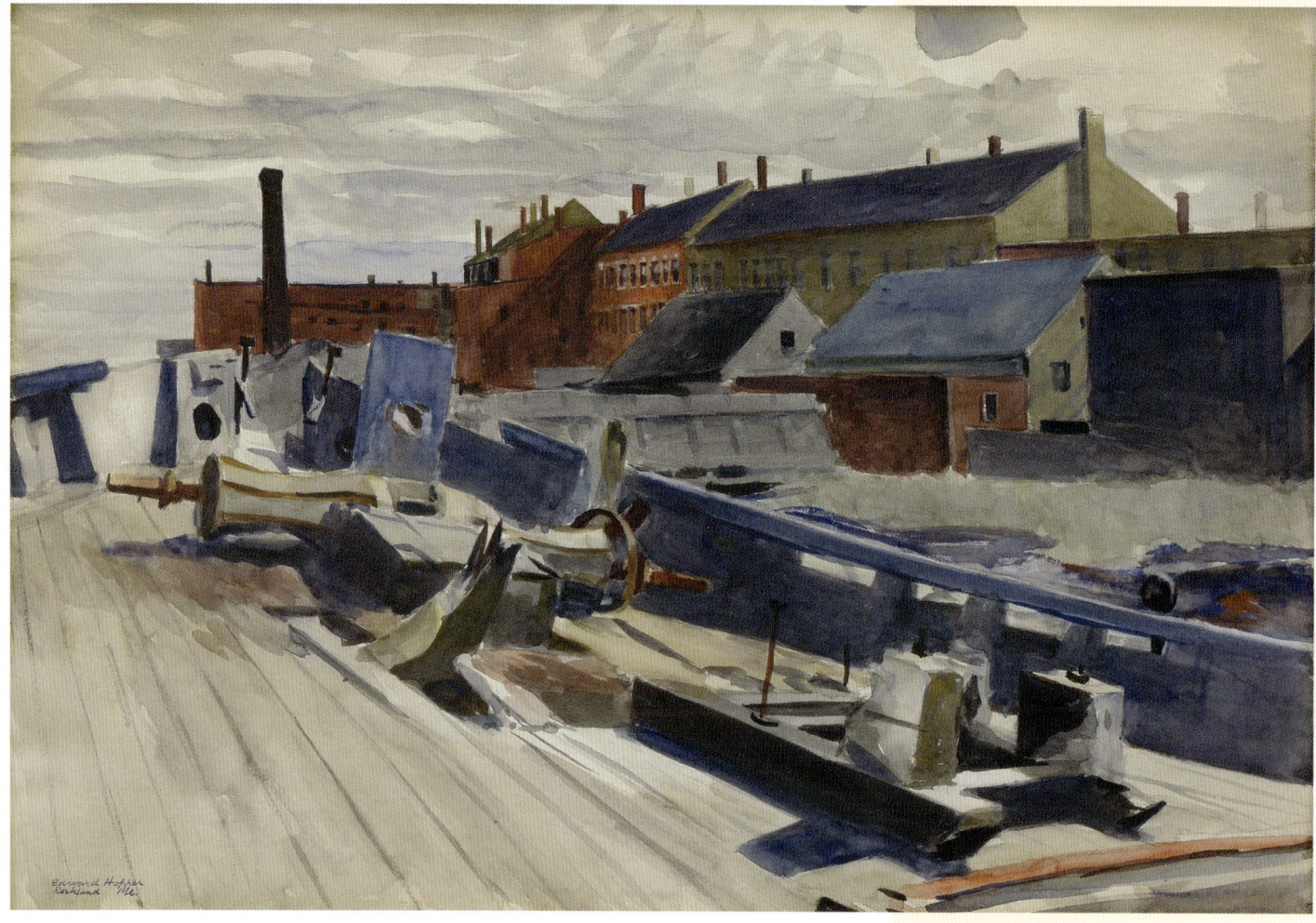

Edward Hopper's Maine painting expeditions began in 1914 when he visited Ogunquit. Later trips took him to Monhegan Island, Portland, and Rockland, where he spent seven weeks in the summer of 1926. In addition to images of the lime quarries and a classic Victorian captain's house, Hopper (1882–1967) made studies of the waterfront, with a special focus on the ragtag assortment of vessels tied up to the docks. In disrepair, the ship in *Schooner's Hull* signals the end of the era of large sailing ships on the Maine coast.

"My watercolors are all done from nature—direct out-of-doors—and not made as sketches," Hopper once noted. His intimate impressions of place have influenced more than a handful of contemporary Maine painters, as we shall see later on.

Edward Hopper
Schooner's Hull, 1926
Watercolor on paper,
13 ⅝ x 19 ⅞ in.
Given in memory of Mr. and Mrs. Robert Wheelwright and in honor of A. Bodine Lamont by the Lieber Family
© 2019 Heirs of Josephine N. Hopper
Licensed by Artists Rights Society (ARS), New York City

Yesterday

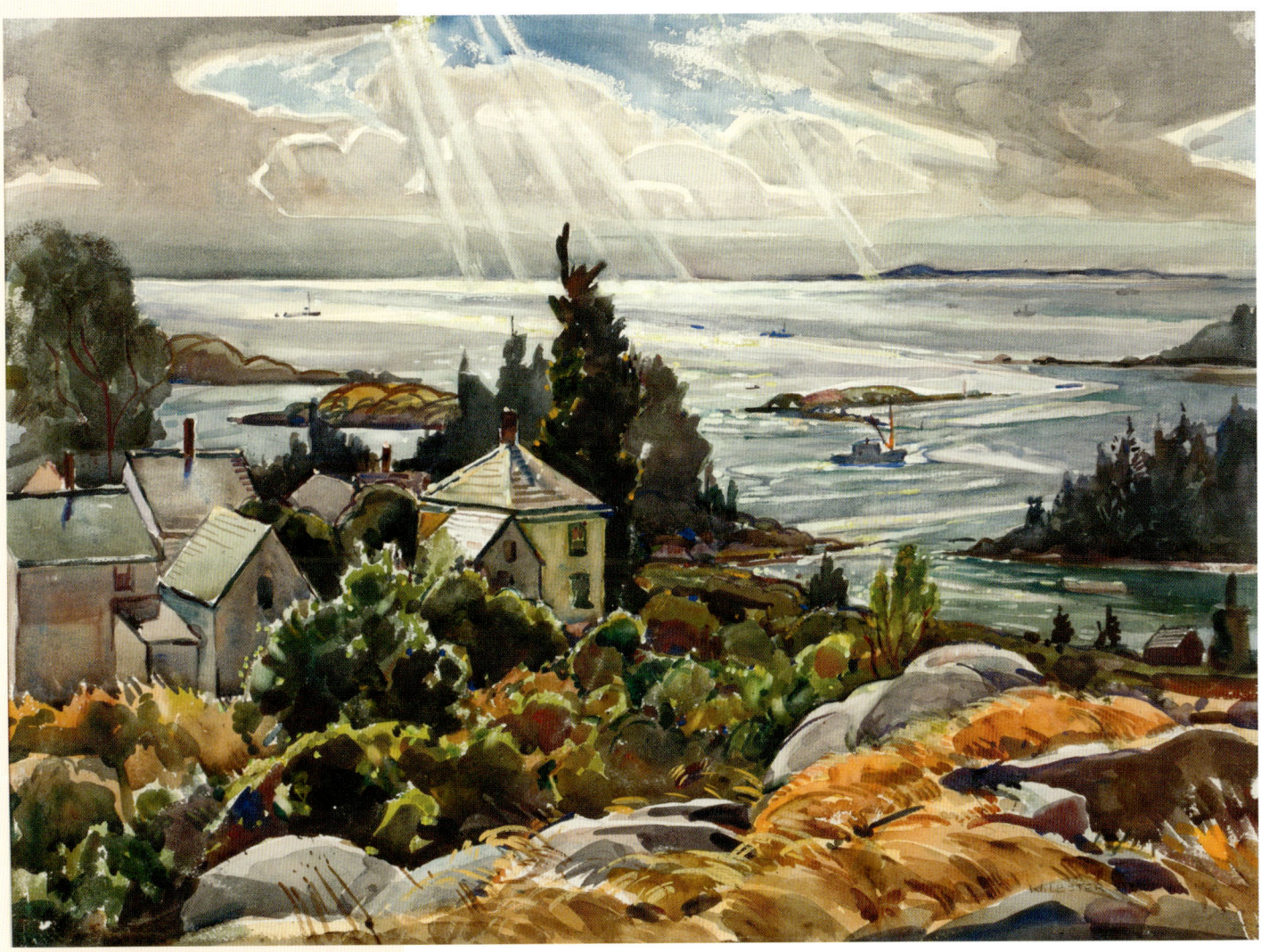

William Lester Stevens
Epic of Vinalhaven, Maine, n.d.
Watercolor on paper, 22 x 30 in.
Courtesy of the Vose Galleries
Boston, Mass.

Hopper's contemporary and fellow realist **William Lester Stevens** (1888–1969) also wielded a deft watercolor brush as witnessed in his painting *Epic of Vinalhaven, Maine*. After spending time hunting the best vantage point, Stevens painted rapidly and with great facility. His wide-angle view features a handful of island houses, fishing boats and a line of glory rays piercing distant clouds, the latter underscoring the "epic" in the title. Stevens taught at Princeton and Boston universities, as well as in Rockport, Mass., where he helped found the Rockport Art Association. The artist told his students, "Don't paint to sell. Paint because you can't help it!"

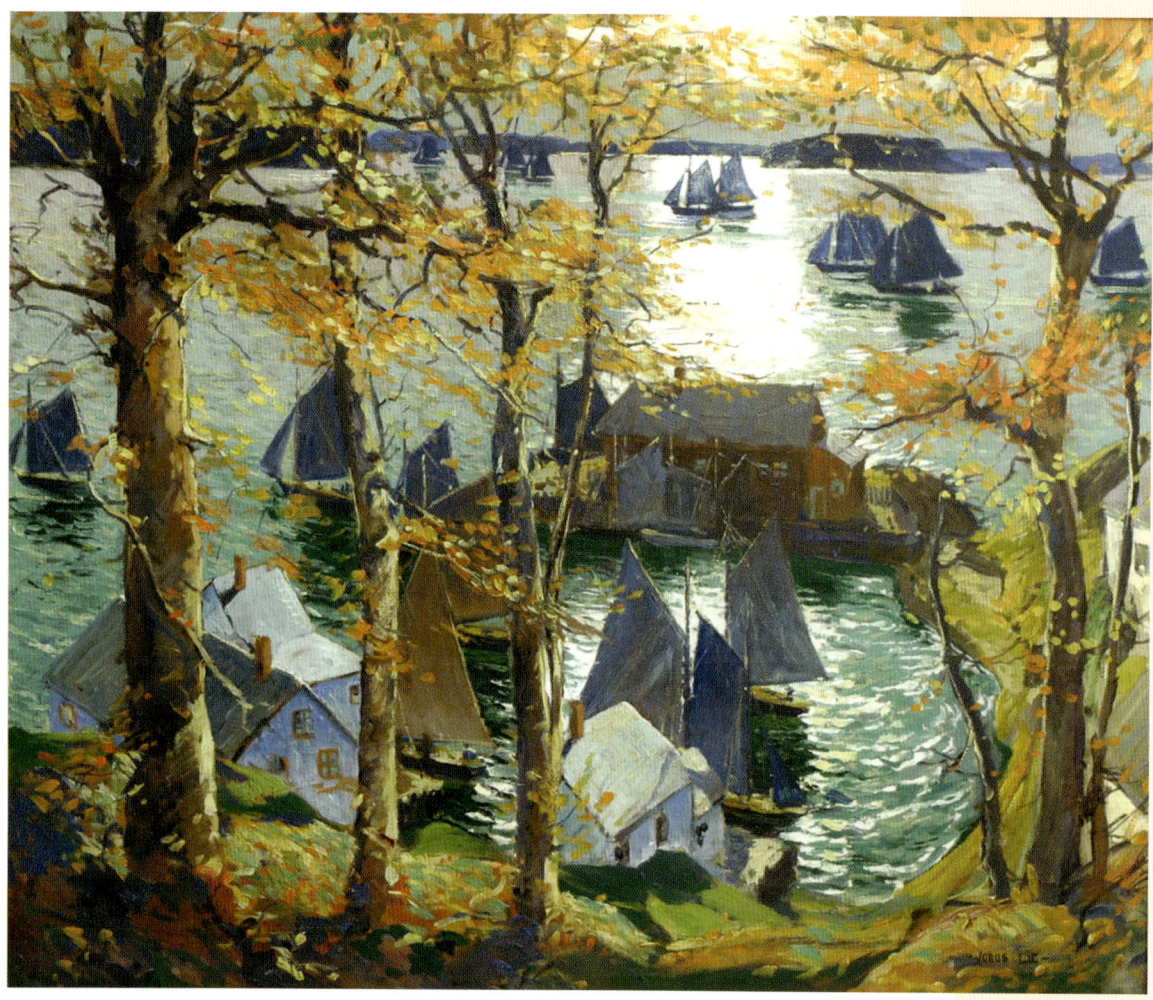

A latter-day impressionist with ties to the Cape Ann art colony, the Norwegian-born painter **Jonas Lie** (1880–1940) brought a romantic eye to his Maine coast vistas. His images of sailboats cruising Penobscot Bay waters celebrate the splendors of summertime outings. A sailor himself—he joined President Franklin Delano Roosevelt on sailing trips from Campobello—Lie was expert at depicting the angular geometries of sails crossing the waters. Other high notes in his career include a series of paintings of the Panama Canal and his prestigious post as the first foreign-born president of the National Academy of Design in New York.

Jonas Lie
Romantic Sunset, Maine, c. 1920s
Oil on canvas
Courtesy of Wikimedia Commons

Yesterday

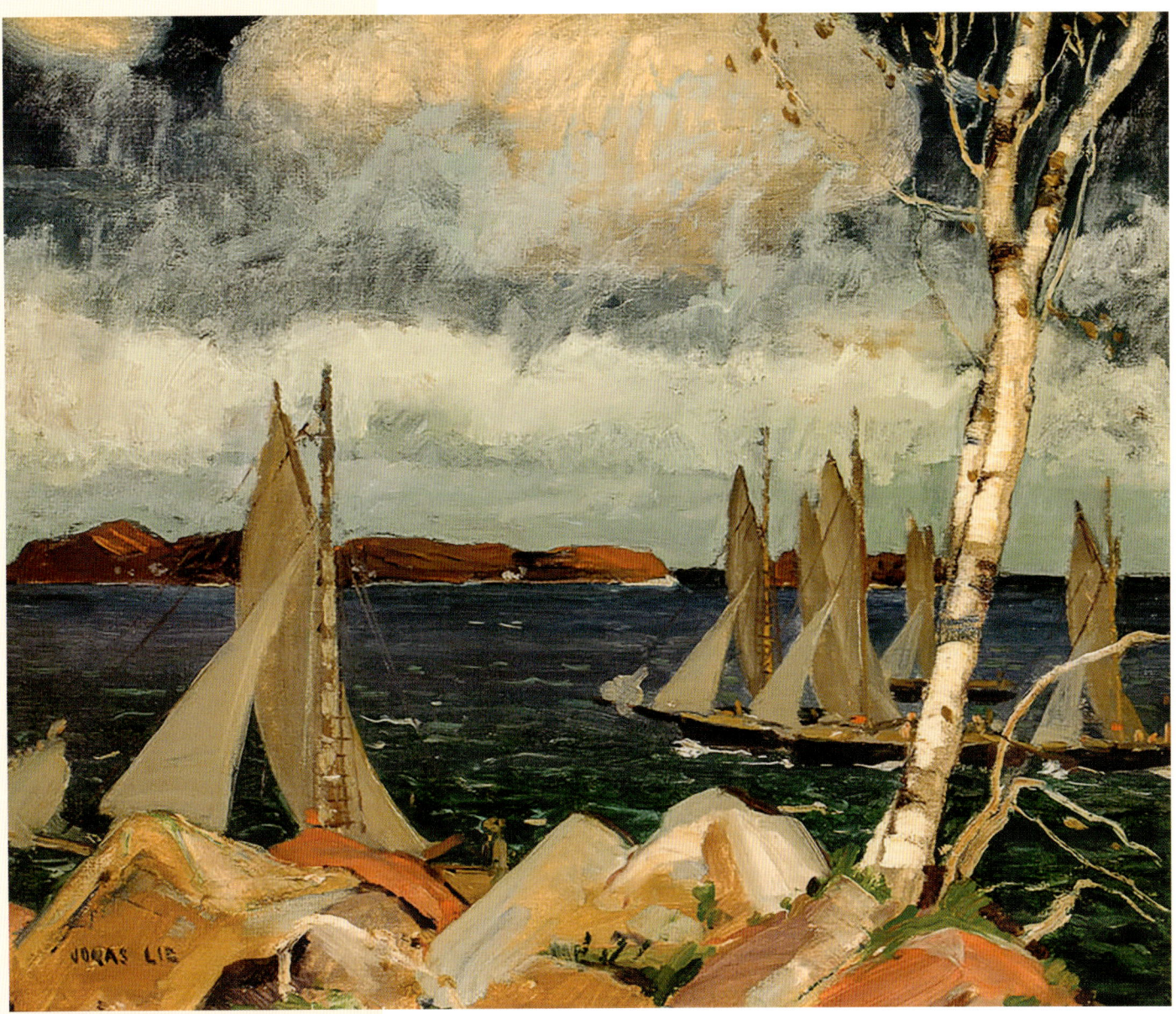

Jonas Lie
Yachting on the Maine Coast,
c. 1920s
Oil on canvas
Courtesy of Wikimedia Commons

The Modernists Come to Maine

American modernism arrived in Maine in the early 1900s when the likes of **William Zorach** (1887–1966) and **John Marin** (1870–1953) started their forays along the coast in search of subject matter. Both artists had exhibited paintings in the landmark Armory show in New York City in 1913 (as had Henri, Bellows, Luks, Kroll, Hopper, and Lie), which introduced many viewers to modern European art—and shocked them by its new visions of what art might look like. Cubism and other ground-breaking styles subsequently inspired American artists to greater experimentation.

When Zorach set up shop in Stonington in the summer of 1919, he used his Cubist-influenced approach to create images of the seacoast town with sailing vessels. Art historian Donelson Hoopes notes that "the enclosed space and crystalline forms of his *Boat in the Early Morning* bore a remarkable affinity to Marin's innovative style."

William Zorach
Boat in the Early Morning, Stonington, Maine, 1919
Watercolor and charcoal on paper
22 x 15 in.
Photo courtesy of the
Zorach Collection, LLC

Yesterday

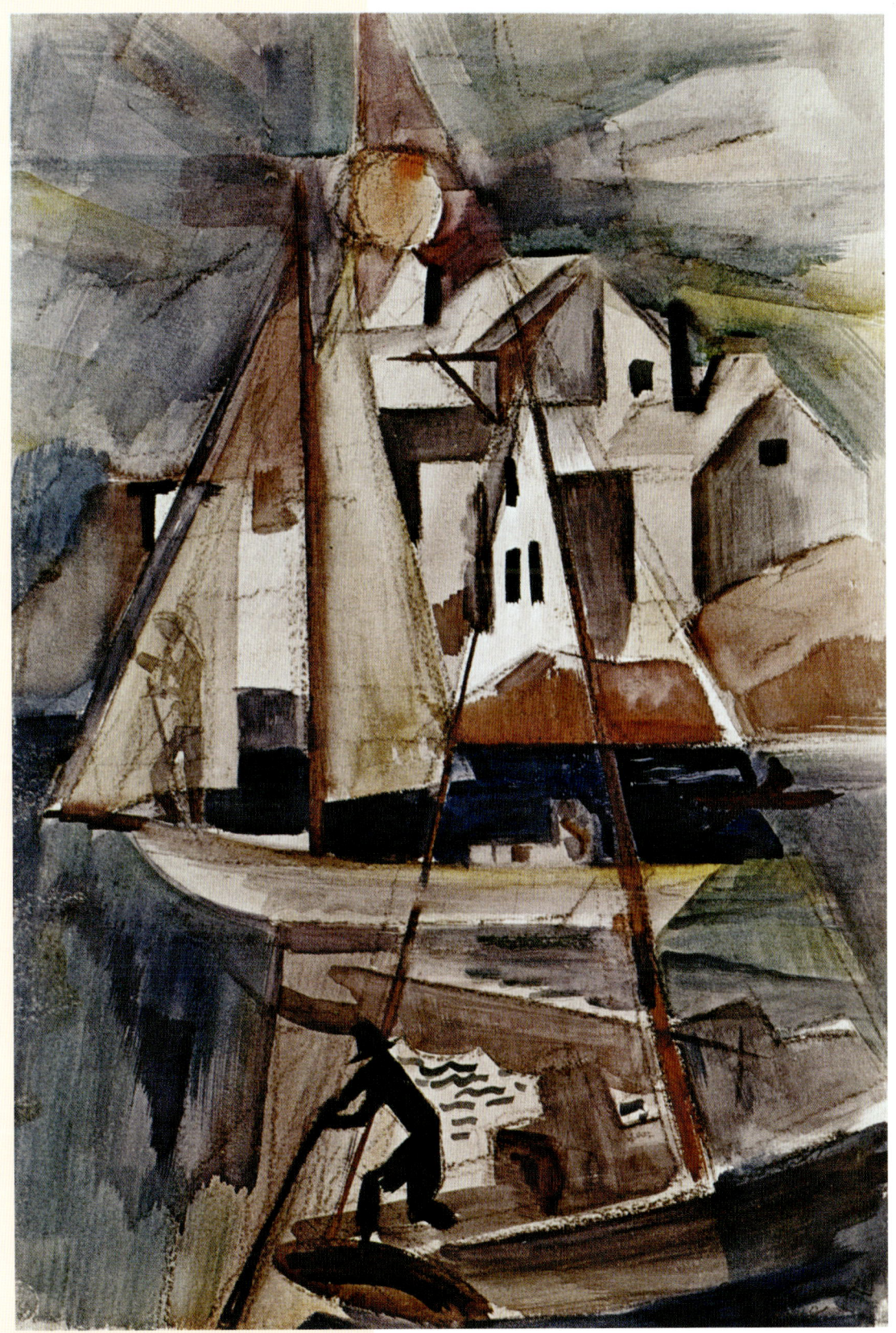

Art of Penobscot Bay

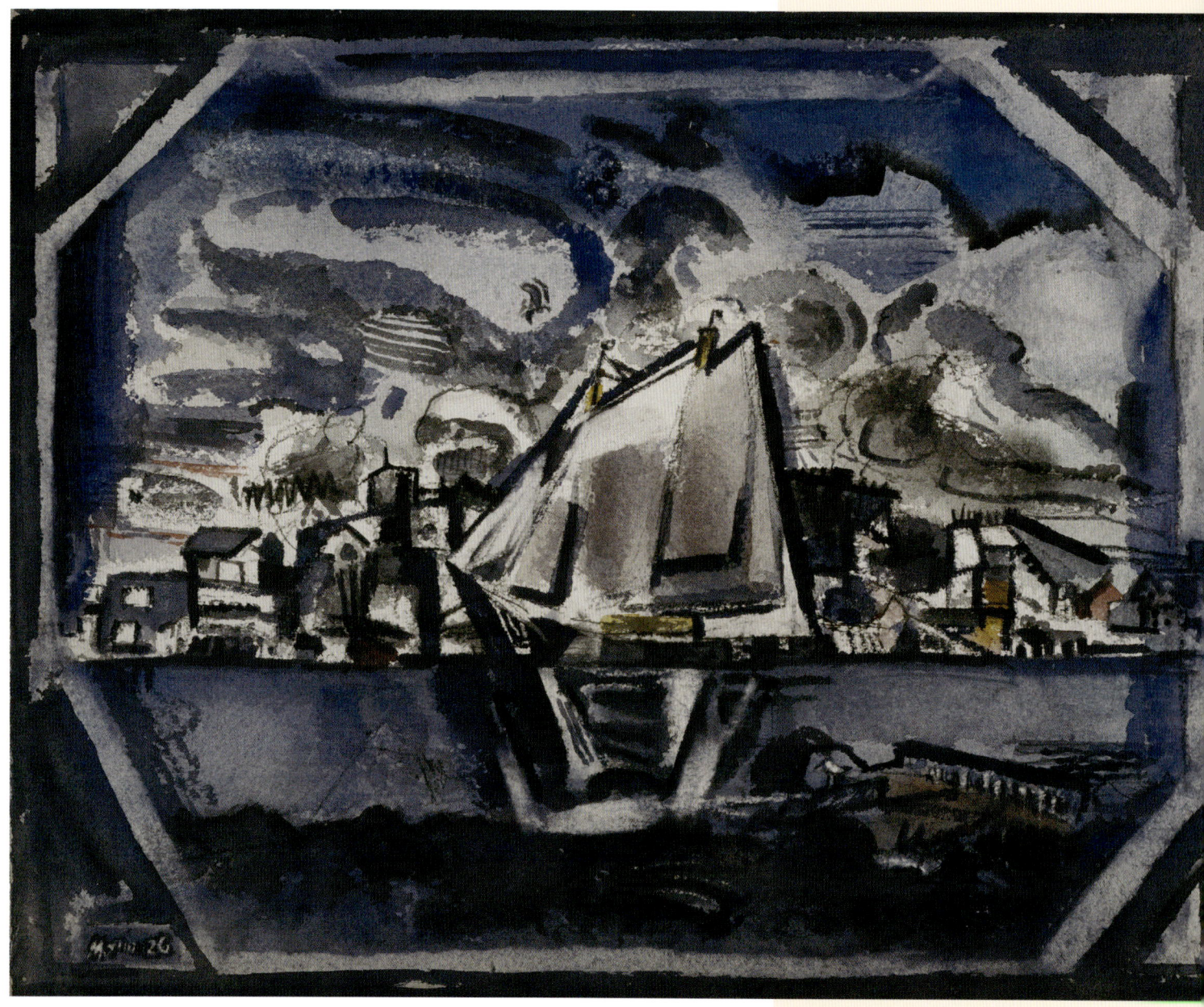

Marin came to Stonington the same summer and immediately took a shine to the place. "Some of the views with innumerable islands are bully," he wrote to his famed New York City dealer, champion of modernist painters and pioneering photographer Alfred Stieglitz. Over the next ten or so years, he returned to paint nearly every summer, never wanting for subjects. "This place has gotten me by the nape of the neck," he wrote Stieglitz on September 11, 1926. "Once I get here, I forget other places, which is a failing I have that I am perfectly aware of."

John Marin
Pertaining to Stonington Harbor, Maine No. 1, 1926
Watercolor, black crayon, and charcoal on cream wove paper,
13 3/8 x 17 1/16 in.
Philadelphia Museum of Art
The Alfred Steiglitz Collection, 1949
Marin, John ©ARS, New York City

Yesterday

John Marin
Movement No. 24—Pertaining to Deer Isle—the Road, 1927
Watercolor, black pencil, and crayon on ivory wove paper,
14 3/8 x 17 5/8 in.
The Art Institute of Chicago
Alfred Steiglitz Collection
Marin, John © ARS, New York City

The titles of several of Marin's watercolor paintings during this time use the phrase "pertaining to" to indicate that what they depict related to a specific place but were not meant to be exact portrayals. *Pertaining to Stonington Harbor, Maine, No. 1*, 1926, for example, offers a classic view of the town from nearby Crotch Island, the cluster of waterfront structures disrupted by the broad sails of a schooner.

Even more inventive is *Movement No. 24—Pertaining to Deer Isle—The Road* (1927). Here Marin adds expressionist energy to his riff on an island byway through dashes of color and linear marks, including a line of telephone poles stitched along the right edge. He painted on site, which lends an immediacy to the image.

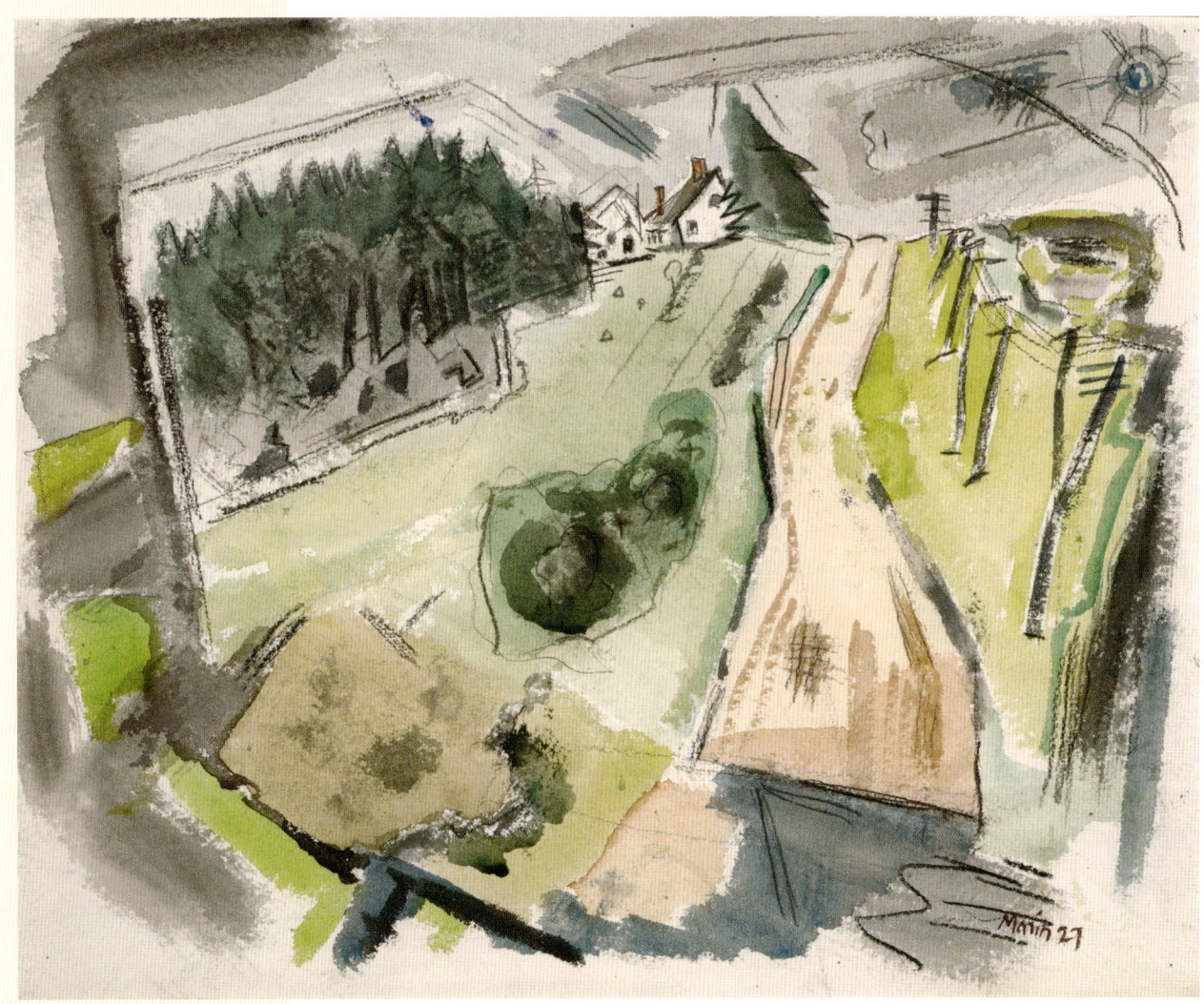

Another member of Stieglitz's stable, **Marsden Hartley** (1877–1943) began his painting life in his home state of Maine and then returned after spending time in New York, the Southwest, Mexico, and Europe. Living an itinerant life, he drifted around Maine, with stays in Georgetown, Bangor, Corea, and West Brooksville.

Hartley spent the summer of 1939 in West Brooksville at Bagaduce Farm, with his friends Claire Spencer and John Evans. While exploring the area, he came upon a logjam near the confluence of the Bagaduce River and Penobscot Bay. In his essay "An Ambivalent Prodigal," writer Randall Griffey wrote that Hartley was drawn to "the repetitive interlocking and overlapping forms that the subject of logging provided, the kind of patterning at which he excelled."

A forthright representation of flotsam and jetsam—a shoe, a barrel, and a lobster trap mix with the clustered logs—Hartley's painting also documents an element of Maine's timber industry. As George Wasson notes in *Sailing Days on the Penobscot*, logs often escaped from river drives and ended up on the shores of the bay, at times creating a navigational hazard.

Art historians often list **Maurice Freedman** (1904–1985) alongside such contemporaries as Hartley, Arthur Dove, and Milton Avery as an American modernist. American modernist artists adopted some of the tenets of contemporary European painting, including Cubist ideas, in their landscape, still-life, and portrait paintings, using the unmixed bright colors of the Fauvists and experimenting with non-objective geometric and organic shapes.

In his painting *Stonington Pier* (c. 1955), Freedman is closest to Hartley: The simplified trees, the faceless fishermen, and the length of rope might have been painted by the Lewiston-born artist.

Marsden Hartley
Log Jam, Penobscot Bay, 1940–41
Oil on Masonite, 30 1/16 x 40 7/8 in.
Gift of Robert H. Tannahill
Detroit Institute of Arts, USA
© Detroit Institute of Arts
Photo by Bridgeman Images

Yesterday

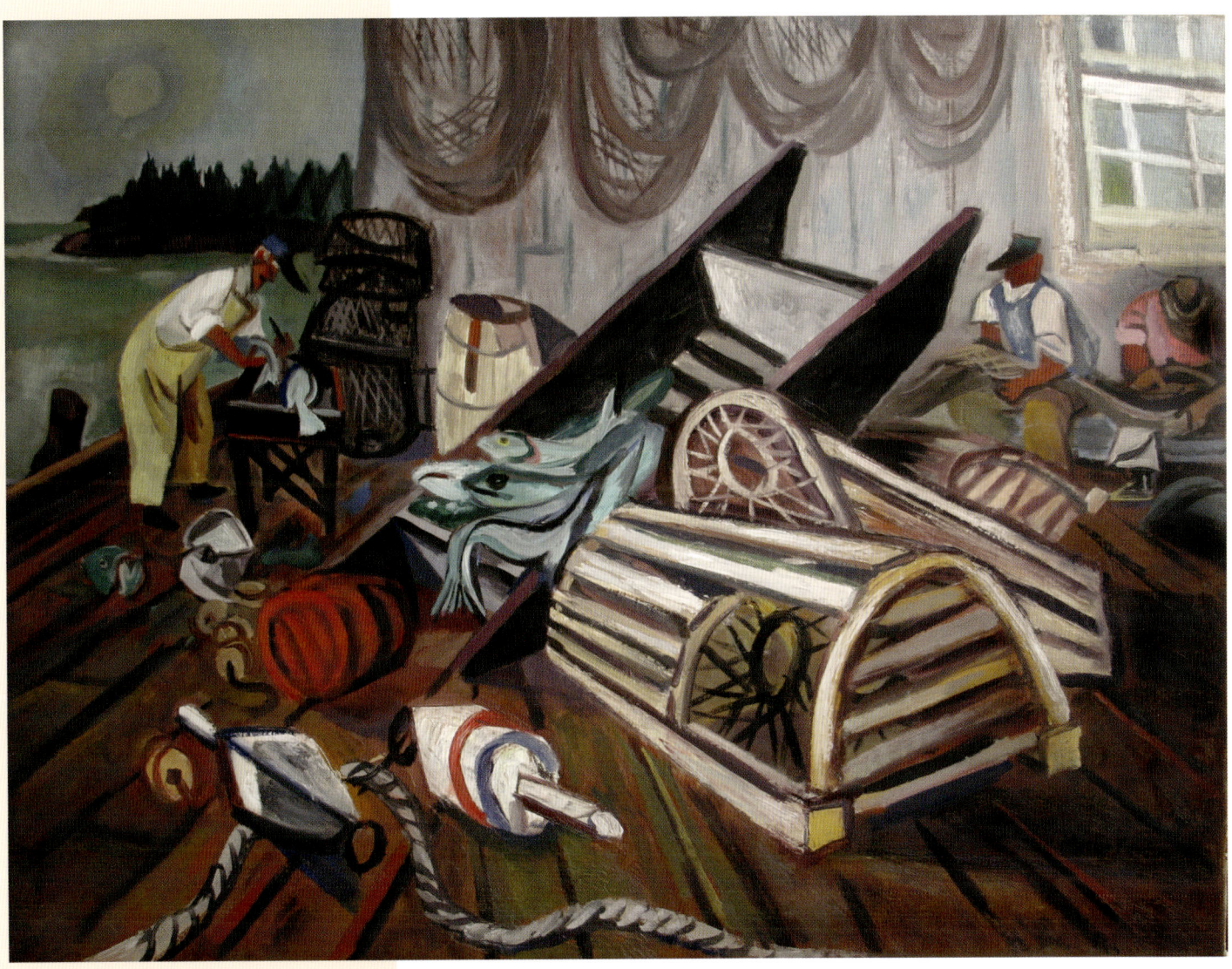

Maurice Freedman
Stonington Pier, 1954
Oil on canvas, 30 x 40 in.
Courtesy of Greenhut Galleries

Stonington Pier offers a full range of marine enterprises—a fisherman cutting fish, lobster traps, and net menders. In an interview with his son Joel, Freedman described how being sensitive to "what's there" was "like a door that suddenly opens and then you slowly walk in." Once inside, the painter would review the colors and forms around him and set out to discover the logic of the scene. "All this is so reassuring to your life," Freedman noted, "that you go on living because it's so beautiful."

The same goes for the viewer of Freedman's *Stonington Pier*. We enter this world he saw and painted in Stonington and find a kind of comfort in the tableau—men hard at work, a bounty of fish, a place where every object is meaningful.

Art of Penobscot Bay

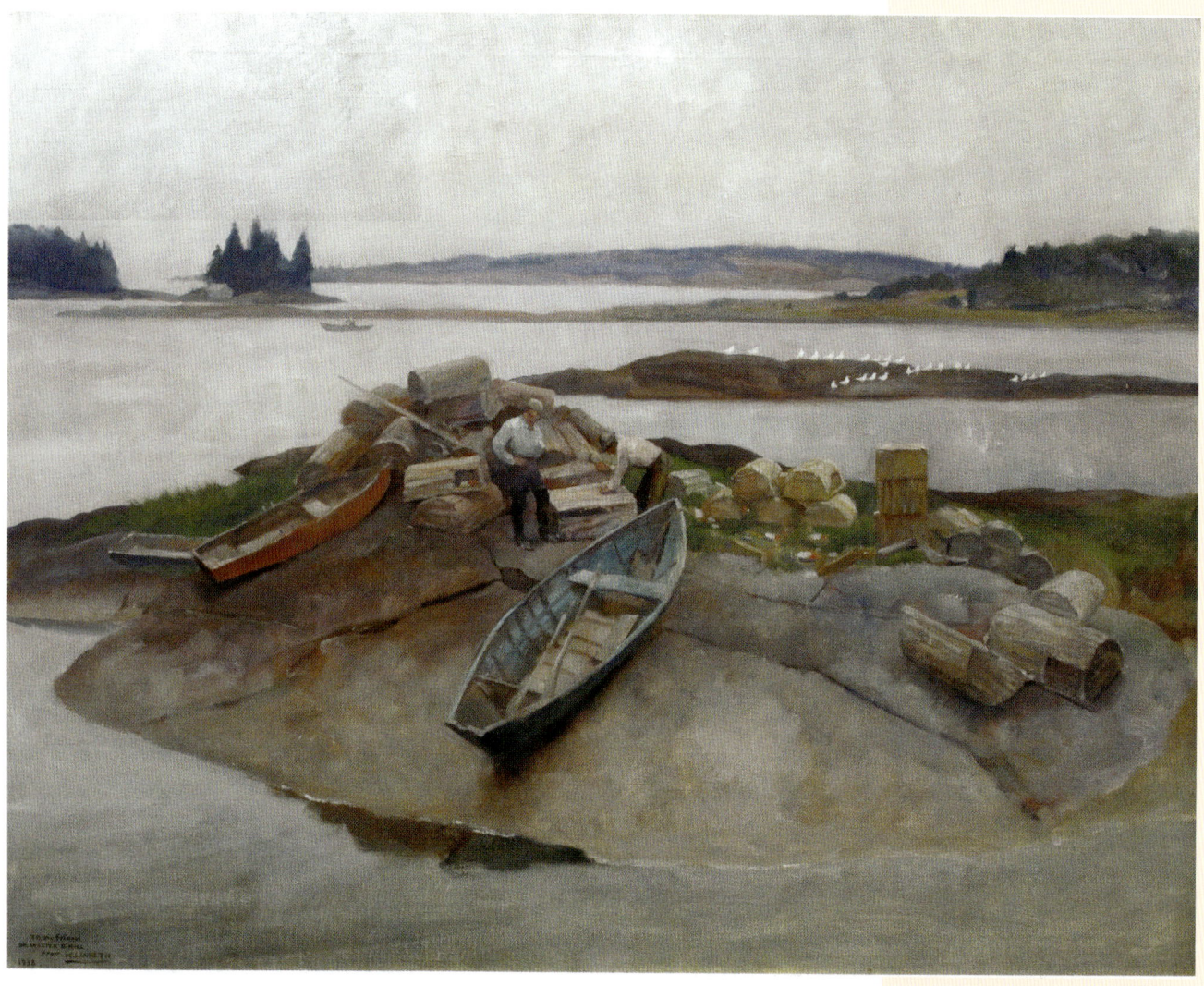

The line of realist painters going back to Frederic Church, Winslow Homer and others gained new proponents on the shores of Penobscot Bay. The renowned illustrator **N. C. Wyeth** (1882–1945), founding father of a line of extraordinary artists that includes his son Andrew and grandson Jamie, often focused on the heroic aspects of Maine coast livelihoods, including the lobsterman who, in his day, hauled traps by hand from small craft. *Mending Traps, Martinsville, Maine* (1938), shows two lobstermen going about their business on a bare ledge outcropping in Mosquito Cove around a coastal bend from Port Clyde. The artist inscribed it "To my friend Dr. Walter D. Hall from N. C. Wyeth, 1938."

N. C. Wyeth
Mending Traps, Martinsville, Maine,
1938
Oil on canvas, 31 ⅞ x 40 in.
DeNormandie Family Collection

Yesterday

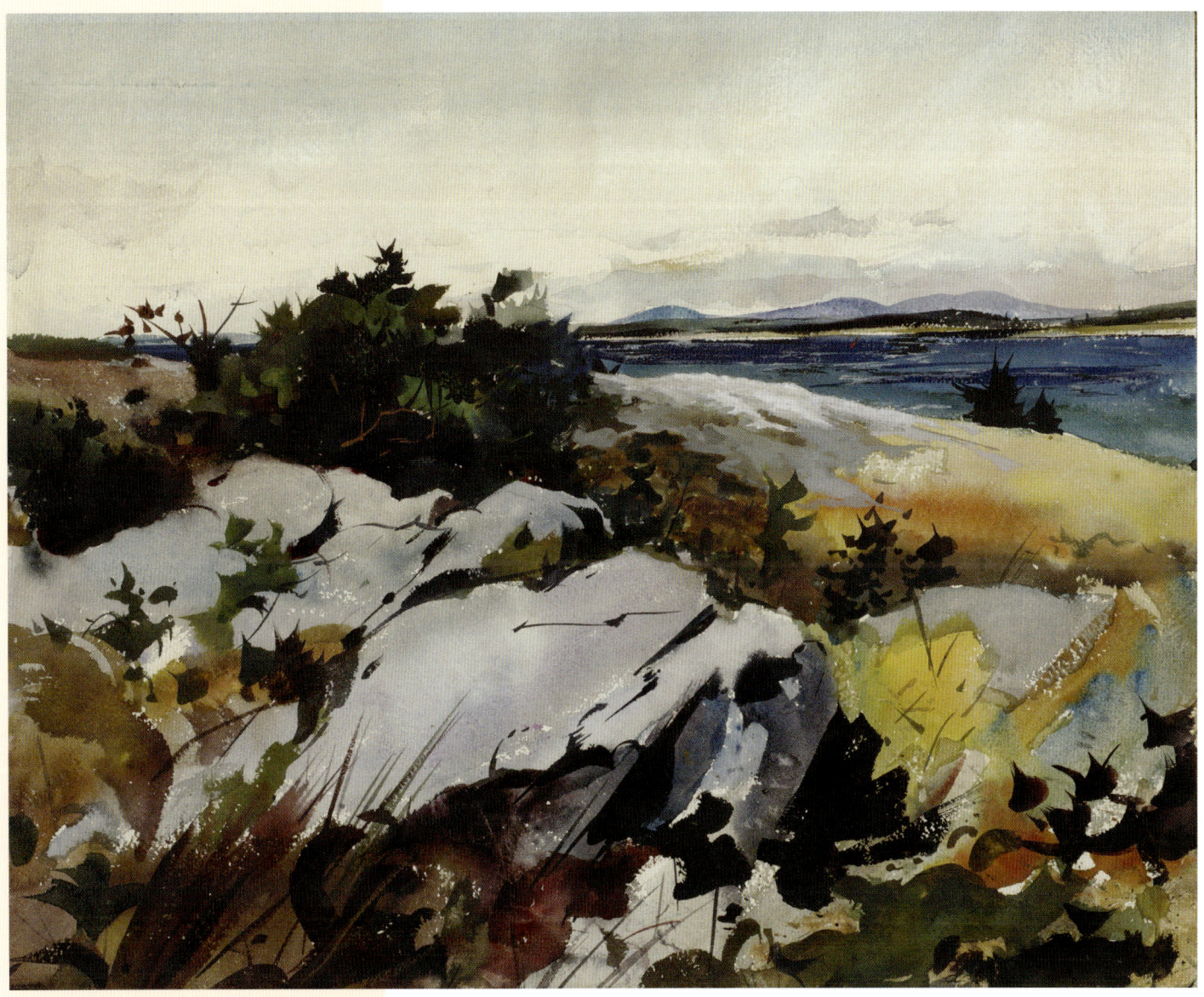

Andrew Wyeth
Camden Hills, Maine, n.d.
Watercolor on paper, 21 x 23 in.
Gift of Margaret G. Decker
Wyeth, Andrew ©ARS, New York City
Francis Lehman Loeb Art Center
Vassar College, Poughkeepsie,
New York

Wyeth purchased a "little storm-beaten homestead" in Port Clyde in 1920 and began summering there in 1930 after making extensive repairs. His son **Andrew Wyeth** (1917–2009) shared his studio and the two went on painting excursions along the coast, where Andrew also fell under the spell of the Maine landscape and its people.

Before Andrew Wyeth established himself as a virtuoso creator of poetic and often enigmatic egg tempera paintings of seaside milieus and Maine folk, he excelled in watercolor, producing studies that earned him comparisons to Homer. The undated *Camden Hills, Maine* exemplifies that early brilliance, the rocky ledge and dark underbrush meticulously limned.

Art of Penobscot Bay

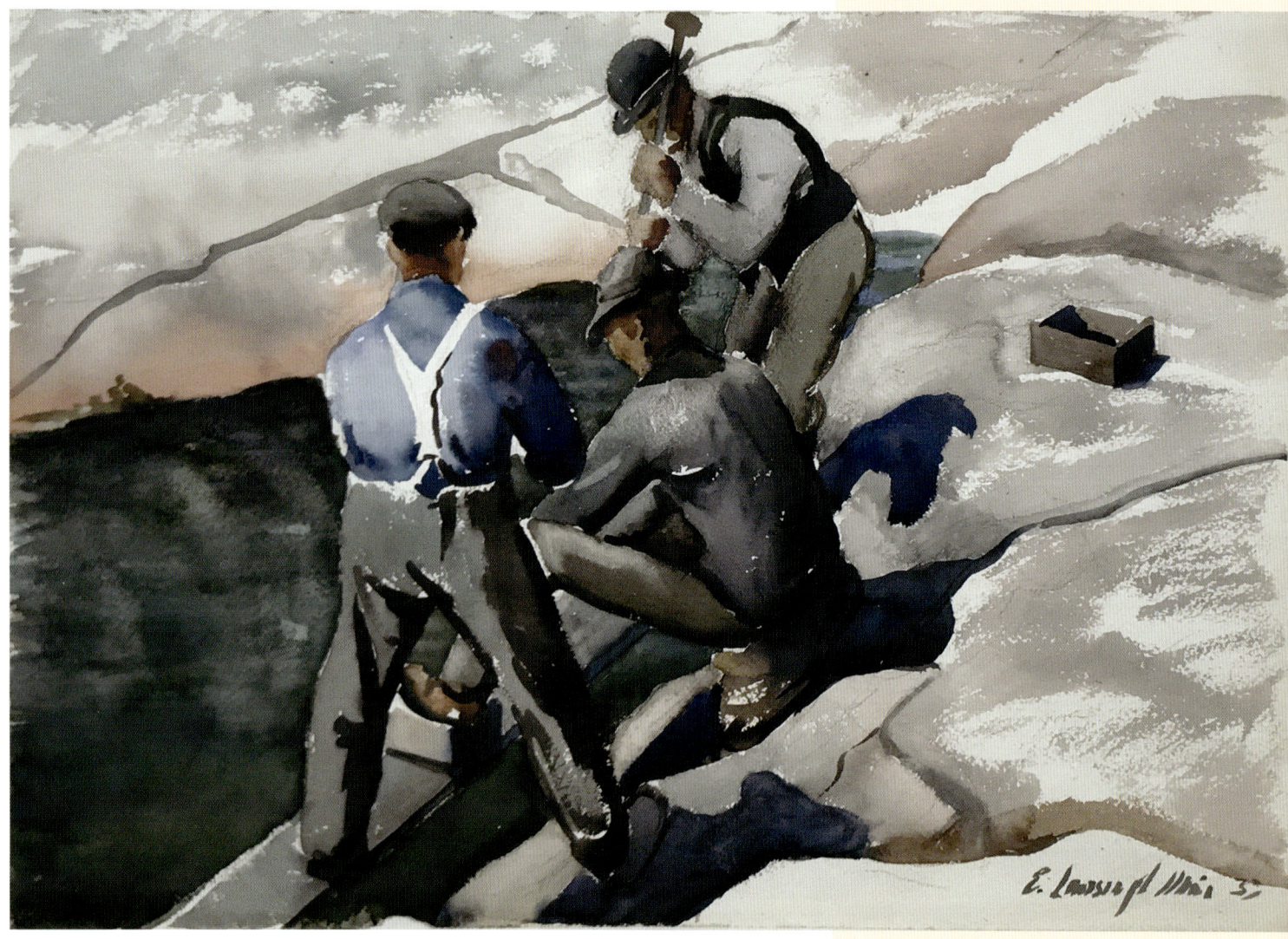

Emily Muir (1904–2003) and **William Muir** (1902–1964) met while attending the Art Students League in New York City in the 1920s. After moving to Stonington in 1939, they wasted no time in absorbing—and painting—their new surroundings. The former's watercolor study of quarriers on nearby Crotch Island dates from that first year. A man in bowler hat and vest raises a hammer while his fellow stone workers prepare for the strike. Granite surrounds them. According to a former island quarry worker, at one time two hundred men worked there, producing finished granite on site.

In addition to being a painter, Muir was also a self-taught architect and designer, as well as an author, lecturer, and conservationist. Island Institute founder Philip Conkling referred to her as a "practical visionary," protecting islands from development.

Emily Muir
Quarriers, 1939
Watercolor on paper,
13 ½ x 19 ½ in.
Bequest of Mrs. Elizabeth B. Noyce
The Farnsworth Art Museum,
1997.3.36

Yesterday

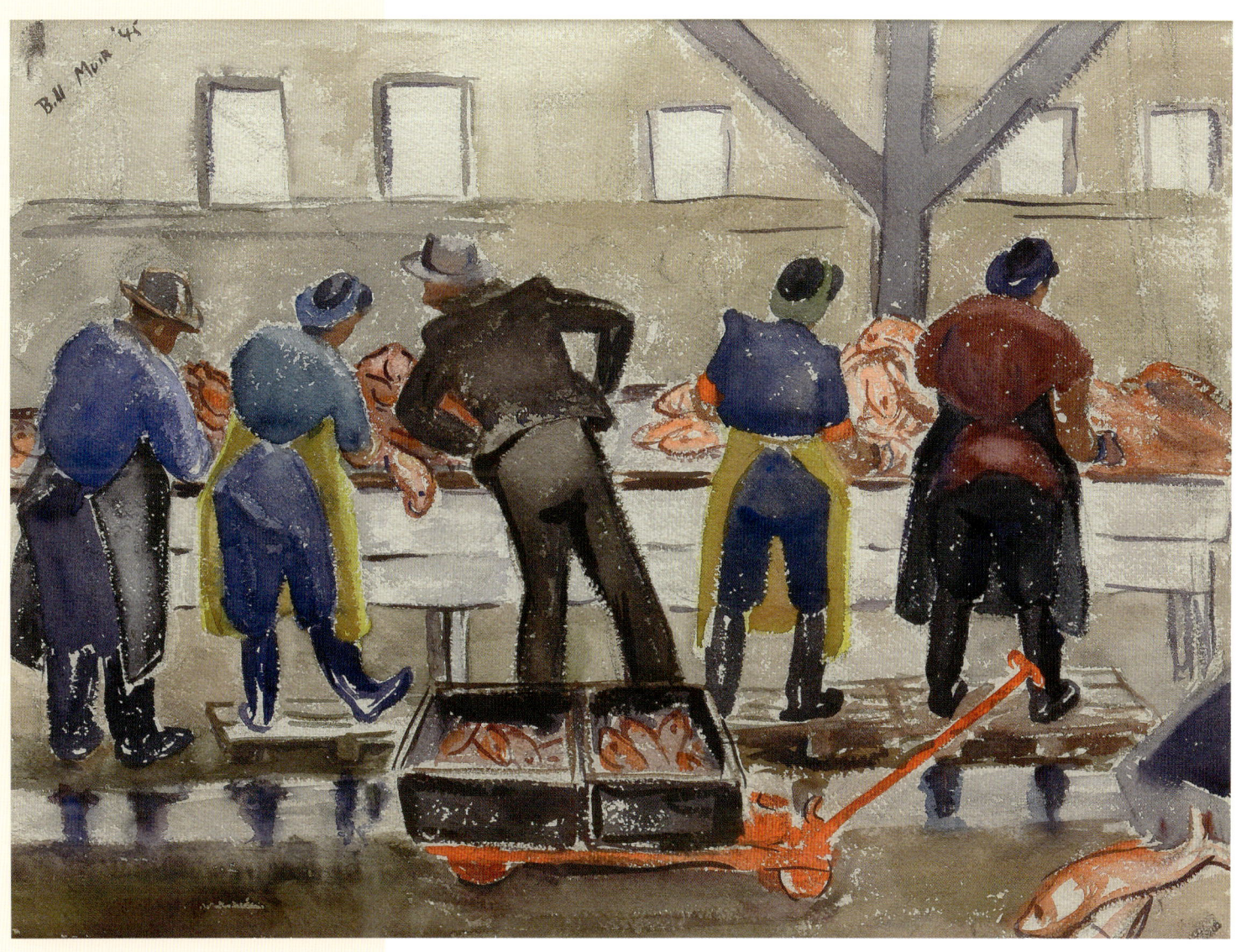

William Muir
Fish Packing Plant, 1945
Watercolor on paper,
14 5/8 x 19 5/8 in.
Bequest of Mrs. Elizabeth B. Noyce
The Farnsworth Art Museum,
1997.3.40

Best known for his sculptures, which include a tribute in bronze to Stonington's stone cutters, William Muir turned to watercolor from time to time to capture the local scene. His *Fish Packing Plant* has an almost comical feel to it as the supervisor leans over to inspect the work of the sardine cutters in their rubber aprons. The year he made the painting, the Stonington cannery was in full gear; today, what was once one of Maine's key industries is all but gone. In 1959, the Muirs helped locate property on Deer Isle for the Haystack Mountain School of Crafts, which moved there from Montville in 1961.

Art of Penobscot Bay

Although best known for his photographs, the globe-trotting **Eliot Elisofon** (1911–1973) also painted, primarily while at his summer home on Vinalhaven, from the 1940s until his death in 1973. Displaying a liveliness that harks back to John Marin, Elisofon's watercolors sometimes depict the local scene—an island fisherman crossing the water, a stack of lobster traps on the shore, a fishing shack bedecked with lobster buoys.

Eliot Elisofon
Vinalhaven, 1944
Watercolor on paper,
12 ½ x 18 ½ in.
Photo by William Trevaskis

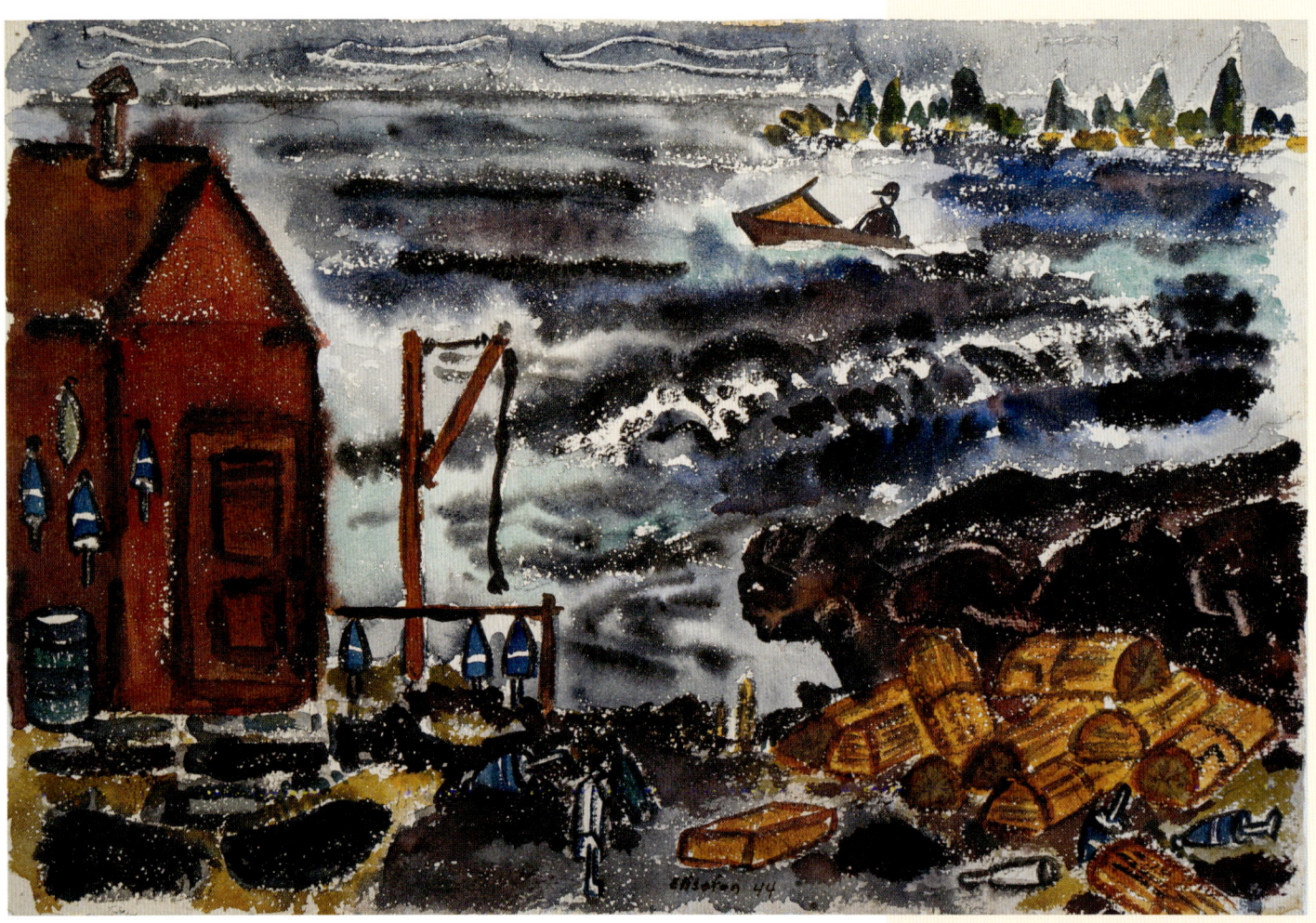

Yesterday

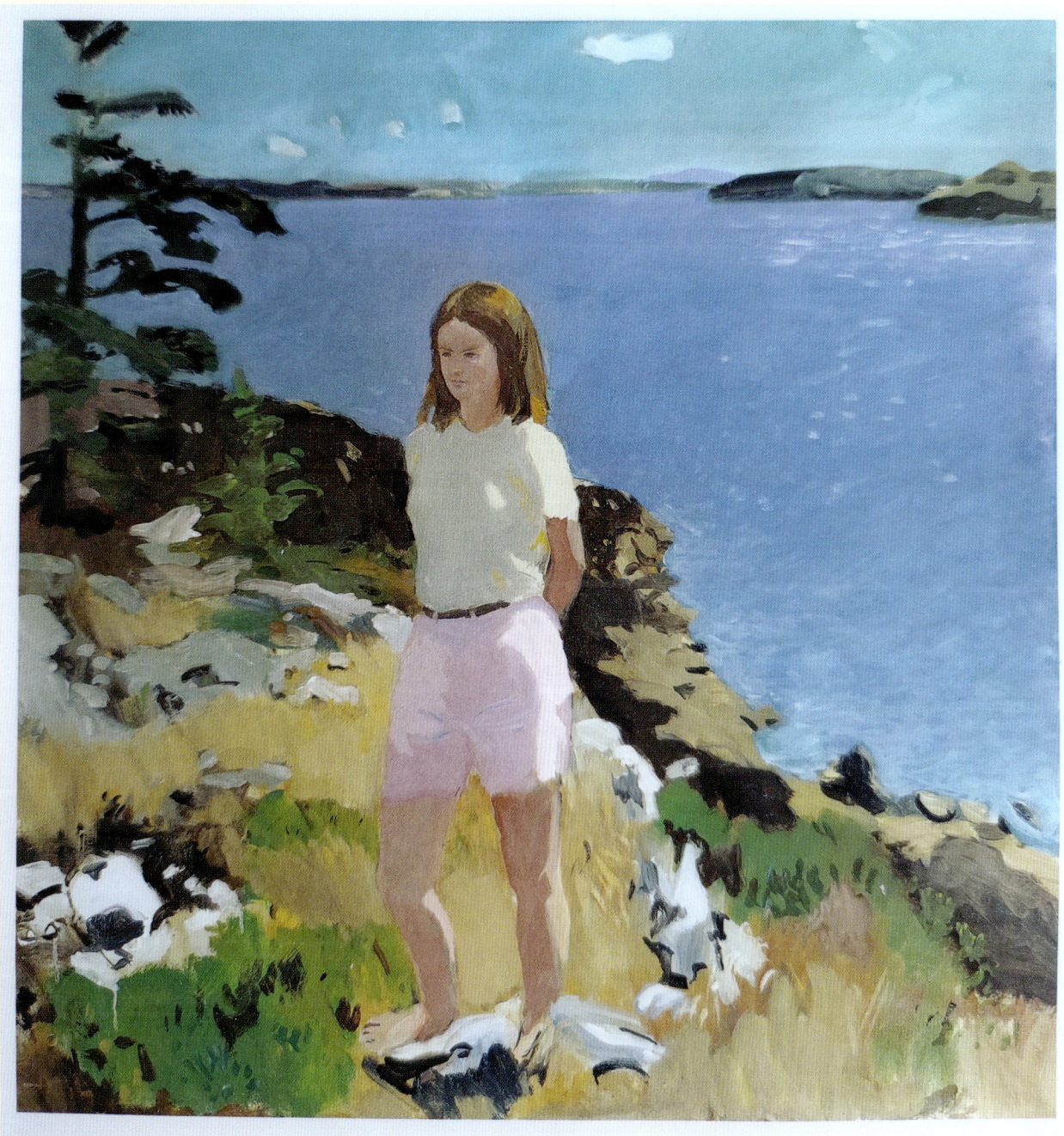

Fairfield Porter
Girl in a Landscape, 1965
Oil on canvas, 45 ½ x 44 in.
© 2022 The Estate of Fairfield Porter/Artists Rights Society (ARS), New York City
United Missouri Bank, Kansas City, Missouri

Fairfield Porter (1907–1975) spent a part of nearly every summer for thirty years on Great Spruce Island in the middle of Penobscot Bay. After his father, James Porter, a businessman and amateur naturalist from Illinois, purchased the 280-acre island in 1912, the family embraced it as a kind of northern Eden, a place that offered freedom to explore and grow—and paint.

Porter practiced what has come to be called "painterly realism" marked by loose, expressive brushwork. He often turned to friends and family for subjects, as in *Girl in a Landscape* (1965), which portrays his daughter Katherine casually posing barefoot before the blue stretches of the bay.

In her review of Porter's 1984 retrospective at the Whitney Museum, the *New York Times* critic Grace Glueck noted how the painter tended to be blunt with the human figure, "yet his carefully composed studies of friends and family members in domestic tableaux can't help projecting the warmth of his observation." She ranked his work "among the finest realist paintings produced in the United States since the end of World War II."

When they built a concrete tennis court on Great Spruce Head Island during World War I, suspicious neighbors thought it was a secret gun emplacement. Porter's painting *A Tennis Game* (1972), documents the leisure time enjoyed by summer islanders. In doubles formation, the four men prepare to play in their spruce-surrounded sanctuary.

With his immersion in painting from life on the island and his deep involvement in the radical art world of New York City, Porter's philosophy as artist and critic found parallels in the precepts of both realism and abstract expressionism. He wrote of the important space between what painters can consciously control and what actually occurs in the process of painting—the importance of surface, spontaneity, painting directly from life, sensations, and vitality.

Fairfield Porter
The Tennis Game, 1972
Oil on canvas, 72 ¼ x 62 ¼ in.
Lauren Rogers Museum,
Laurel, Mississippi.
Purchased in part with funds from
Mississippi Arts Commission, 73.78

Yesterday

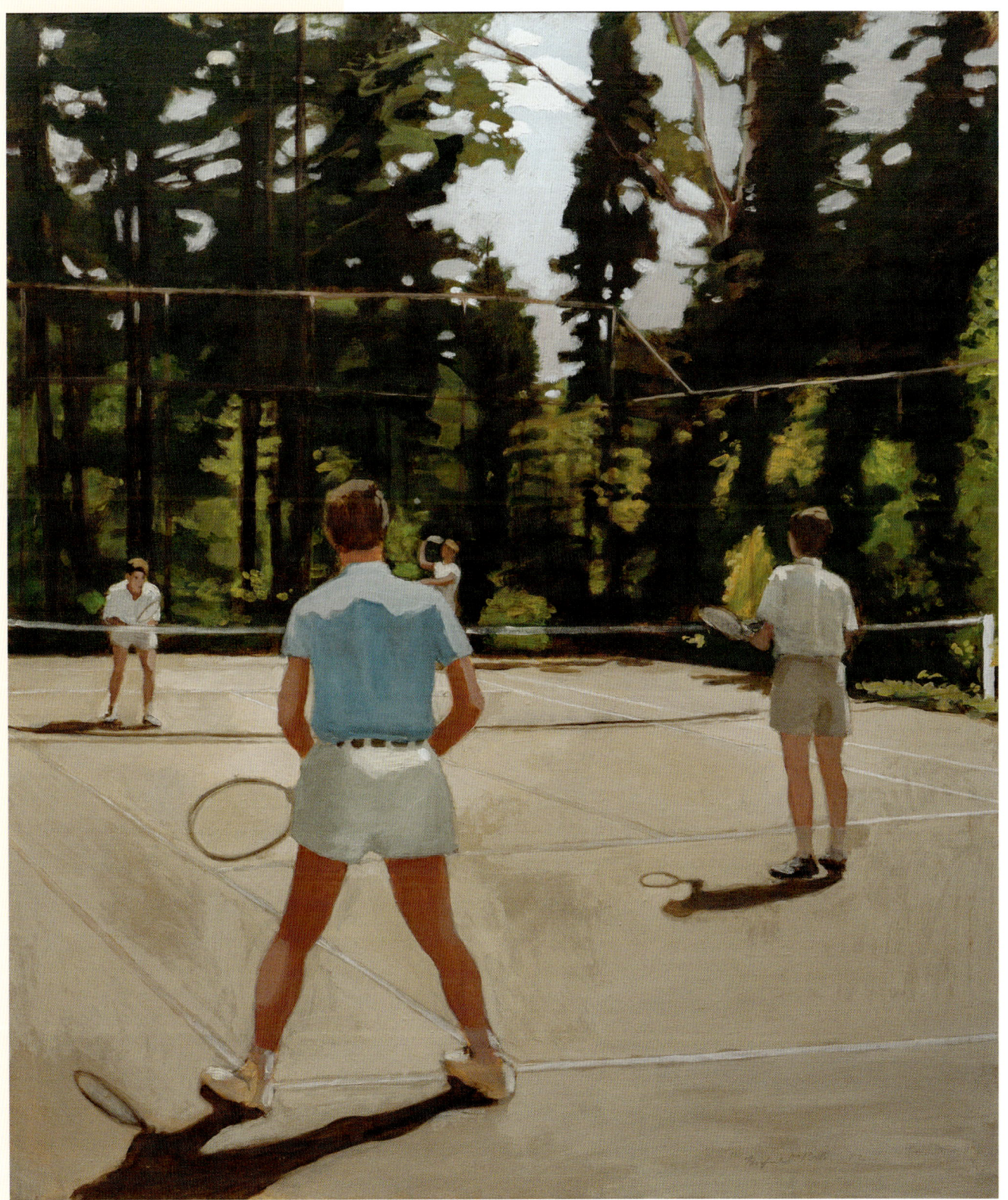

43

Art of Penobscot Bay

A contemporary of Porter, **William Kienbusch** (1914–1980) started painting in Maine and Penobscot Bay in the 1940s. Like Porter he drew the elements of his subjects from nature. He spoke of his work as "a translation, a language, to communicate a world." Like Porter, he admired the work of Willem de Kooning, a leader in the field of Abstract Expressionism.

In his essay "The Diversity of Our Times, 1940–1963," part of the landmark survey *Maine and Its Role in American Art: 1740–1963,* art historian James Carpenter placed Kienbusch's abstract paintings at the "opposite pole" from Andrew Wyeth's realist work. Influenced by Abstract Expressionism and his heroes Hartley, Marin, and Arthur Dove, Kienbusch brought new energy to Maine subjects, including islands, bell buoys, sea grass, and ledges. In doing so, he never lost touch with the landscape, always retaining contact with what Carpenter called "the world of visual experience."

Once the home of a granite quarry industry and now part of the Outward Bound School, Hurricane Island was Kienbusch's favorite place in Maine. He would hire a lobsterman on Vinalhaven Island to drop him off for the day so he could wander the abandoned island, taking photos with his Brownie camera and making quick drawings to use as prompts for paintings made in his summer digs and his New York City studio. He likened the experience to a dream—"an epiphany of nature," as art historian Donelson Hoopes put it, writing about Kienbusch's first visit to the island in 1951.

Kienbusch found motifs everywhere in the ruins of the island. *Across Four Pines, Hurricane Island* highlights the power of his vision. In the painting, the rich blue of Penobscot Bay serves as backdrop to a view from the island, the four pines in the title framing a way to the sea. Kienbusch creates movement through sweeps of the brush—the island is a living thing.

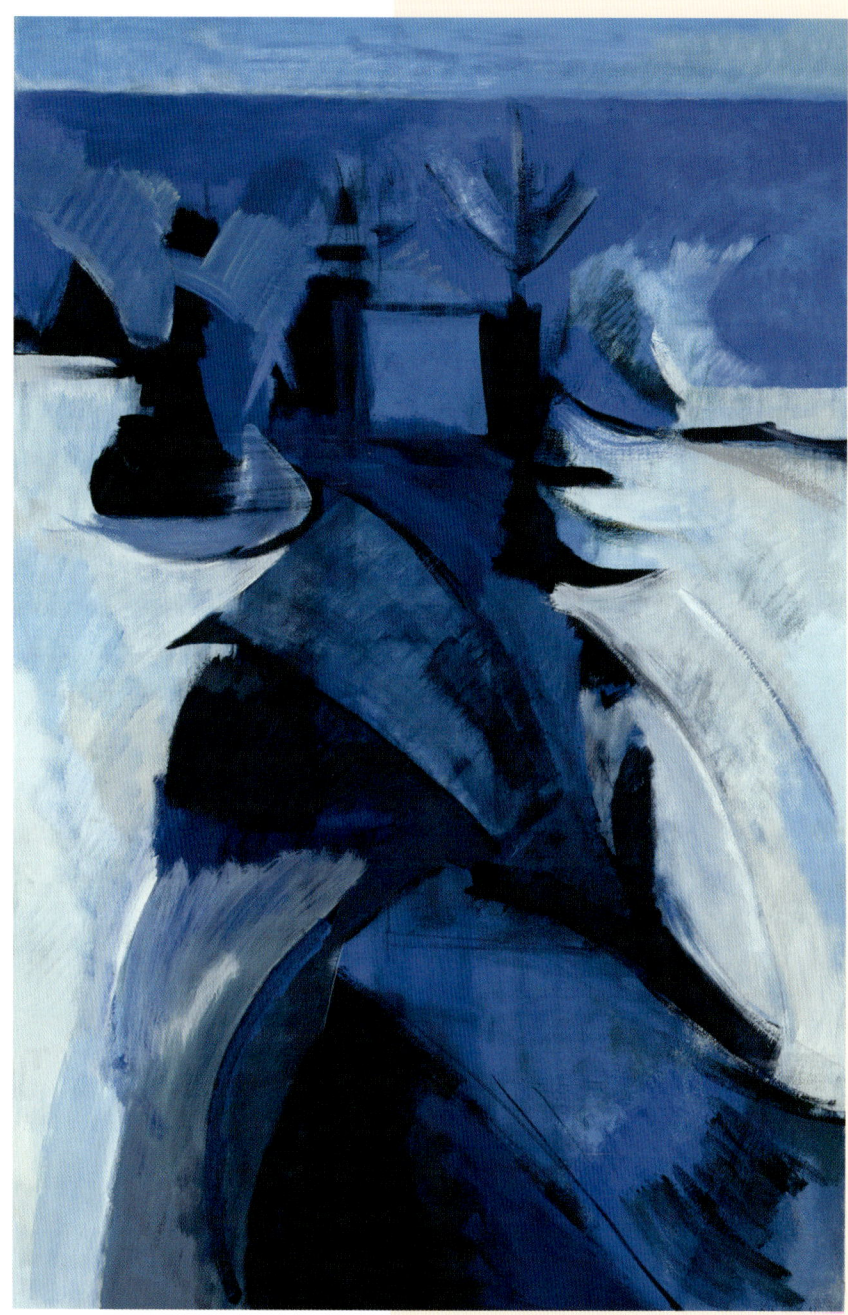

William Kienbusch
Across Four Pines (Hurricane Island), 1956
Casein on paper mounted on composition board, 40 5/8 x 26 7/8 in.
Gift of the Sara Roby Foundation
Smithsonian American Art Museum, Washington, D.C.
1985.30.33

Yesterday

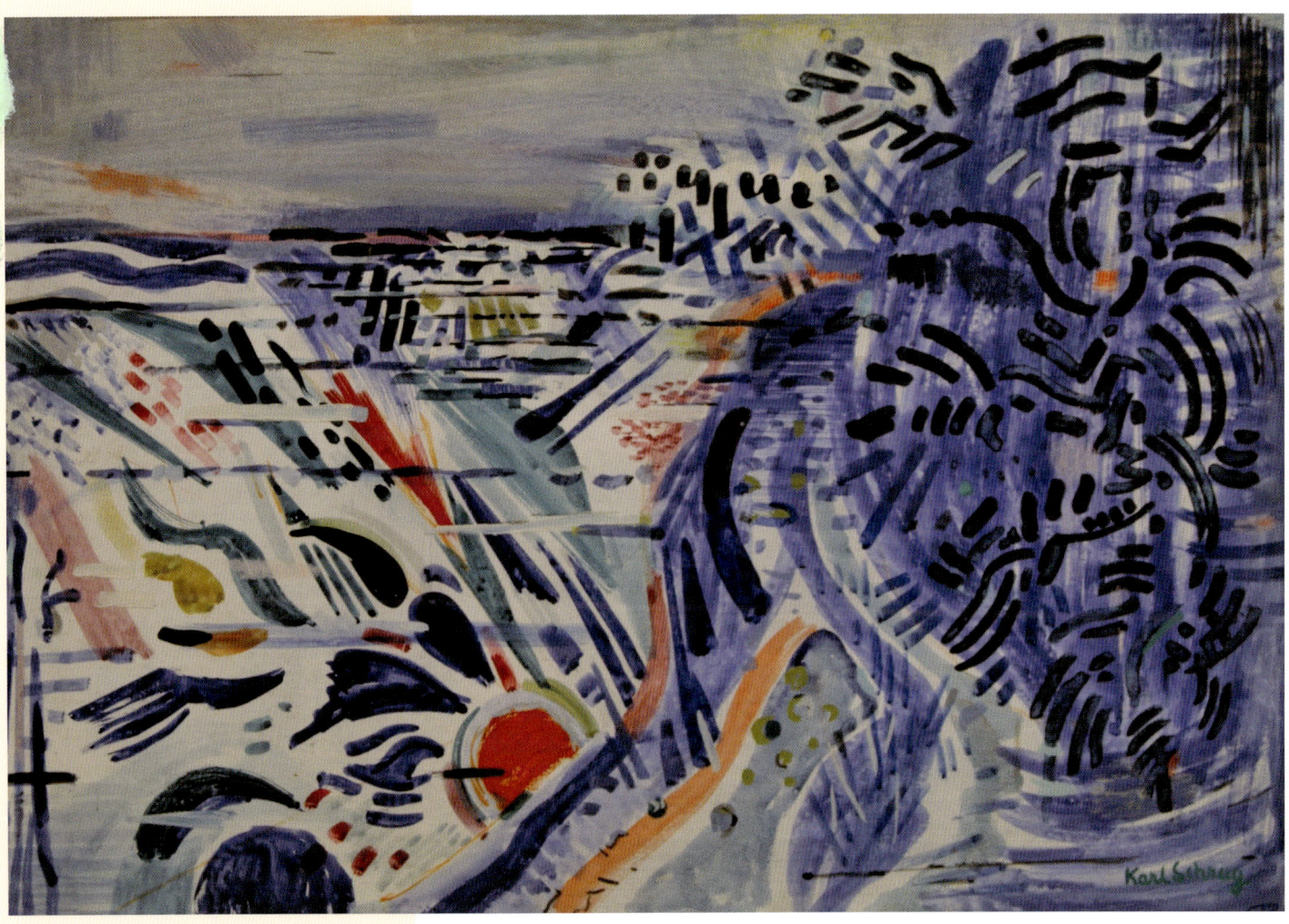

Karl Schrag
Spirit of Ocean, c. 1960
Gouache on paper, 28 x 38 in.
© Karl Schrag LLC
Photo by Katherine Wangh

Kienbusch's friend **Karl Schrag** (1912–1995) found similar visual stimuli on Deer Isle, his seasonal home for nearly forty years and a major muse. In an interview for the Archives of American Art in 1970, the German-born artist noted he shifted from Massachusetts to Maine because he felt the latter's landscape was "stronger … more outspoken."

Schrag began his annual summer sojourns from New York City to Maine in 1945, gradually finding his way down the coast before settling in Deer Isle in 1959 in a 150-year-old house on a thirty-five-acre farm (he converted a barn into a studio). His paintings and prints are highly linear and rhythmic, evoking the movement of wind and sea through channels of light. His *Spirit of Ocean* exemplifies his personal response to the elements, a kind of free verse visual poetry.

"Inspired by summers at the coast of Maine," Schrag wrote in 1966, "I wanted to show the immensity of the sea, to find a visual parallel for the fragrance of grasses, for the sound of the sea and of falling rain, and to express the influence of the moon upon the ocean."

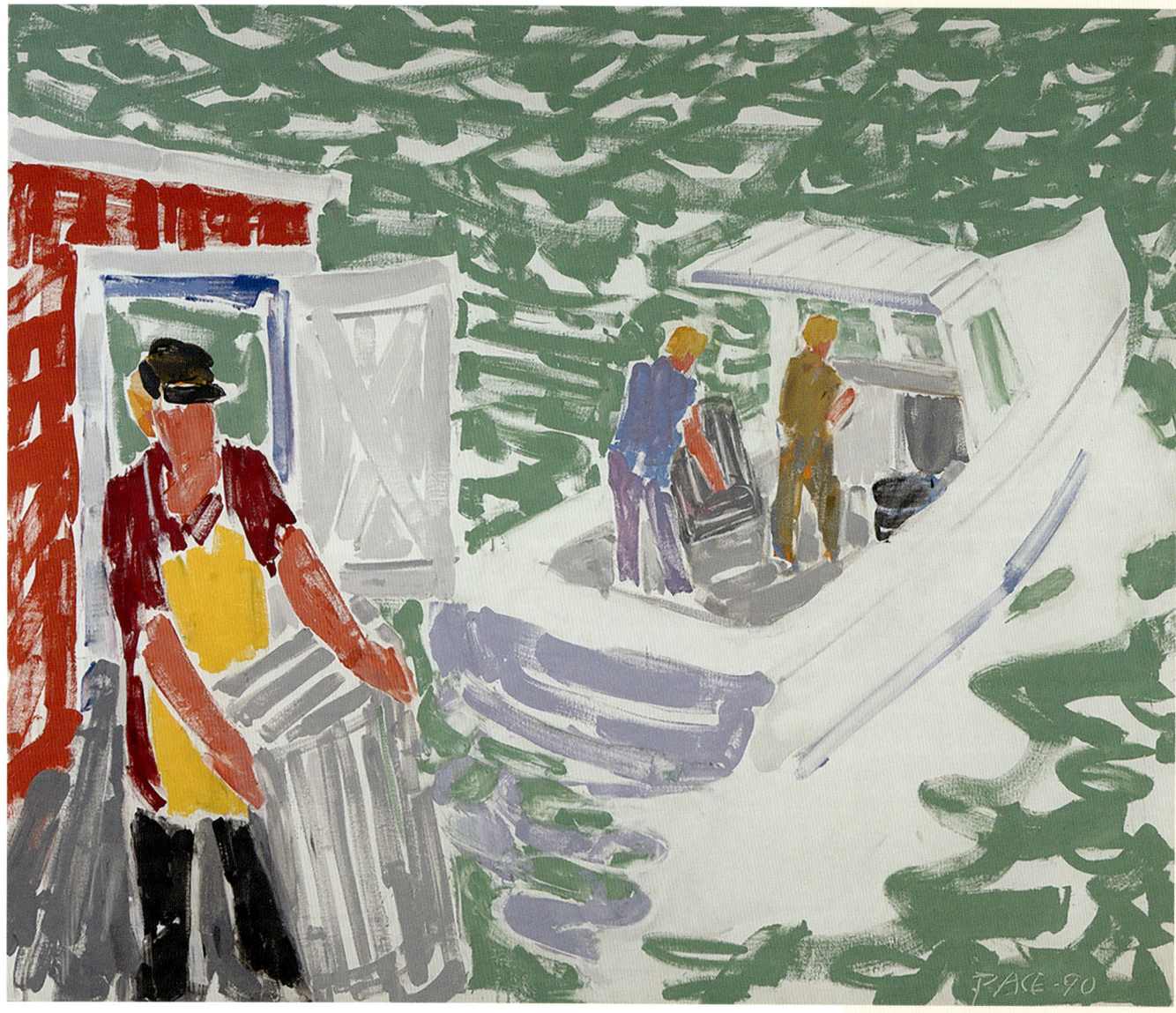

Fellow New Yorker **Stephen Pace** (1918–2010) had a home and studio in nearby Stonington. Like Schrag, Pace felt the liberating force of Abstract Expressionism, but in the end, he used large brushes, big canvases, and fast, forceful gestures to turn that energy to representational subjects, wishing to transform but not relinquish reality.

Stonington is one of the most active lobstering ports in the world. Captivated by the bustle, Pace frequented the town's waterfront, the docks, and the lobster co-op. Using a pastel palette similar to that of his life-long friend Milton Avery and a lively loose brush, he captured the action in his singular style.

When Pace and his wife Pam moved back to his boyhood home in southern Indiana later in life, they donated their home in Stonington to the Maine College of Art.

Stephen Pace
Leaving Co-Op Pier, 1990
Oil on canvas, 60 x 72 in.
© Stephen and Palmina Pace Foundation
Photo courtesy of Dowling Walsh Gallery

Yesterday

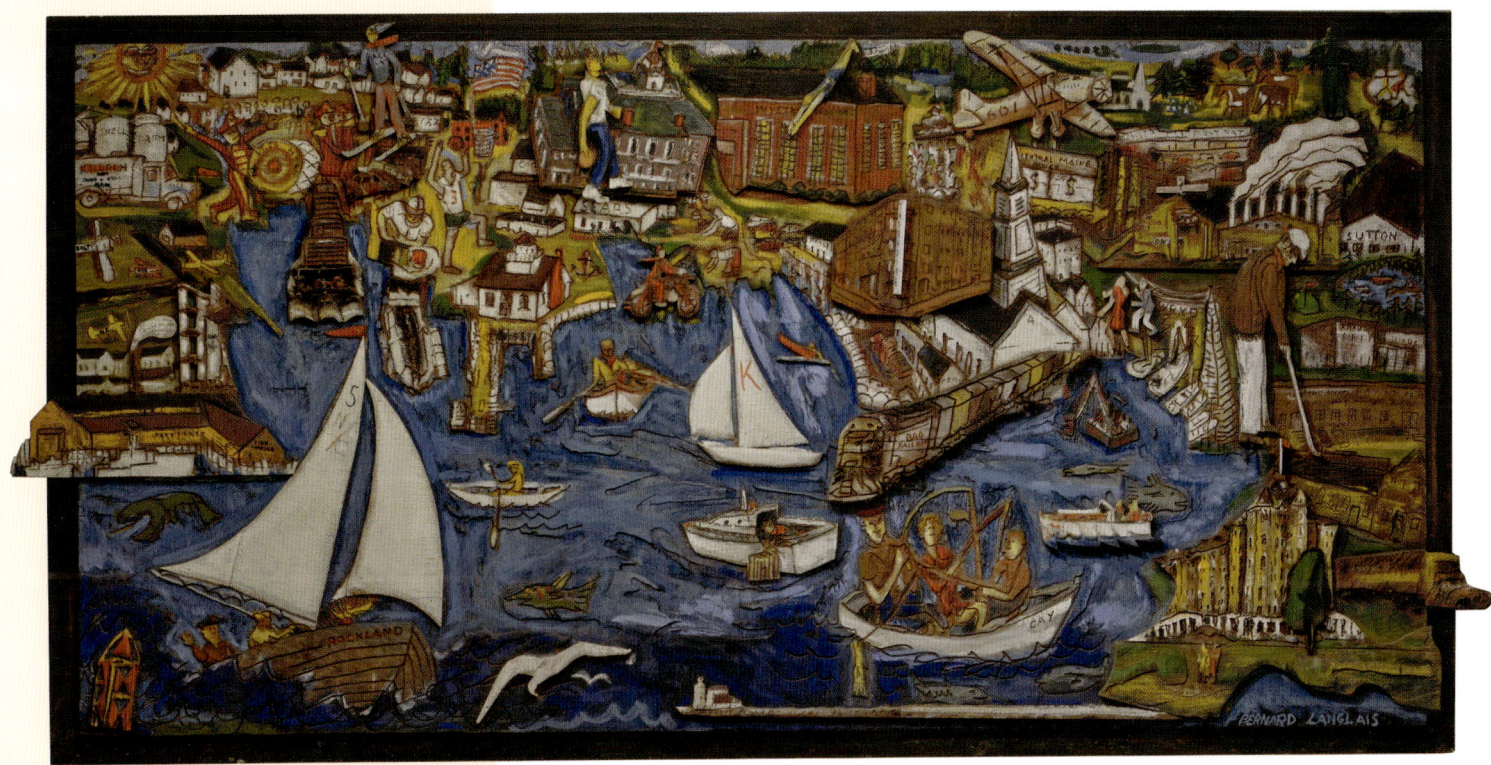

Bernard Langlais
Rockland, Maine
Carved and painted wood on panel,
48 x 98 in.
Gift from the Arlene and
Walter Meranze Collection
The Farnsworth Art Museum,
2019.3

Sculptor **Bernard Langlais** (1921–1977) took to wood relief to present the hurly-burly world of Rockland. The frieze-like carved and painted assemblage from the 1970s stretches ninty-eight inches across—and beyond as several elements, including a tractor trailer, overreach the frame. He highlighted a variety of landmarks, including the "Wyeth Museum," a tongue-in-cheek reference to the Farnsworth Museum, which holds one of the largest collections of Wyeth art in the world.

Born in Old Town, Langlais made a name for himself in New York City in the 1950s through inventive wall constructions. He abandoned the stressful and fickle art scene in 1966 to retreat to a farm in Cushing overlooking the St. George River. There he set about transforming his eighty-acre property, which today is managed by the Georges River Land Trust, into an informal sculpture park. Following his death in 1977, an initiative combining art preservation and land conservation helped secure him a lasting legacy, enhanced in recent years by the Langlais Art Trail. Like so many artists before and after him, he found a place to make art at his own pace and pleasure.

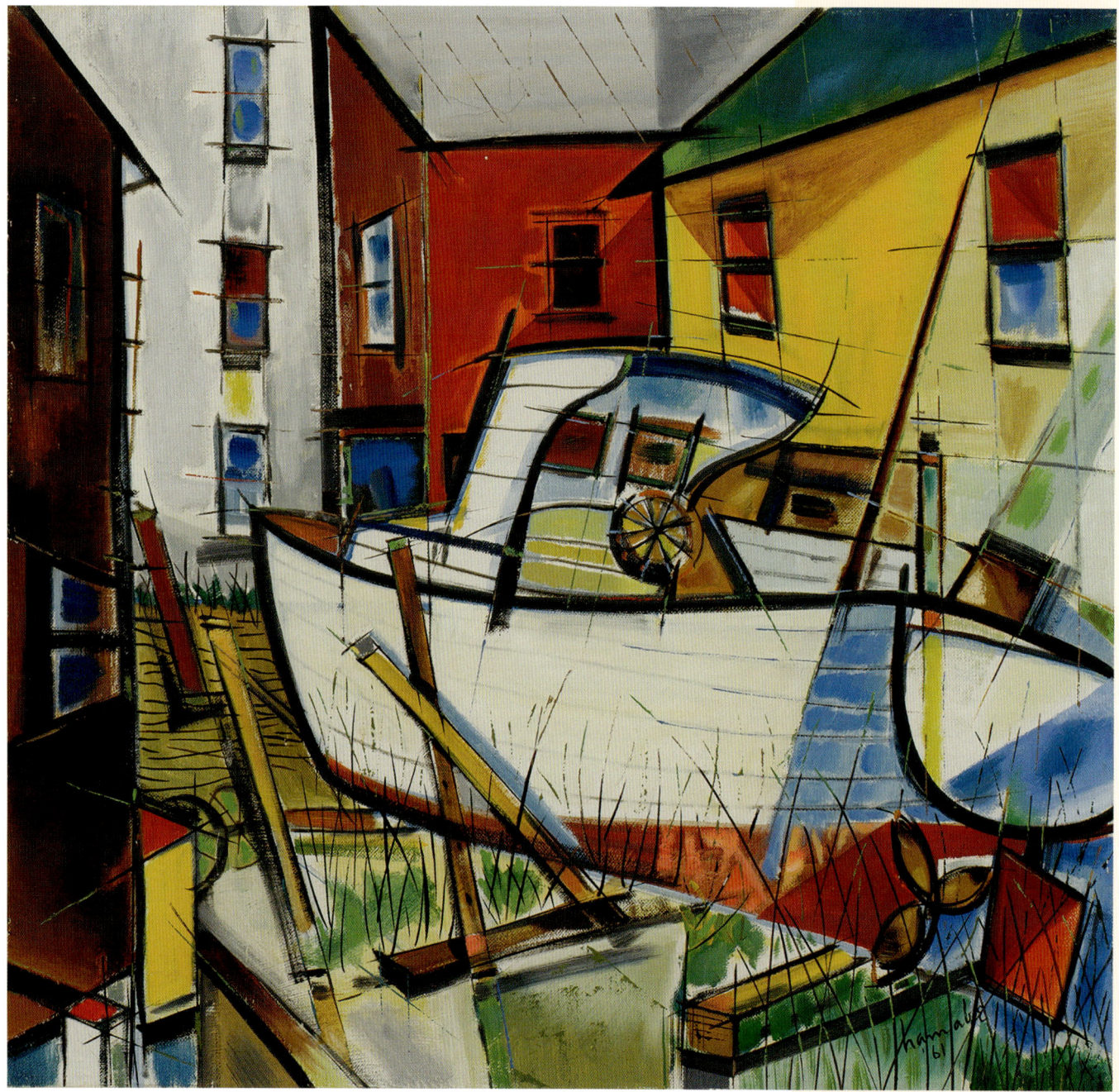

Francis Hamabe (1917–2002) did likewise, moving to Maine in 1947 after serving in World War II and finishing his art studies at the Rhode Island School of Design. The Maine coast became a constant source of inspiration. Throughout his life, Hamabe was an artistic jack-of-all-trades, bringing art—joy, really—into so many lives with so many creative talents: painter, puppeteer, printmaker, potter, professor, art editor, draftsman, calligrapher, and cartoonist.

Francis Hamabe
Castine Wharf, 1961
Oil on canvas, 23 ½ x 24 ½ in.
Gift of Waldo Peirce
Bates College Museum of Art

Yesterday

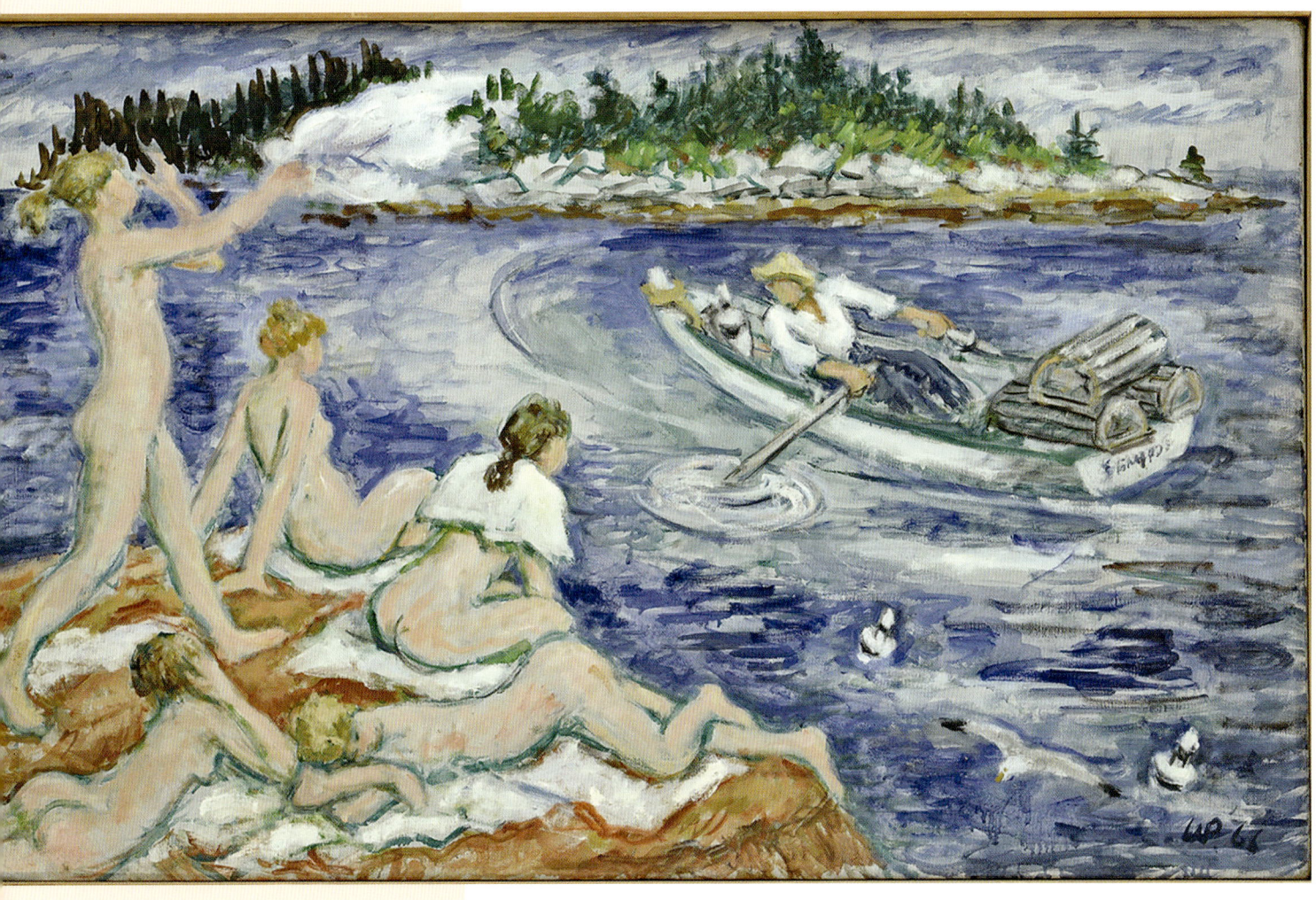

Waldo Peirce
Sirens of Searsport, 1966
Oil on canvas, 22 x 36 in.
Inscribed "For Karen Peirce from Papa"
Courtesy Morphy Auctions, Denver, Penn.

Hamabe was especially taken by harbors and working waterfronts, sometimes turning to a kind of American Cubism to represent them. In *Castine Wharf*, he uses linear and geometric means, plus a rich color scheme, to build the image of a lobster boat propped up in a grassy lot.

The painting was a gift to the Bates College Museum of Art from Hamabe's friend and fellow painter, Bangor-born **Waldo Peirce**. Peirce lived in Searsport for nearly a quarter century, painting his family and scenes of the world around him, including Penobscot Bay. Sometimes referred to as "the American Renoir," the larger-than-life painter, who hobnobbed with Ernest Hemingway, often brought a sense of humor to his Maine paintings as can be seen in his *Sirens of Searsport*. In a nod to the *Odyssey*, a lobsterman rows past a rocky ledge, trying to ignore five naked and flirtatious female sunbathers.

Art of Penobscot Bay

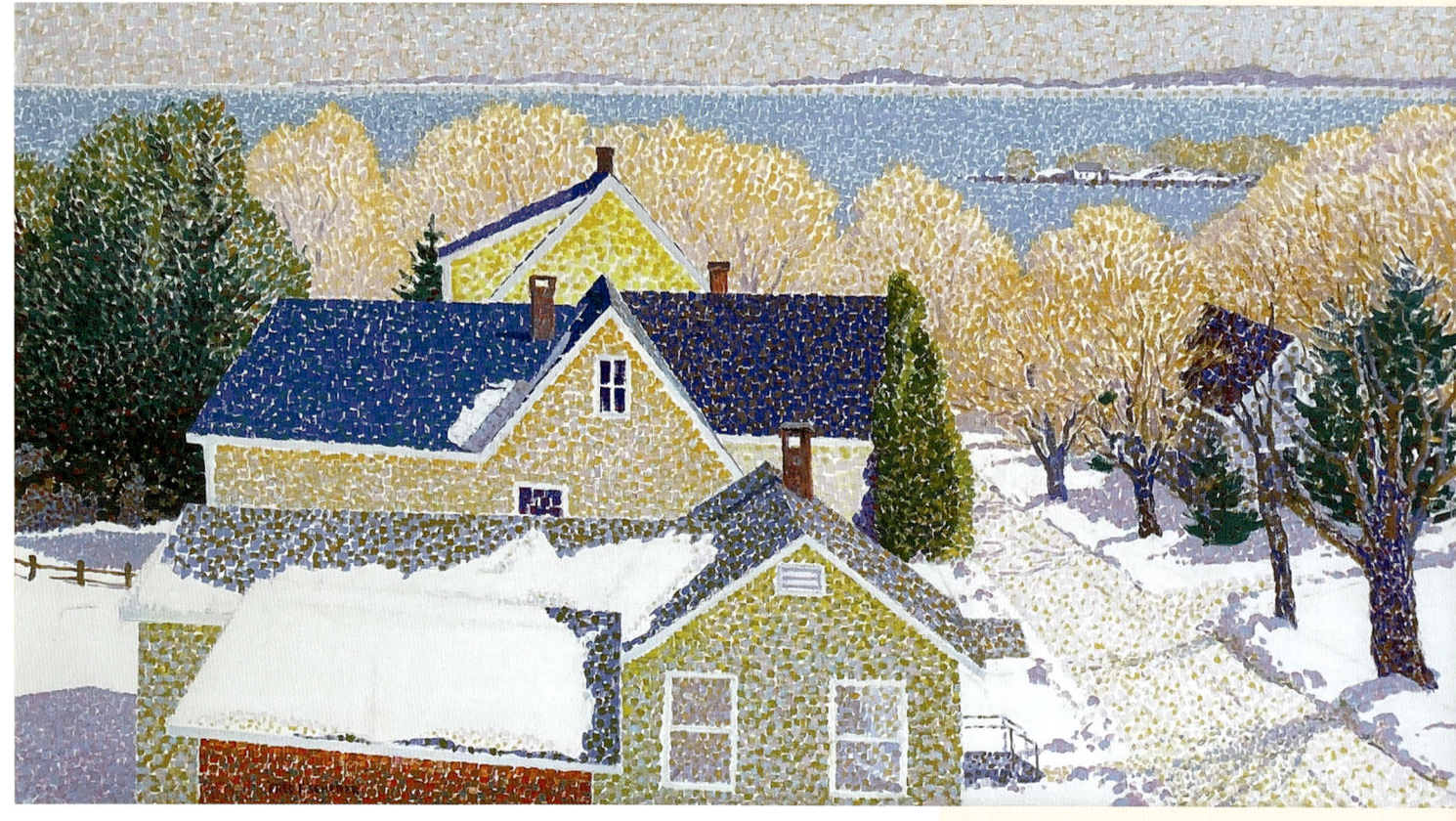

Fred F. Scherer
Camden Roof Tops, 2002
Oil on linen, 26 x 49 in.
Collection of Gianna Robinson

If Peirce brought an impressionist quality to his Maine paintings, **Fred Scherer** (1915–2013) and **Imero Gobbato** (1923–2010) turned to varieties of pointillism, a nineteenth-century French style of painting using small dots of color in patterns, to paint their views of Camden. Scherer, who was famous for the dioramas he helped create for the American Museum of Natural History in New York City, retired to Friendship, in the 1970s. There, he painted local scenes while serving as a consultant to the Maine State Museum in Augusta. His *Camden Roof Tops* presents a stunning, mosaic-like winter view of Penobscot Bay.

Born in Milan, Italy, Gobbato emigrated to America after World War II, eventually settling in Camden. In addition to his illustrations for children's books, he painted views of the Maine coast, often emulating the French pointillists Seurat and Signac. His *Camden Harbor* features a host of different boats, with sails taking up much of the canvas.

The variety of post-war aesthetics brought to bear by artists inspired by the magnificence of Penobscot Bay would expand and proliferate as the twenty-first

Yesterday

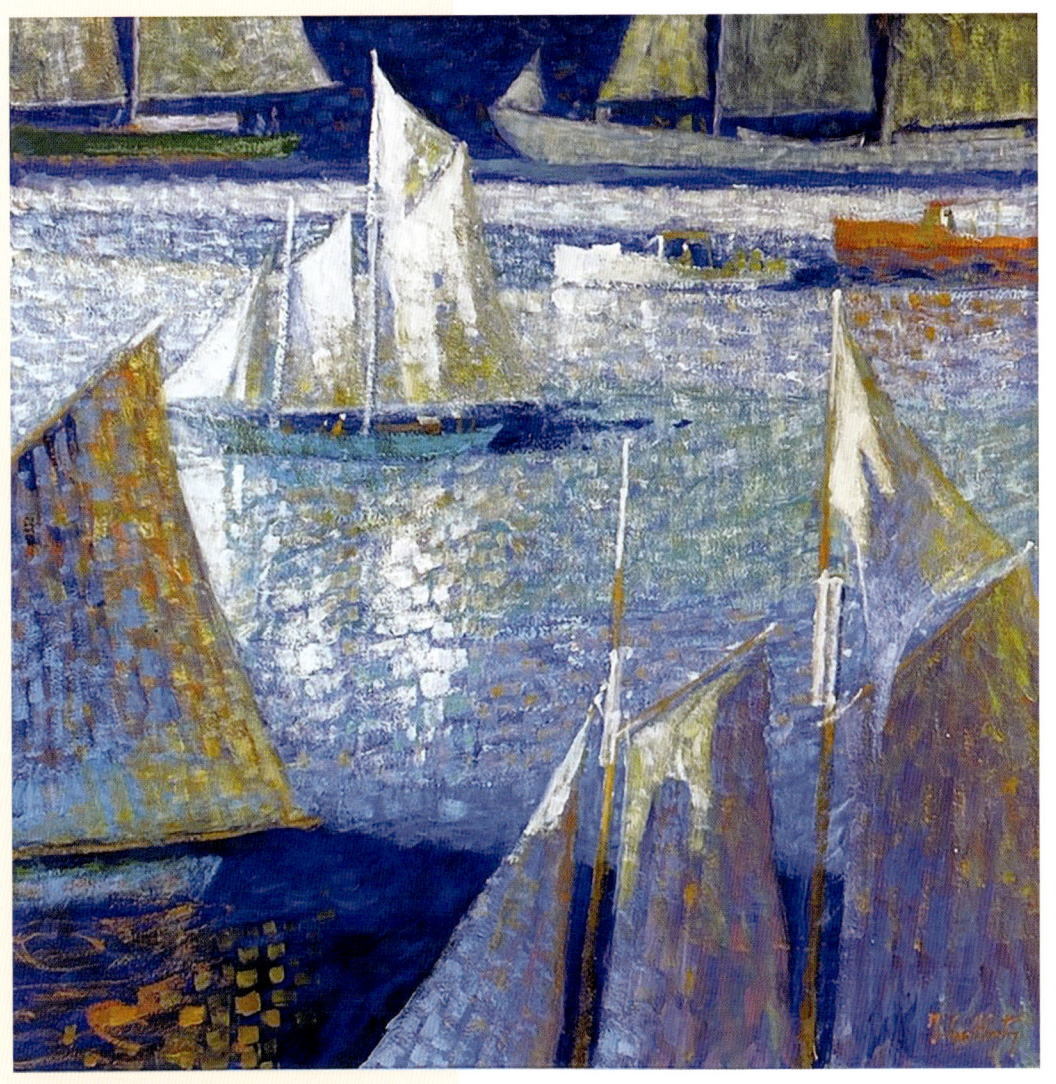

Imero Gobbato
Camden Harbor, c. 1990s
Oil on canvas, 39 x 39 in.
Courtesy Harbor Square Gallery, Rockland, Maine

century approached. Abstract expressionism, impressionism, and realism would continue to influence painters even as they pursued new avenues of representation. As Christopher Huntington noted in an essay for the landmark exhibition "Maine: 100 Artists of the 20th Century" at Colby College in 1963, these –isms were for the most part "little more than a point of stylistic departure for the artists who move in a direction dictated by nature herself"—and by an "unlimited respect for the land and sea."

The challenge of finding an authentic voice has increased thanks to new art techniques, materials, and technologies; think computer art programs, tablets and iPads, social media, websites, and beyond. In the face of these innovations, artists have both extended existing art styles and reacted against them.

While painters continued to establish and return to seasonal residences in Maine, others became year-rounders, leading to a fuller portrayal of the coastal reaches, towns, and islands that make up Penobscot Bay. The paintings that follow reflect a remarkable variety of experiences of self-discovery and an ongoing passion for place.

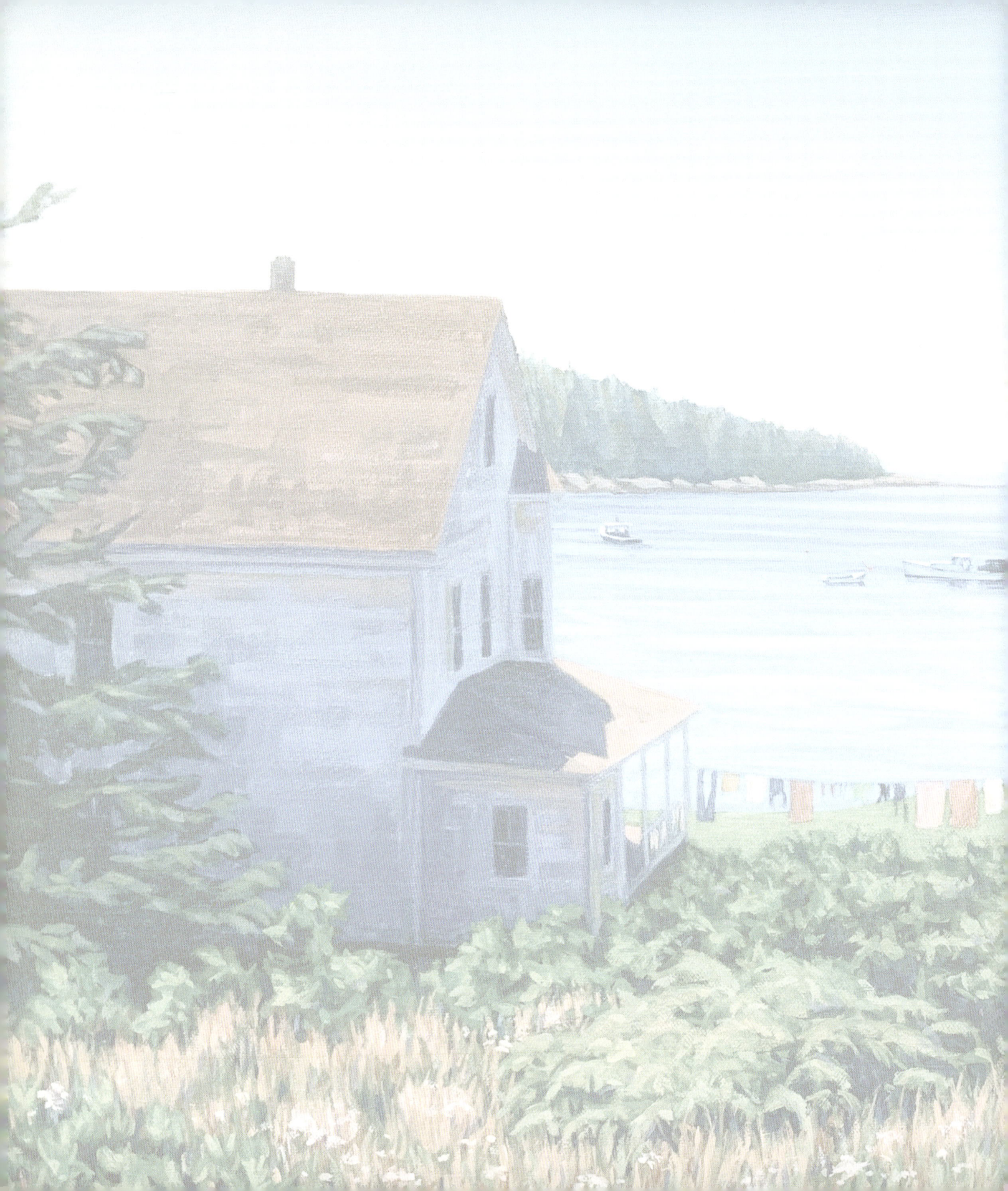

Today
The 21st Century

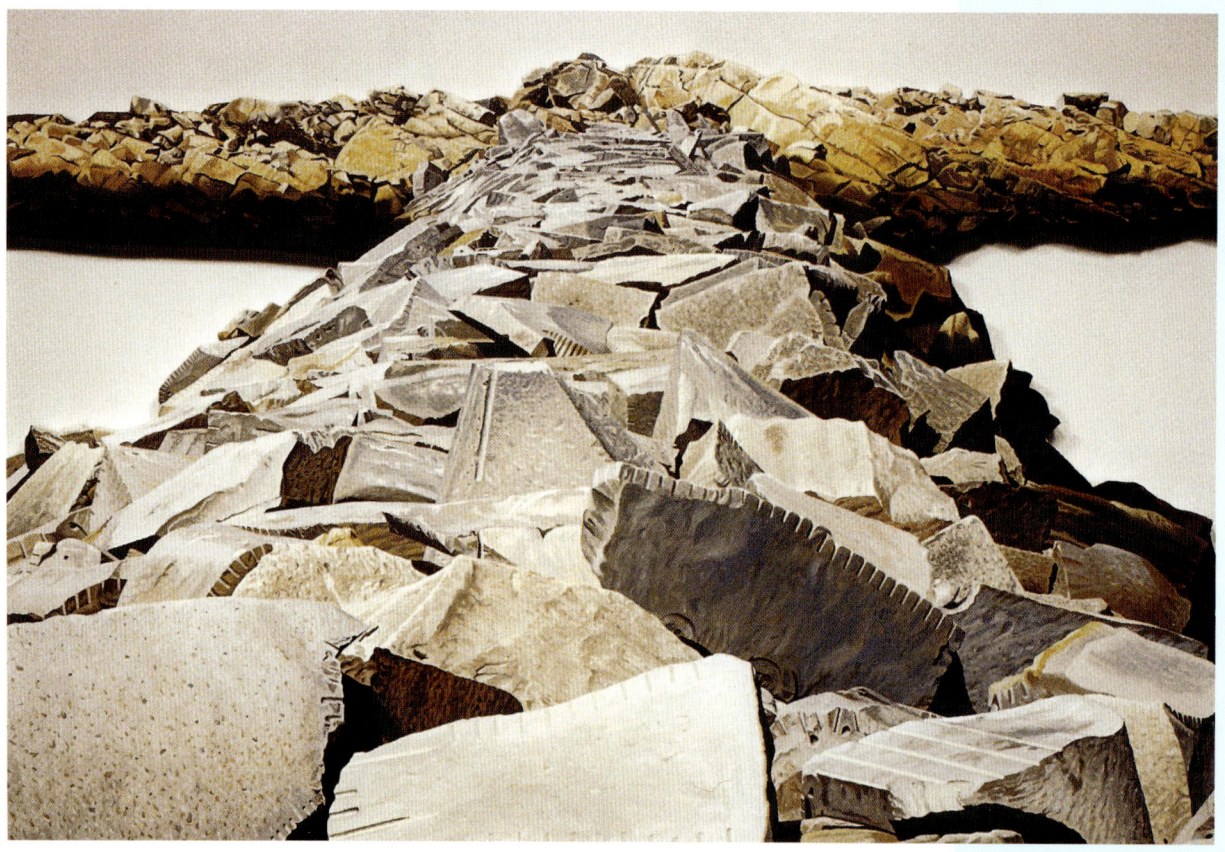

Sam Cady
Breakwater, Matinicus, 2000
Oil on shaped canvas,
41 ¾ x 64 in.
Collection of Farnsworth Art Museum
Museum purchase with support from the Friends of the Farnsworth Collection and the Artist's Resource Trust, 2003.10

Our journey begins at the outer edge of Penobscot Bay and the island that guards it—Matinicus. From the Abenaki language, the name means "far out island," a fitting description as Matinicus has the distinction of being the farthest inhabited territory off the East Coast of the United States.

Despite its remoteness, Matinicus has lured—and inspired—painters. **Sam Cady** from Friendship, Maine, took advantage of a friend's cottage to spend a week drawing, photographing and "soaking the island in." On a walk to the far shores, Cady was struck by the breakwater, the "chaos and order" of it, every granite shape different, with drill marks providing evidence of construction, plus "the beauty of light, shape, color, texture." His shaped painting offers a dramatic view of what he calls a "symbol of protection and collective power for good use."

Loretta Krupinski's *View from the Second Tower, Matinicus Rock Light, 1904* (2012), one of a series of remarkable maritime paintings based on historical photographs, offers another image of protection, an impressive beacon that oversees a wide expanse of Penobscot Bay. In her work the South Thomaston realist seeks to preserve the past. As she told the late art historian Stephen May, she relishes the sense of "stepping back in time, stepping inside my painting."

Loretta Krupinski
*View from the Second Tower,
Matinicus Rock Light, 1904*, 2012
Oil on canvas, 28 x 22 in.
Courtesy Bayview Gallery,
Brunswick, Maine

Today

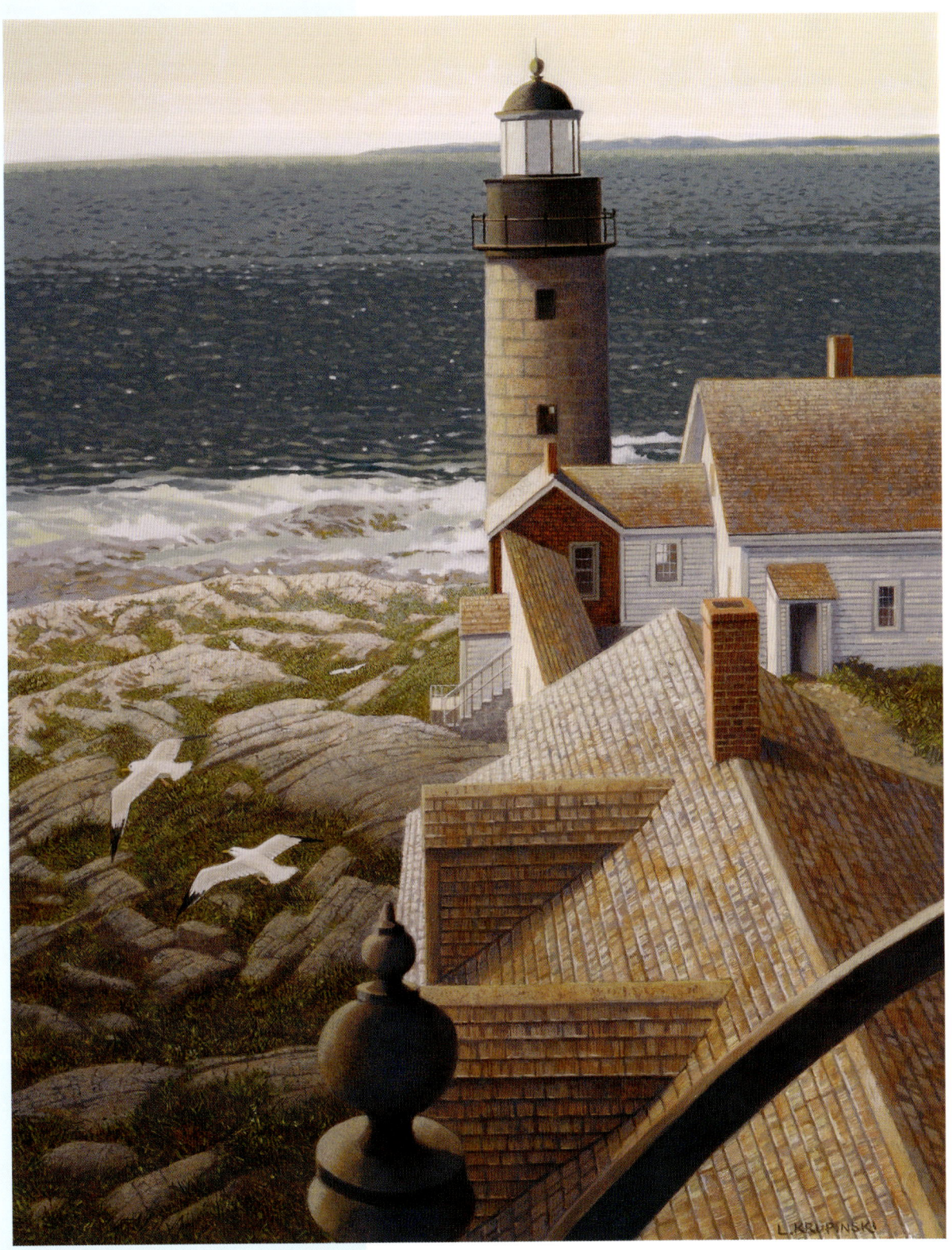

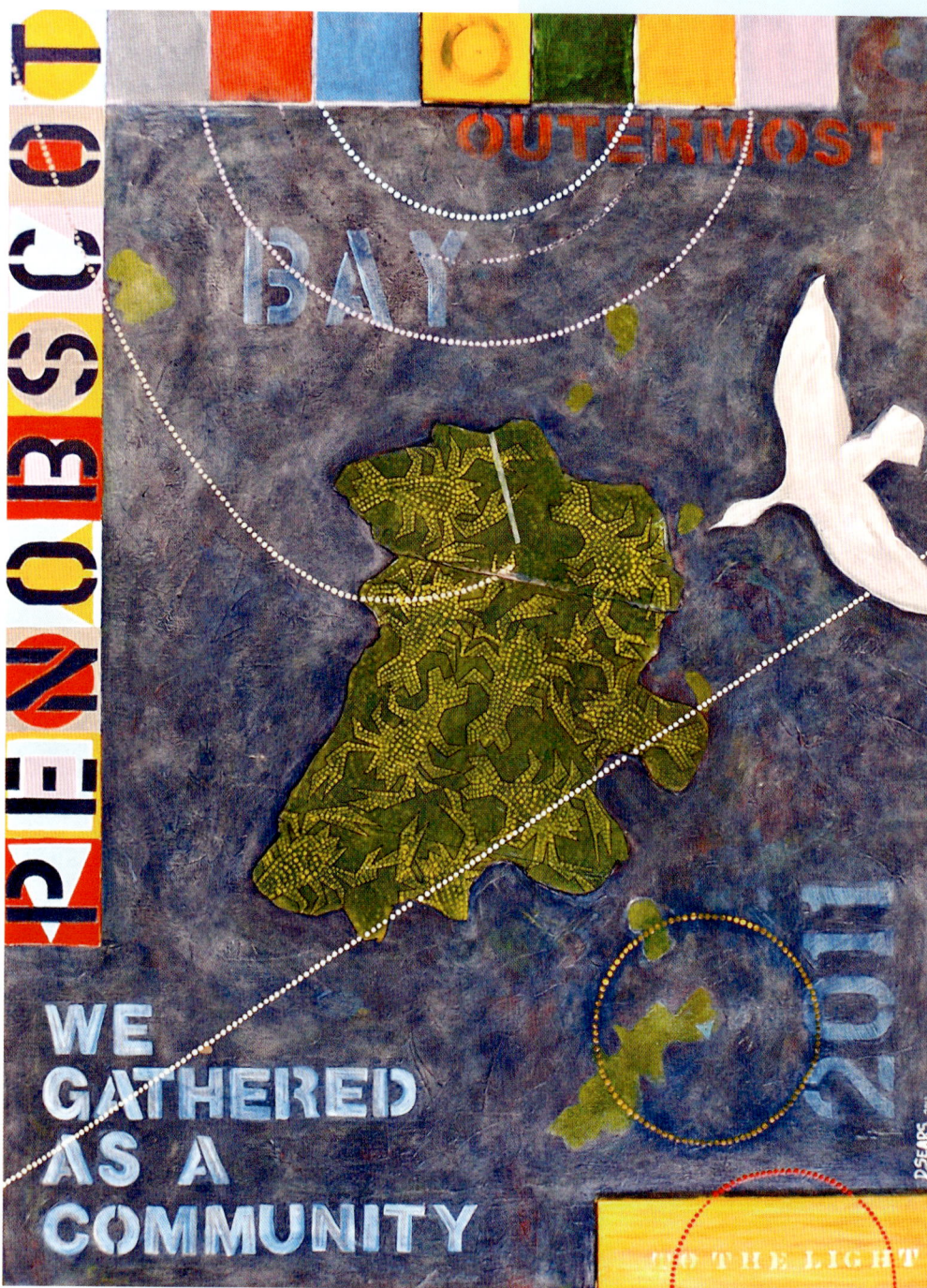

David Sears's *To the Light / We Gathered as a Community* was prompted by the death of Penobscot Island Air pilot Don Campbell. As he attempted to land on Matinicus on October 5, 2011, Campbell's plane was knocked from the air by a fierce wind. "Our good friend Don was killed instantly," wrote island resident Eva Murray in a tribute in the *Penobscot Bay Pilot* newspaper.

In the wake of the crash, the islanders "gathered as a community," as Sears stenciled on his painting, to mourn Campbell. In a style reminiscent of Jasper Johns and Robert Indiana, Sears created a stunning memorial, with the island at its center.

Ten-acre Wheaton Island helps protect the harbor at Matinicus. In the first decade of the twenty-first century, the Philadelphia-based painter **Bo Bartlett** purchased it, but said, "You don't really own an island, you're just a steward of it while you're gifted with it, and you're happy to look after it."

Look after it—and paint it: The island has inspired a number of Bartlett's paintings, including *Approaches to Penobscot Bay* (2019). A figure wearing a sun-bleached visor sits on a bare ledge, her back to us, gazing at the horizon. The title evokes the outer margin of the bay where one might keep watch for distant sails while the image captures those moments when we are alone with the ocean, undisturbed.

David Sears
To the Light / We Gathered as a Community, 2011
Acrylic on canvas, wood, and cardboard, 48 x 36 in.
Collection of Eva Murray, Matinicus Island

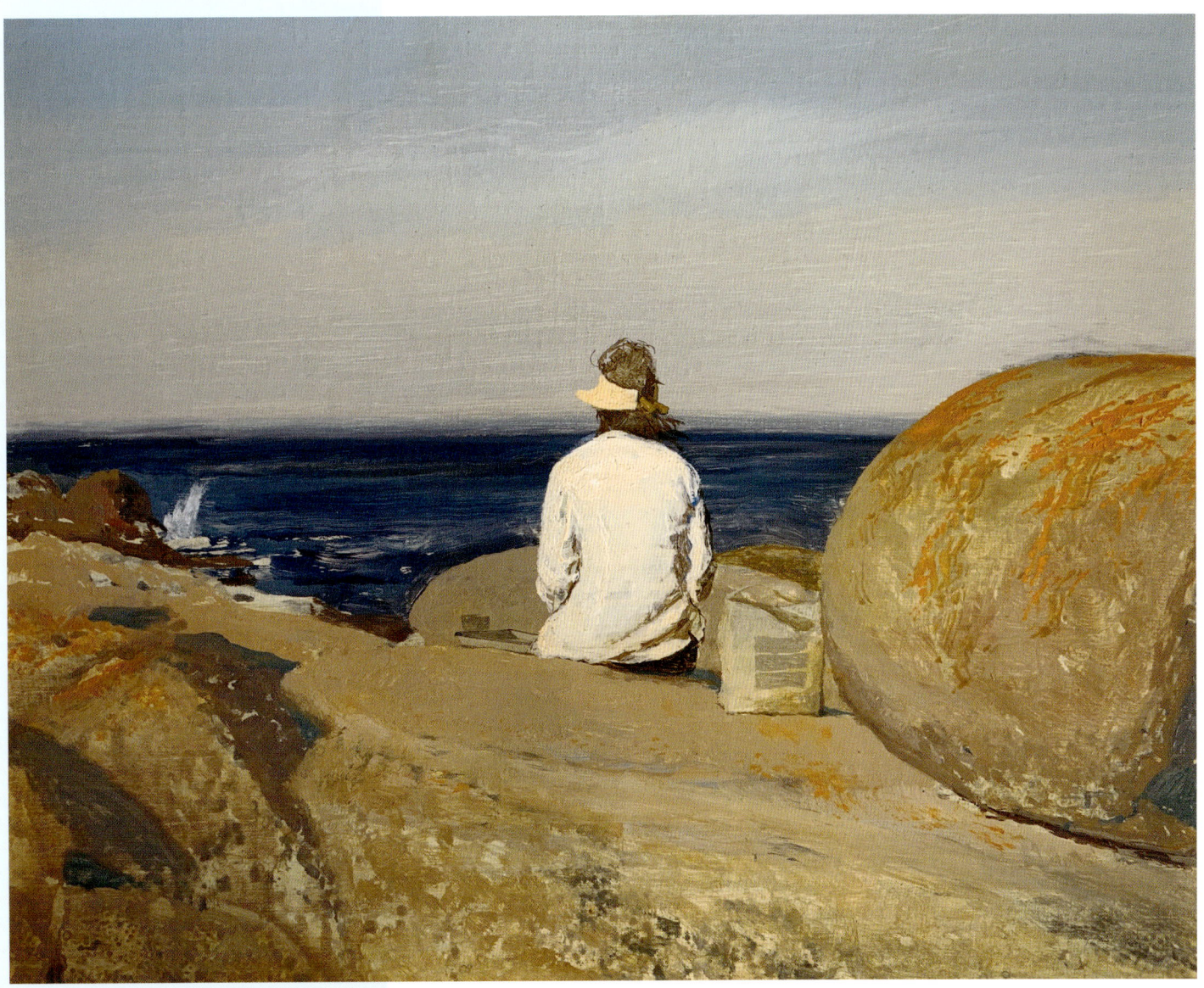

Bo Bartlett
Approaches to Penobscot Bay,
2019
Oil on linen mounted on panel,
16 x 20 in.

Art of Penobscot Bay

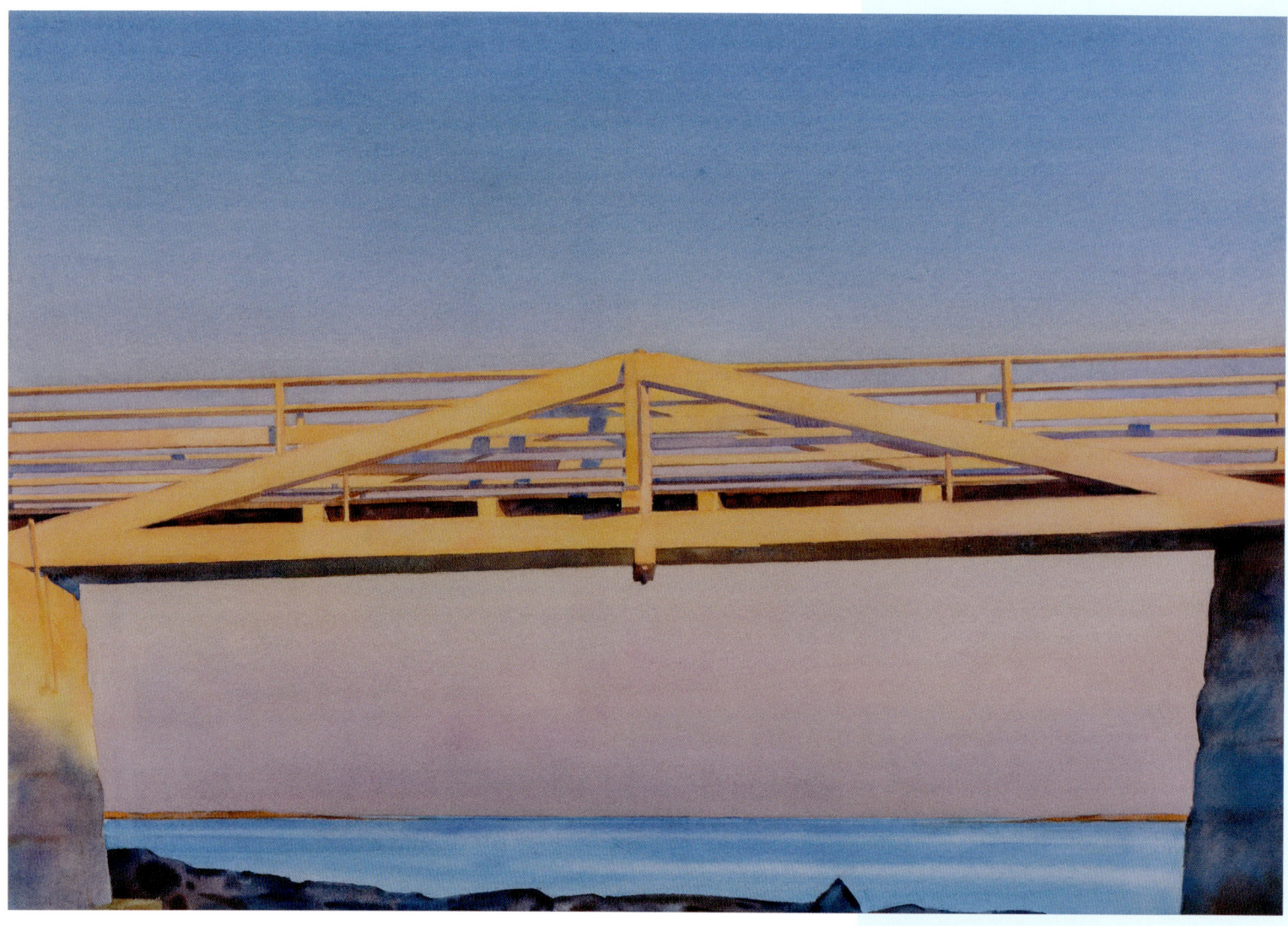

On the mainland, not far from the ferry to Matinicus, is the town of Owls Head. The brilliant watercolorist **David Dewey** considers himself fortunate to live there, a locale that allows him to experience "the entire Penobscot Bay."

Capturing the luminous Maine light as its bathes geographic and architectural landmarks along the coast has been the source of Dewey's vision, which "always begins observationally in real time," he says. The care taken in Dewey's paint application gives the sense of nuanced perfection. In *Marshall Point: Setting Sun*, the walkway to the lighthouse glows in late afternoon light. The structure might be a gateway to the bay, its cross bars and granite stanchions framing the view beyond.

David Dewey
Marshall Point: Setting Sun, 2014
Watercolor, 27 by 39 ⅛ in.
Courtesy Caldbeck Gallery,
Rockland, Maine

Today

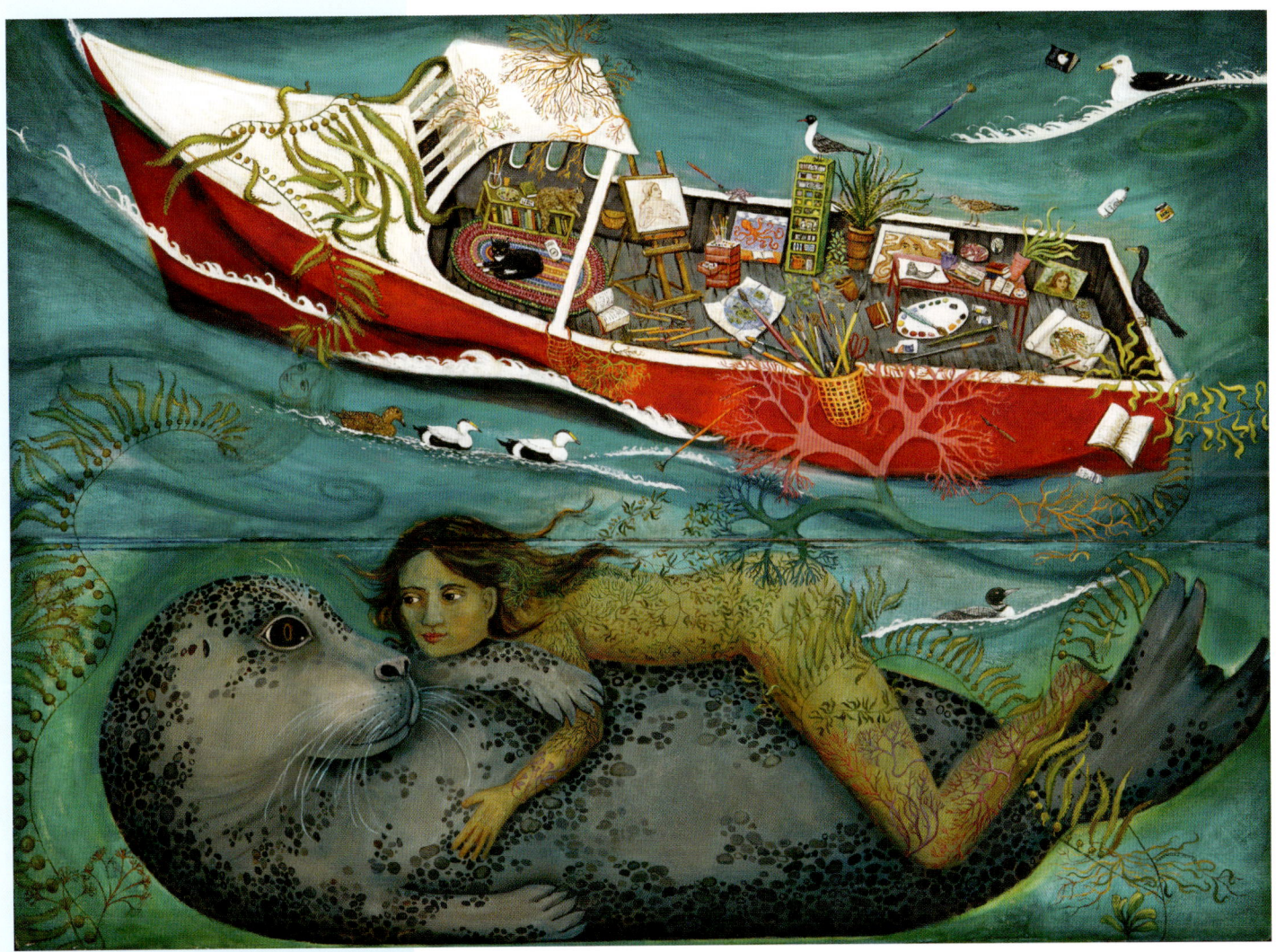

Irene Olivieri
Studio of the Sea, 2019
Oil on wood, 29 ½ x 49 in.

Painter **Irene Olivieri** lived for a year or so in the keeper's quarters at the Marshall Point Lighthouse. The popular tourist site draws many visitors, and the painter sometimes felt put upon. After a lobsterman gave her a ride out on Penobscot Bay one day and she found herself surrounded by forested islands and all manner of wildlife, Olivieri fantasized setting up a studio on an old lobster boat. "On hot summer days," she writes, "I could take breaks by swimming with the seals—and no one could come knocking on my studio door." Her *Studio of the Sea* fulfills that vision and is a marvelous addition to the range of realism on our journey.

Art of Penobscot Bay

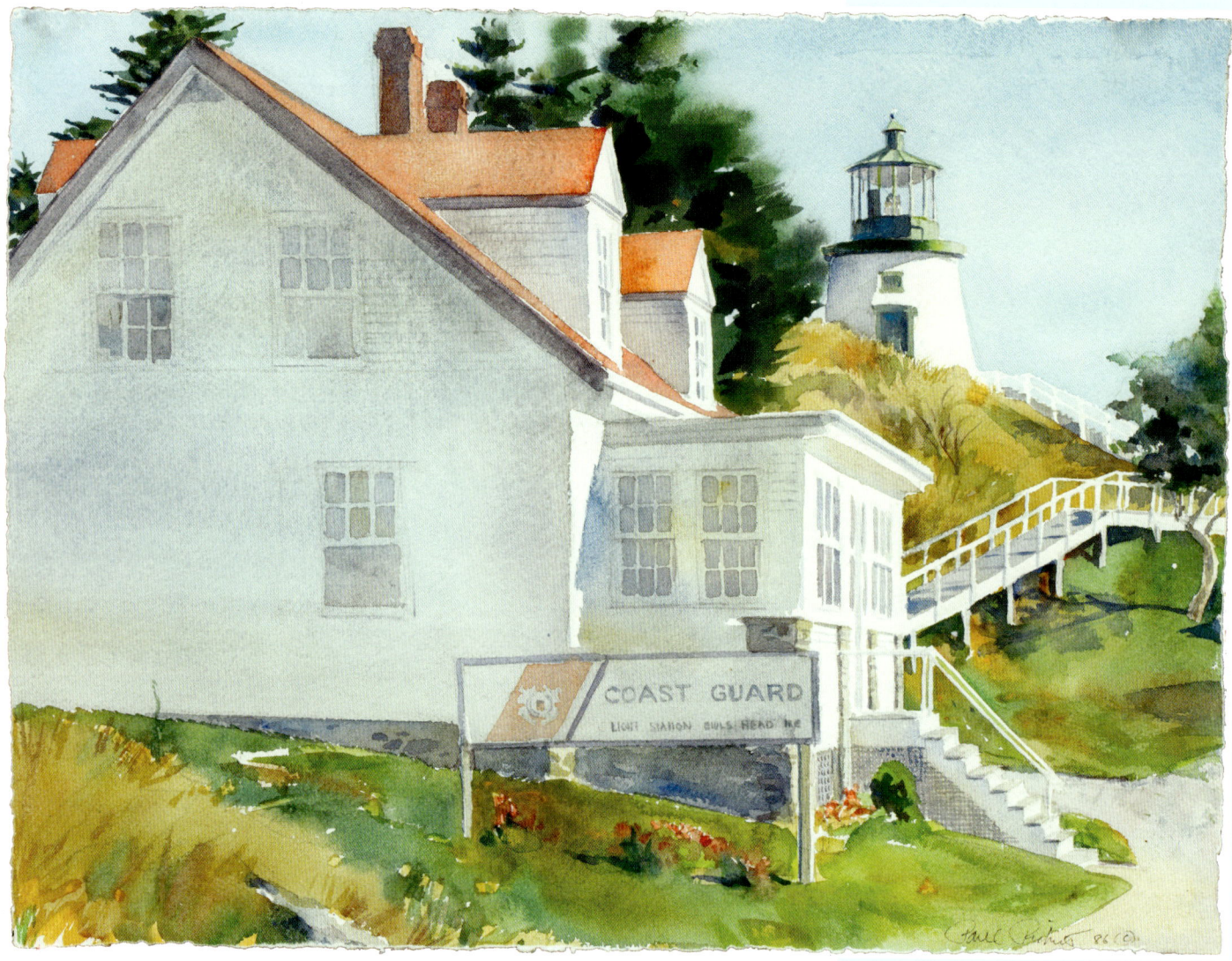

Watercolorist **Paul Rickert** (1946–2023) made his seasonal home in Maine for nearly a half century. Eliot Porter's book *Summer Island* about Great Spruce Head Island factored into his decision to move to Brooksville. From there, he roamed the coast, paints in hand, ready to respond to a scene at a moment's notice. He relished the architecture of Maine, which includes the Owls Head Coast Guard station that is located below the lighthouse. The preciseness of shadows in the painting is signature Rickert.

Paul Rickert
Coast Guard Station at Owls Head Light, 1987
Watercolor, 12 x 16 in.
Photo by Norman Johanson

Today

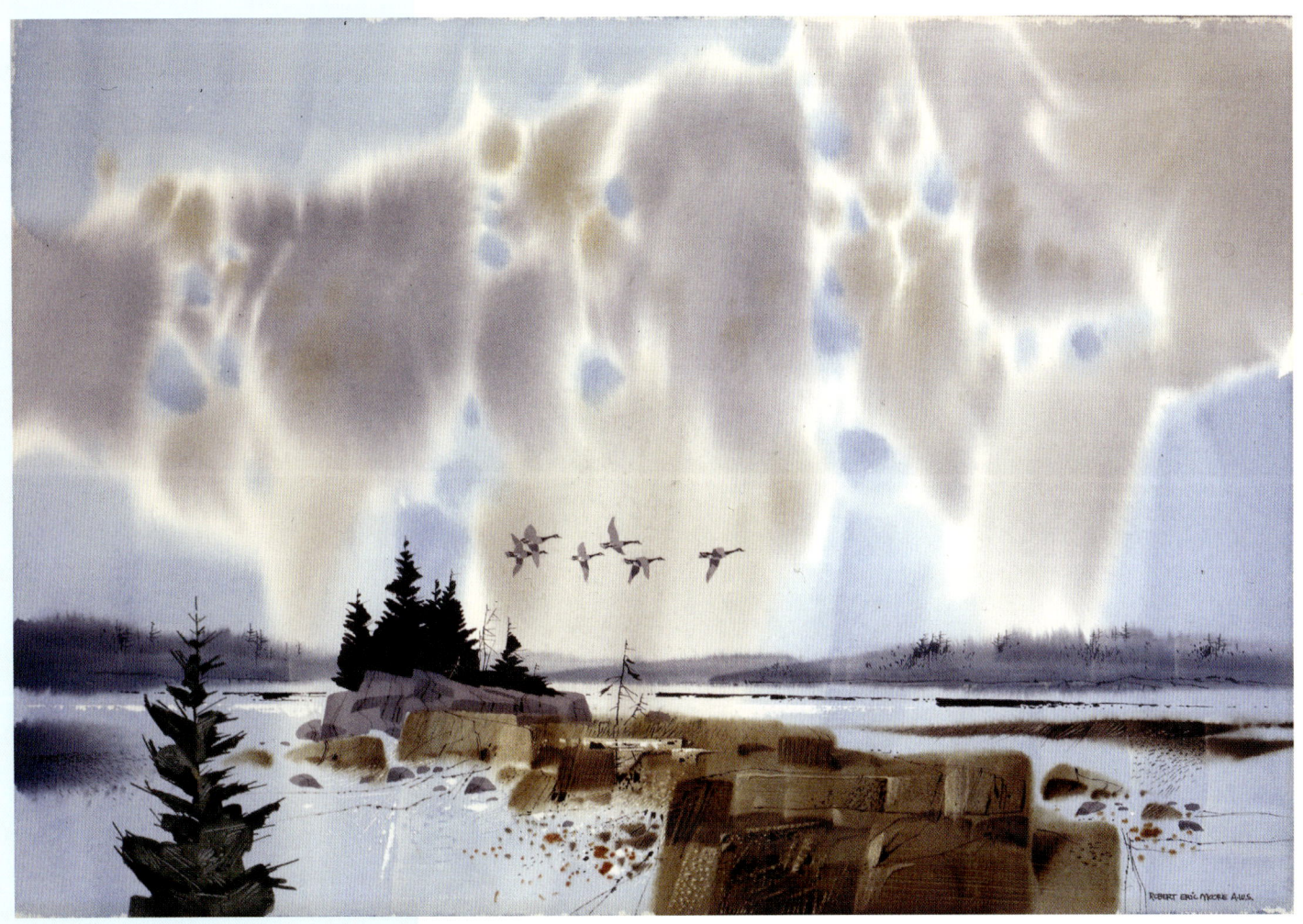

Robert Eric Moore
Geese at Owls Head, 1986
Watercolor, 15 x 22 in.
Courtesy DC Moore Gallery,
New York City

Robert Eric Moore (1927–2006), who lived many of his later years in Waldoboro, painted watercolors in the vein of such New England scene standard bearers as Eric Sloane, Carol Thayer Berry, and Andrew Wyeth. His *Geese at Owls Head* represents a quintessential Maine coast vista. The background cloudscape recalls the aurora borealis in its eerie sweeping configuration—just one of an array of watercolor effects Moore deployed.

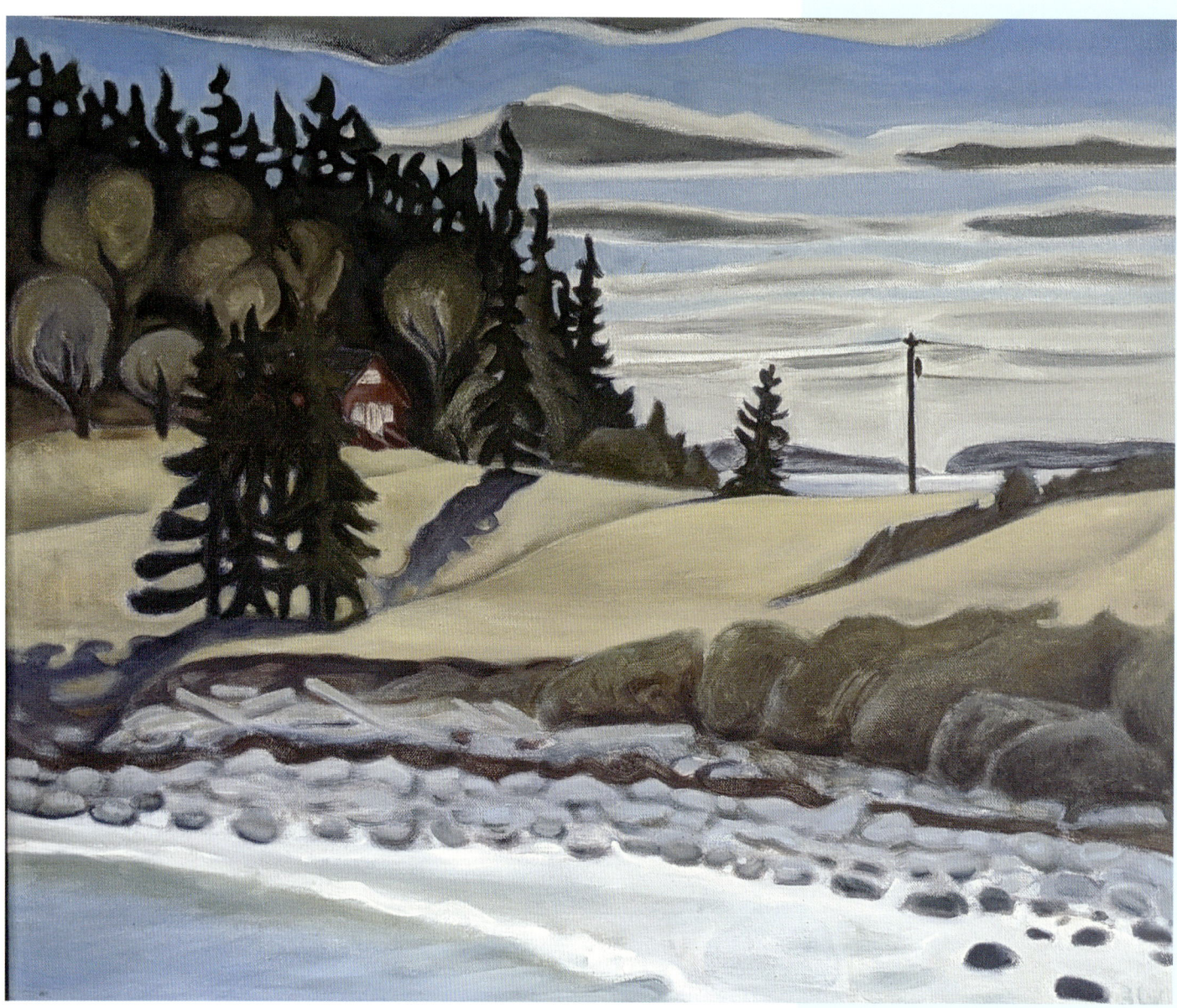

Phoebe Bly
Mosquito Head, 2006
Oil on canvas, 20 x 24 in.
Private collection

Based in Tenants Harbor, **Phoebe Bly** grew up going to nearby Martinsville Beach, to the sandy west side of Mosquito Head. Her back-to-the-land parents collected truckloads of seaweed for their organic gardening business in the 1970s. As a landscape painter, Bly is "acutely aware" of change. Since she painted her view of Mosquito Head in 2006, houses have been built in the field and the beaches made private. At the same time, erosion is cutting away at both sides of the head, turning it

Today

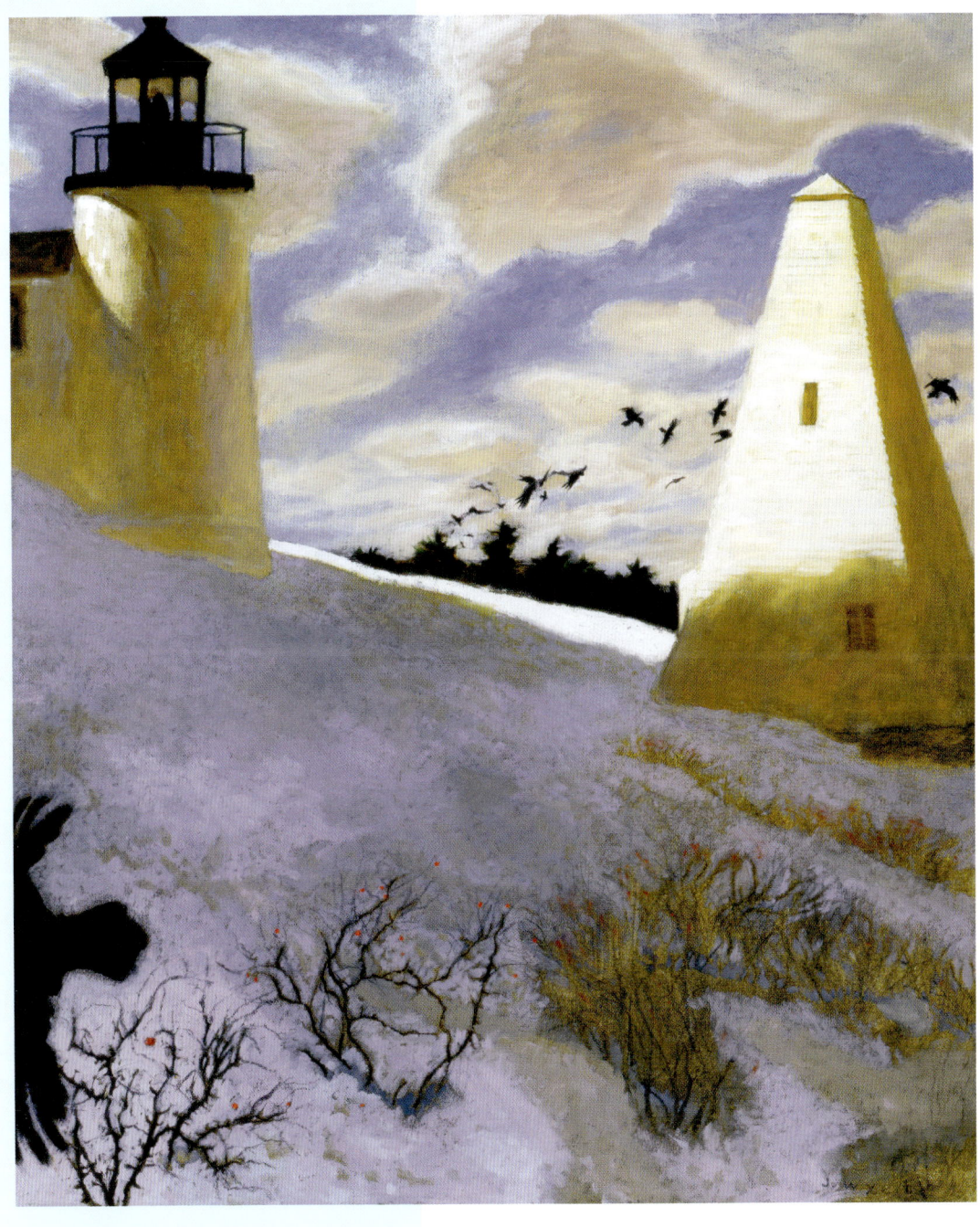

Jamie Wyeth
A Murder of Crows, 2003
Oil on canvas, 36 x 30 in.
Courtesy Jamie Wyeth/ARS,
New York City

into an island. Her painting becomes a record of a place in time. She likes to quote Andrew Wyeth: "One's art goes as far and as deep as one's love goes."

Jamie Wyeth once said of Maine, "It's in my makeup, my DNA. I couldn't survive without it." His Maine includes Southern Island, his part-time home base and site of the Tenants Harbor Light, one of eight privately owned lighthouses in the state. In Wyeth's canvas A *Murder of Crows* (2003) the lighthouse and the obelisk-shaped bell house frame a flock of the dark birds, one of their comrades left in the snow. It might be a scene from Alfred Hitchcock's *The Birds*. Art historian Christopher Crosman once noted how many of Wyeth's bird portraits "bespeak an ornithologist's knowledge of bird-ness but only insofar as an ornithologist might be seduced by form, texture, structure, color, balance and movement—the aesthetic components of art, nature and even culture."

Southern Island lies on the west side of Two Bush Channel, the southwestern entrance to Penobscot Bay. From that geographic point, we head north and east to the city of Rockland.

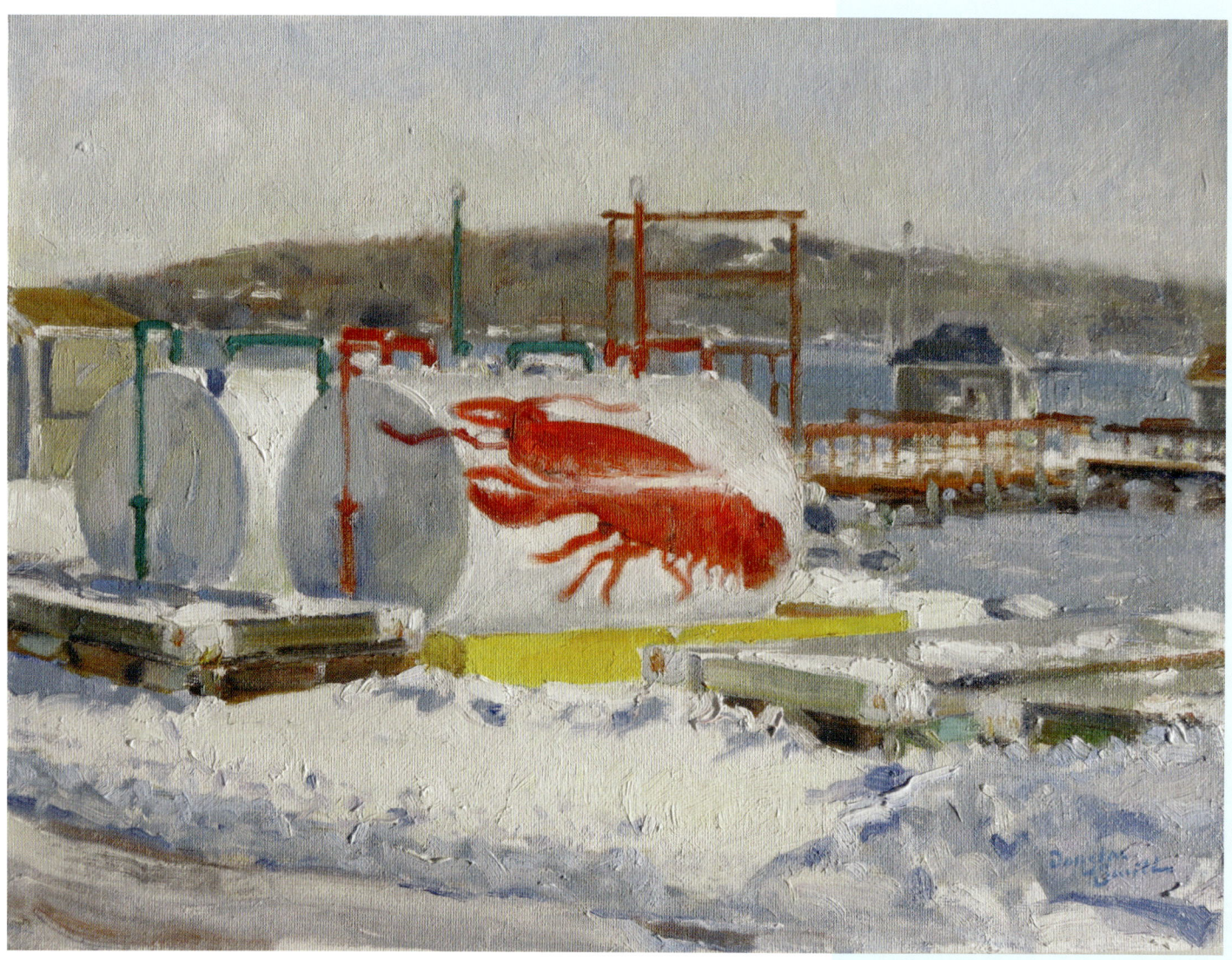

Douglas Smith
Fuel Tanks with Lobster, Rockland, 2012
Oil on panel, 12 x 16 in.

Rockland's waterfront is among the most industrious on the coast of Maine and painters have taken notice.

On a winter day **Douglas Smith**, who lives in the "Lobster Capital of the World," set up his easel on a stack of wooden floats to paint a view of a group of fuel tanks on the harbor. The yellow tank enclosure and bright red *Homarus americanus* pop against the snowy landscape.

"Though the air was cool," Smith recounts, "my down vest and painting coveralls kept the chill at bay and the sunshine remained constant throughout the one-time

Today

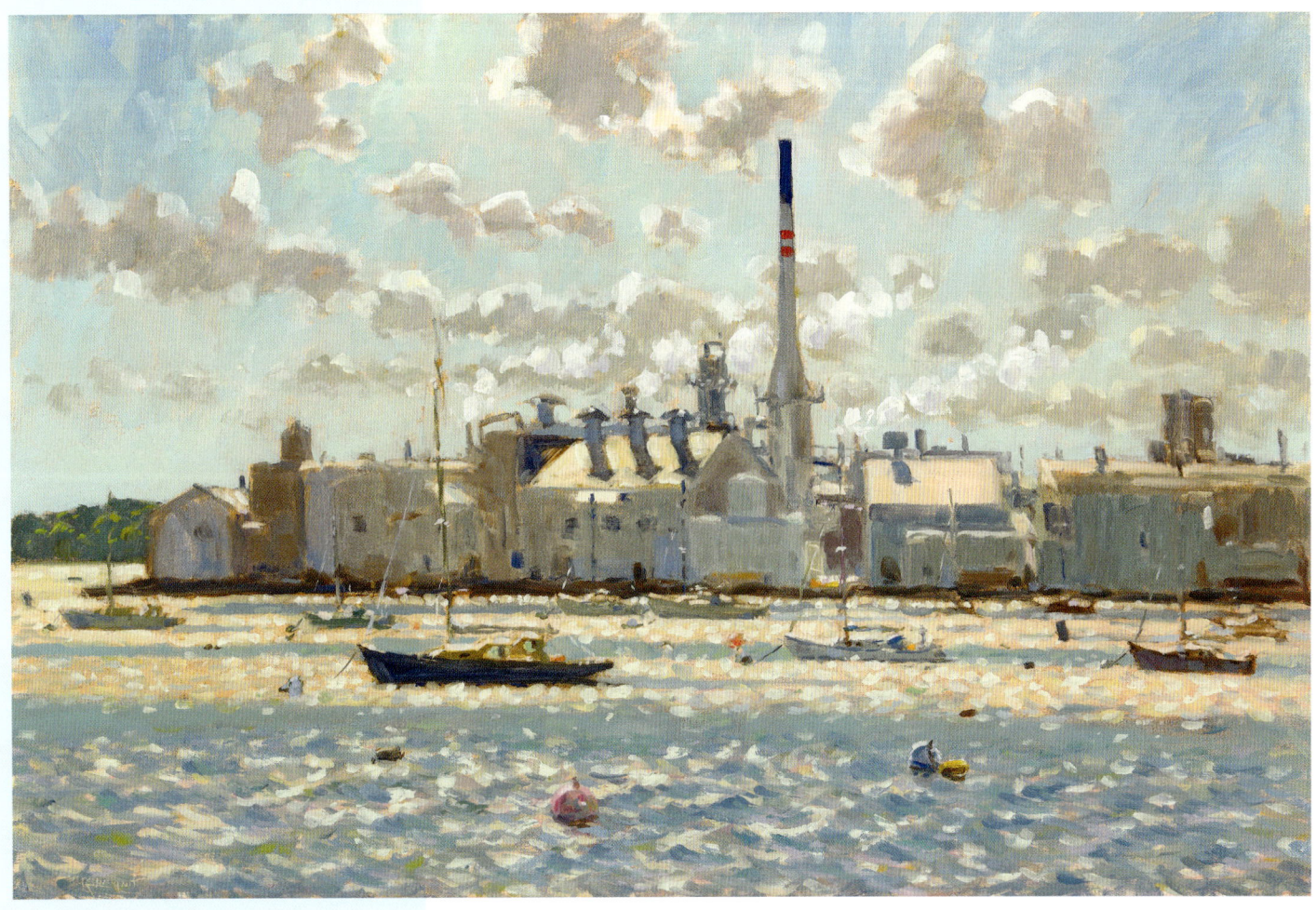

Björn Runquist
Morning at Lermond Cove, 2018
Oil on linen, 20 x 30 in.
Collection of the artist
Photo by Alan LaVallee

painting session." He placed wool socks over his hands and shoved the paint brushes inside, a trick he learned from seeing a photo of Aldro Hibbard (1886–1972) painting on location in winter.

Born in Stockholm, Sweden, **Björn Runquist** arrived in Maine via New York, France, London, and Connecticut. Now residing on Clark Island in St. George, he frequents coastal towns and harbors in search of subject matter.

As much as he loves Maine's colorful history, Runquist is also interested in the "very real life of work." His painting *Morning at Lermond Cove* (2018) offers a sunlit view of the seaweed processing plant on Rockland Harbor. He has painted this prospect more than once, attracted by the smokestack reaching towards the sky and the play of light on the buildings, clouds, and water.

Art of Penobscot Bay

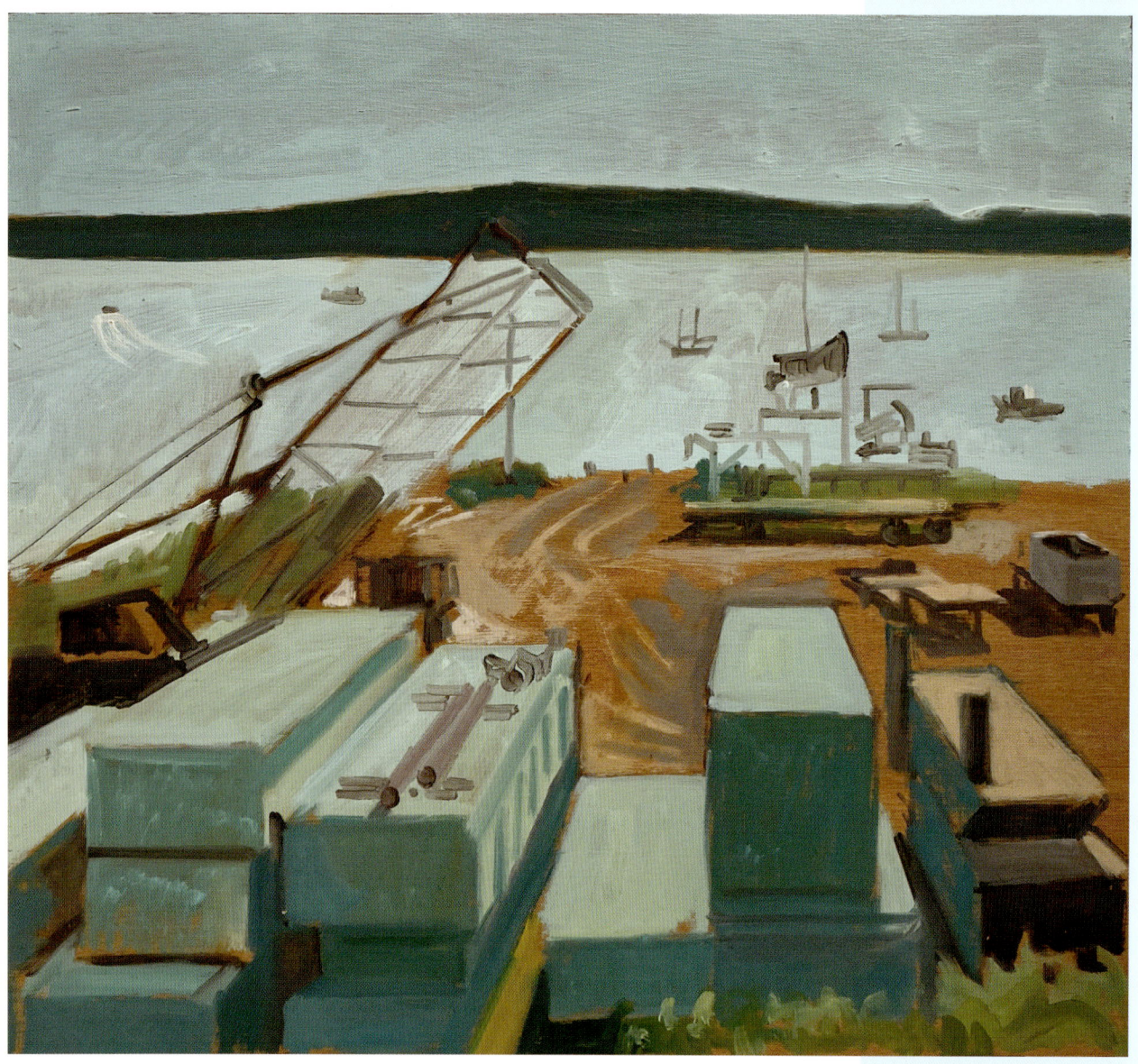

Lois Dodd
Prock Marine, 1999
Oil on panel, 14 ¾ x 16 ½ in.
Courtesy Caldbeck Gallery,
Rockland, Maine

Among Rockland's most venerable waterfront businesses is the Prock Marine Company. Founded in 1938, the construction company offers engineering services ranging from dredging to shoreline stabilization. The place also provides a coastal motif for painters, including **Lois Dodd**. Dodd is one of Maine's most heralded painters, thanks to her persistence of vision and her dedication to helping artists. She is known for intimate landscapes with flowers, figures, and houses inspired by her surroundings in Cushing.

In painting expeditions along the coast with friends, Dodd sometimes parks on the shoulder of Route 1 near Prock Marine and sets up her easel above the facility.

Today

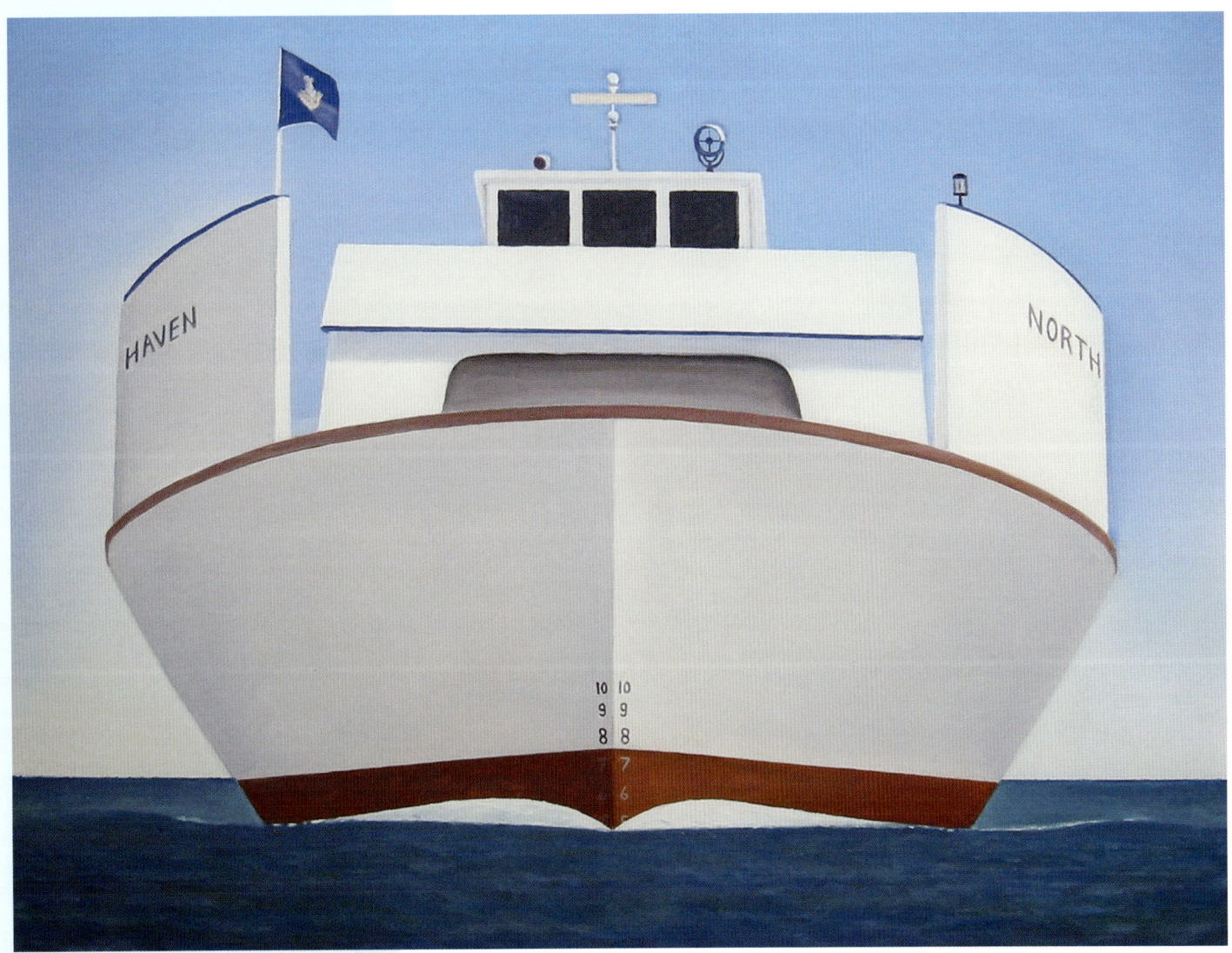

Sam Minot
North Haven Ferry, 2004
Oil on canvas, 16 x 20 in.
Collection of Chellie Pingree

In one of several paintings of the site, Dodd includes stacks of sectional barges and a crane. Hers is an impromptu image of coastal enterprise.

From Rockland, ferries depart bound for several Penobscot Bay islands, including Matinicus, North Haven and Vinalhaven. Bucksport resident **Sam Minot**, whose family has deep roots on North Haven, provides a head-on view of the island car ferry. The painting speaks to the power of modern-day transportation, the broad hull evenly cleaving the water. The painting hangs behind Maine Representative and North Haven islander Chellie Pingree's desk in her Washington, D.C., office.

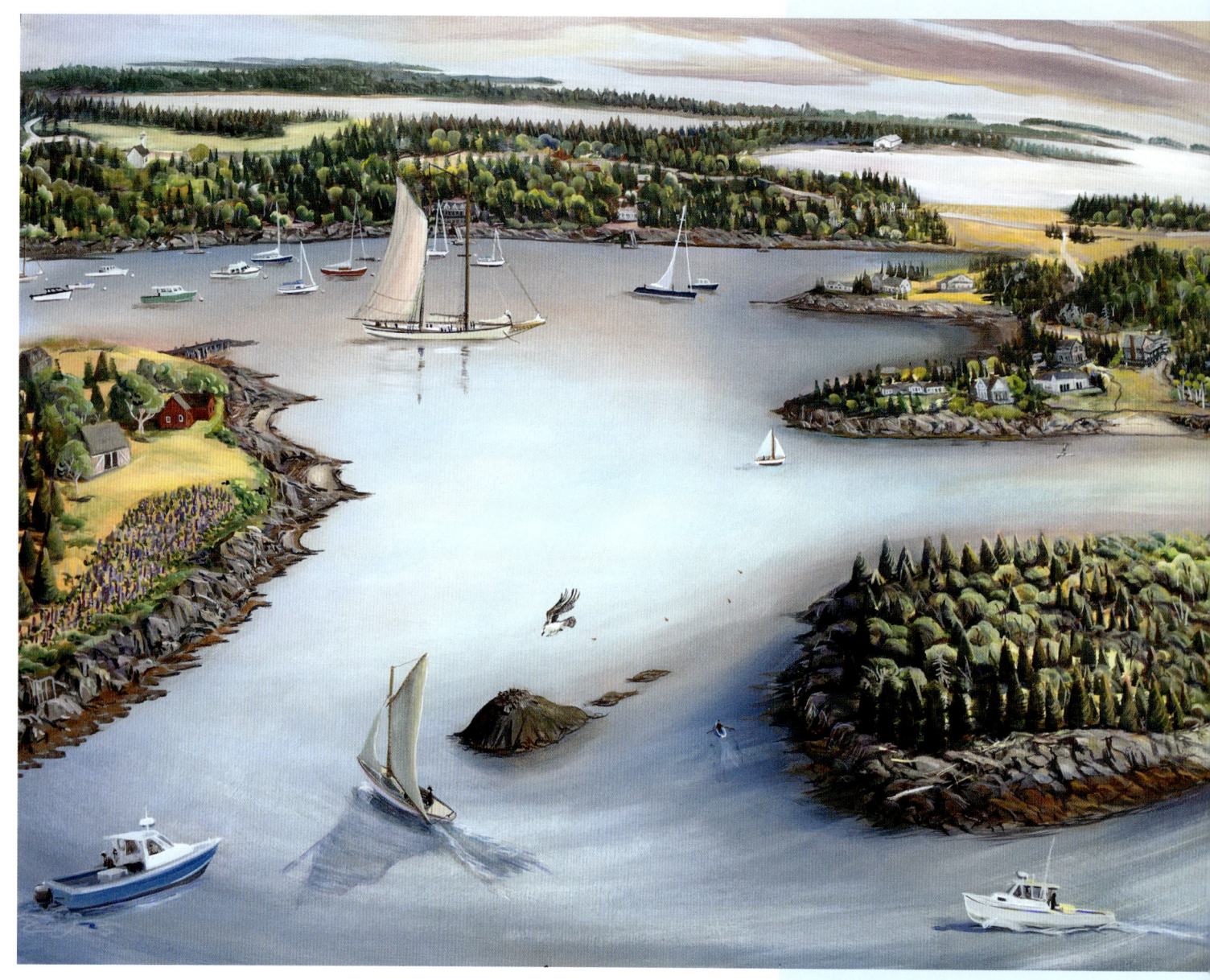

Amy Peters Wood
Coming Home, 2021
Egg tempera on cradled panel,
36 x 48 in.
Collection of Linda Cabot and
Ed Anderson

Today

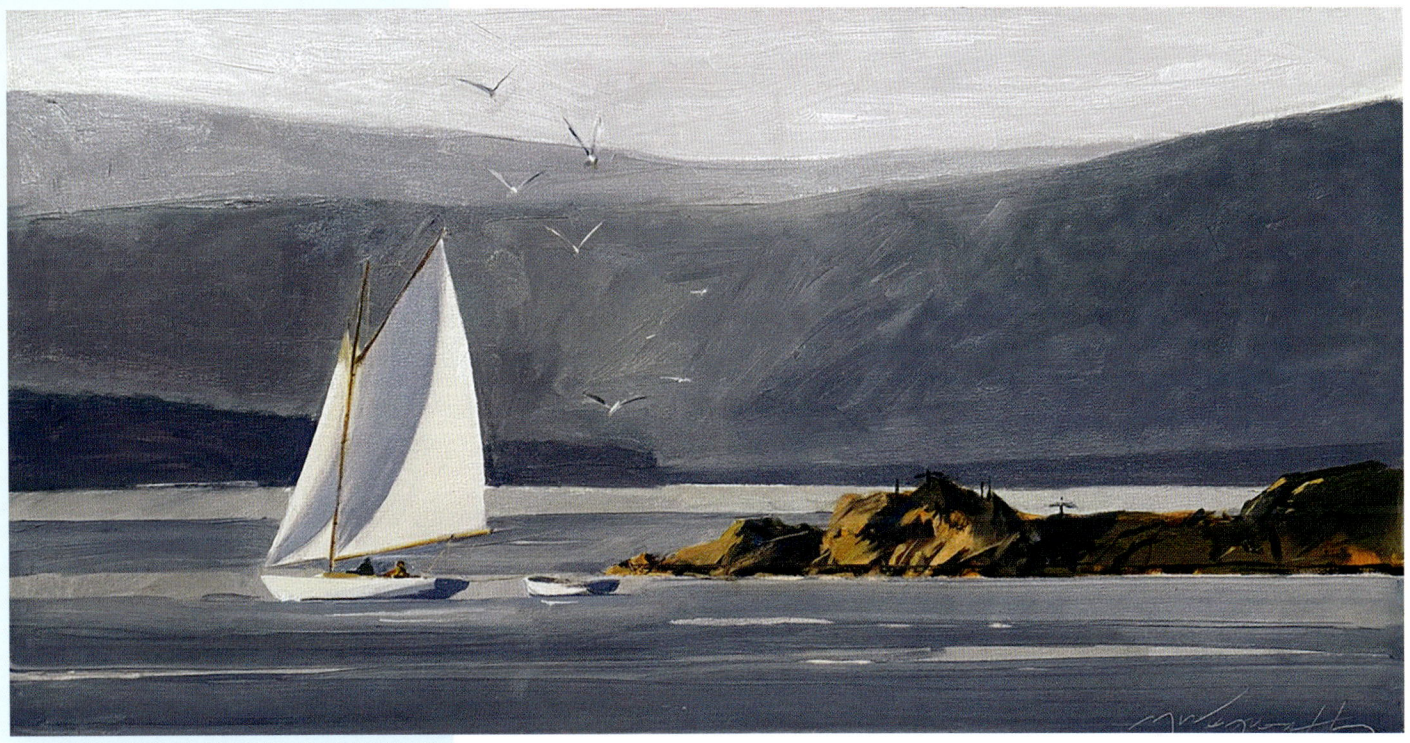

Michael Weymouth
Leaving Pulpit Harbor to a Chorus of Cormorants and Gulls, 2020
Oil on canvas, 12 x 24 in.

"There is no greater joy than rounding the bend of North Haven and seeing the entrance to Pulpit Harbor," says **Amy Peters Wood**. She brings this sentiment to life and light in her egg tempera painting *Coming Home* (2021). Like Minot, she has ties to this "refuge" island that go back generations, a place her family "will forever call home."

Michael Weymouth often uses Great Spruce Head Island as his base for explorations among the midcoast islands, drawn to the "ever-changing colors, hues, and values that are part of the Penobscot Bay palette." *Leaving Pulpit Harbor to a Chorus of Cormorants and Gulls* (2020) shows a sailboat leaving the North Haven harbor with the Camden Hills looming beyond. Weymouth believes capturing the forces of nature with paint "must come from the artist and the energy with which the scene is painted"—the energy and the emotional connection.

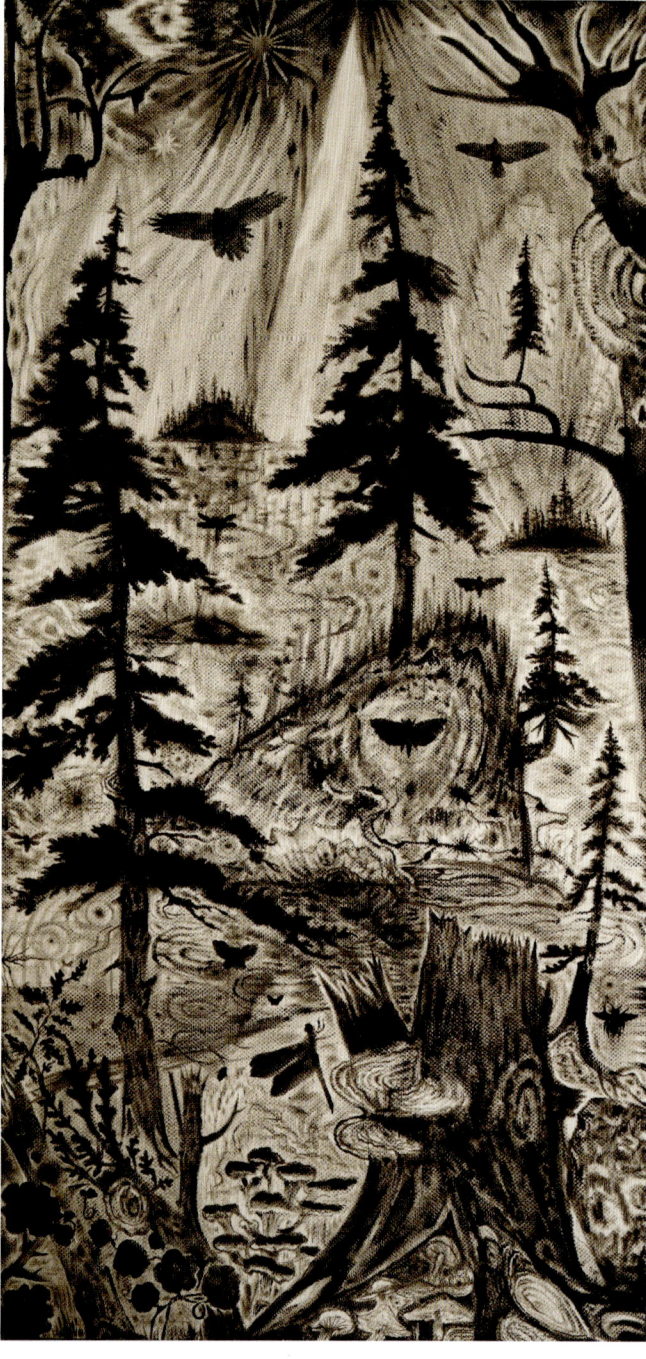

David Wilson
Last September, 2021
Acrylic on monk's cloth,
72 ¼ x 36 in.
Photo by William Trevaskis

In the years **David Wilson** has made his home on North Haven, he has immersed himself in the landscape. *Last September* (2021) is part of a set of paintings called "Black Watch" that incorporate memory, a sense of place, and "an indelible urge to draw trees over and over." Wilson takes liberties with the view, shifting islands, seeking, in his words, to "offer an opening to a place beyond." The large, narrow vertical canvas has an unusual surface, monk's cloth, which adds to its mystery.

Today

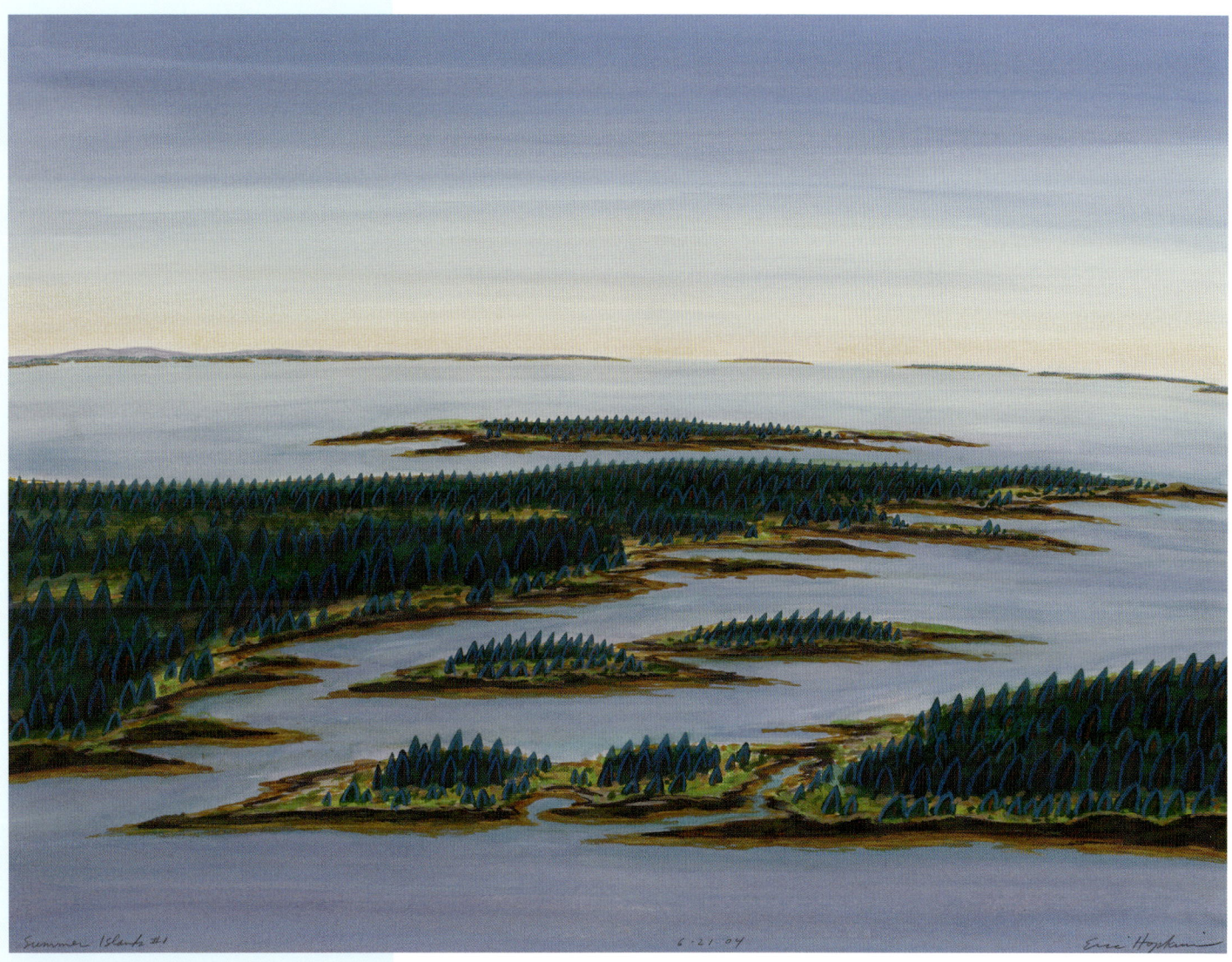

Eric Hopkins
Summer Island #1, 2004
Watercolor on paper,
21 ¾ x 29 in.
Bates College Museum of Art,
Jane Costello Wellehan Collection

Eric Hopkins grew up on North Haven and maintains a studio on the island. A passion for flying led to his signature aerial images of Penobscot Bay. By taking to the air, he found a new way to approach his home bay and to capture the curvature of the earth.

"Fly above [North Haven and Vinalhaven] and you will see that their contours have the beauty of a composition by an abstract-expressionist painter," wrote critic Gorham Munson. He might have been describing Hopkins's watercolor *Summer Island #1* (2004), which the painter calls "a familiar composite of the sights I've seen and the feelings I've felt as I fly around Penobscot Bay." The painting is all about "the interactions of land, water, and sky through time, space, and place"—nature's designs as seen from on high.

Art of Penobscot Bay

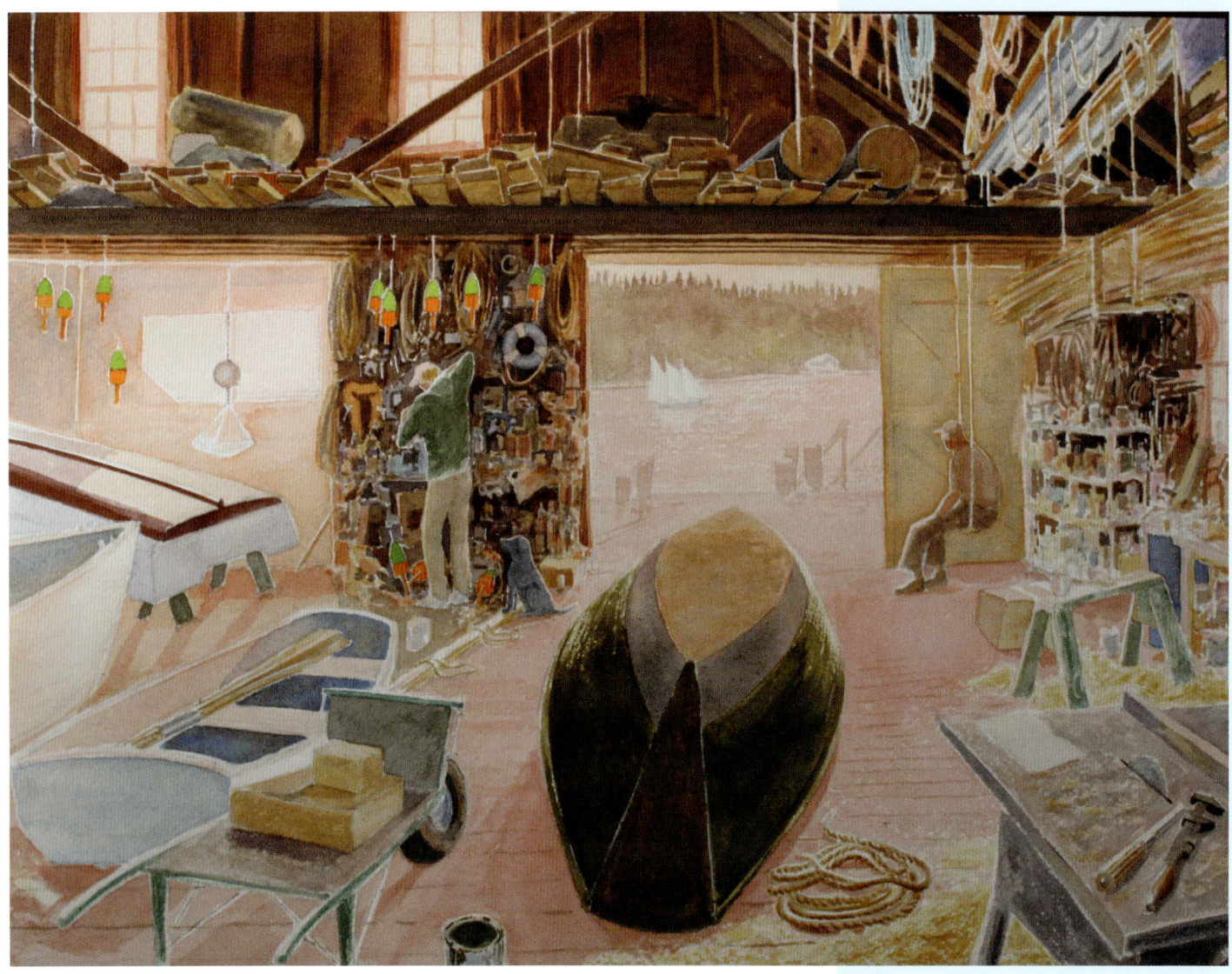

"My paintings," writes Wiscasset-based painter **Seaver Leslie**, "generally celebrate local culture and traditions." His watercolor *J. O. Brown Boatyard (North Haven)* (2012) pays tribute to a legacy of wooden boat building. Owned and run by the same family who began it, the boatyard has built lobster boats, launches, and sailing vessels for well over a century. The craft made there are "archetypal designs that have existed on Maine waters for centuries," Leslie explains, "which puts the boats and the builders in harmony with the past and the present, land and sea." The yard's narrative history is balanced by the visually ordered clutter and the fascinating juxtaposition of dark and light spaces.

Seaver Leslie
The J. O. Brown Boatyard, North Haven, 2012
Transparent watercolor, 11 x 14 in.
Private collection

Today

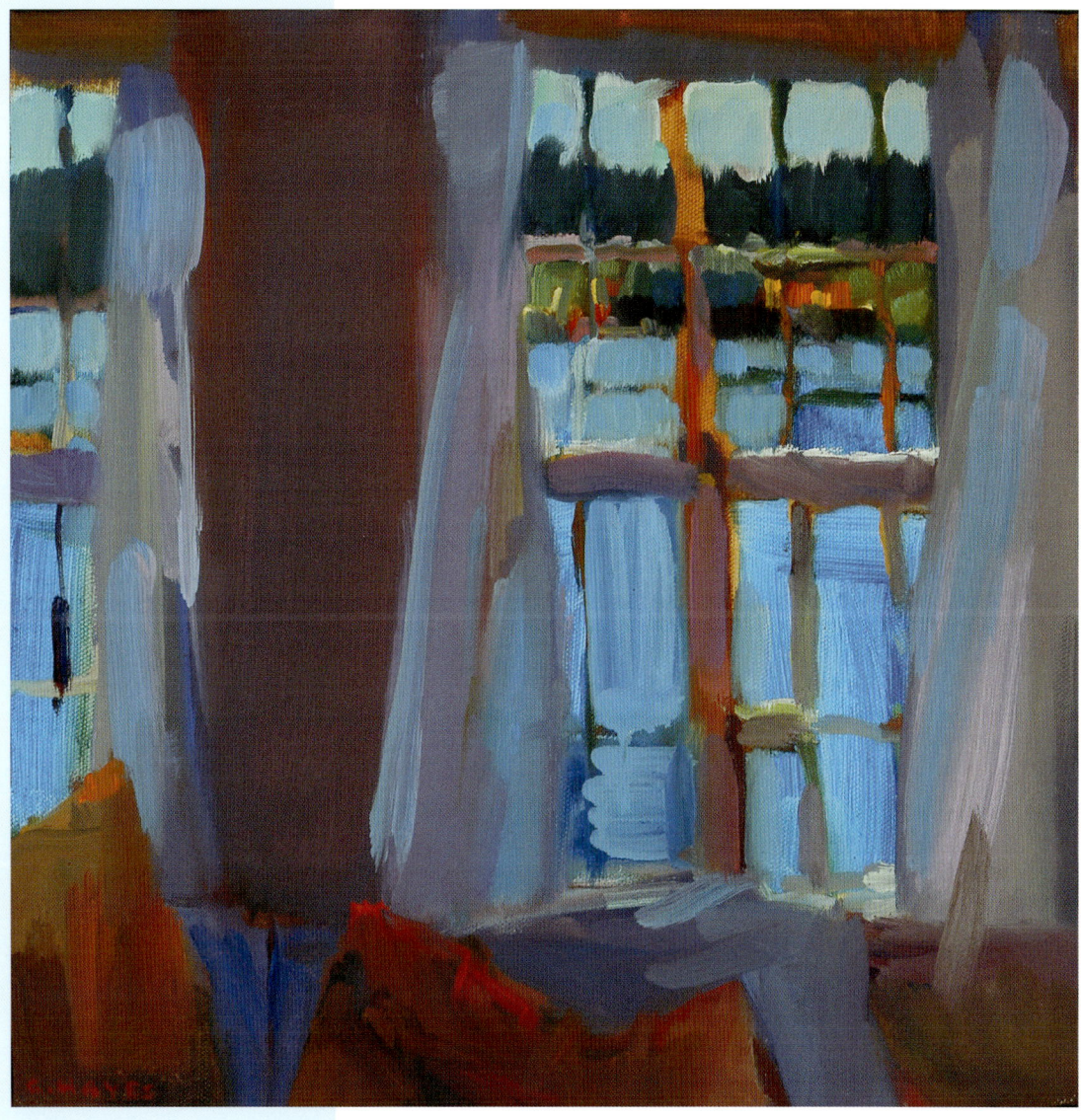

Connie Hayes
Blue on Arrival, VH, 2005
Oil on canvas, 12 x 12 in.

Near North Haven lies Vinalhaven. The island has served as a major muse for **Connie Hayes**, who can jump on the ferry from her home in Rockland and head across the water to renew her acquaintance with the largest island in Penobscot Bay.

Hayes's *Blue on Arrival, VH* (2005) is the view through the window of a cottage in Dogtown, Old Harbor, where the Vinalhaven ferry once docked. For more than ten years, when the painter returned in June to the cottage with her art and food supplies, "the grid of windows and waving curtains greeted me." The day of this painting, she recounts, "delivered bright sun and cobalt blue water, demanding my attention." The intimacy of this work comes through in the combination of her exquisite sense of color and intuitive touch.

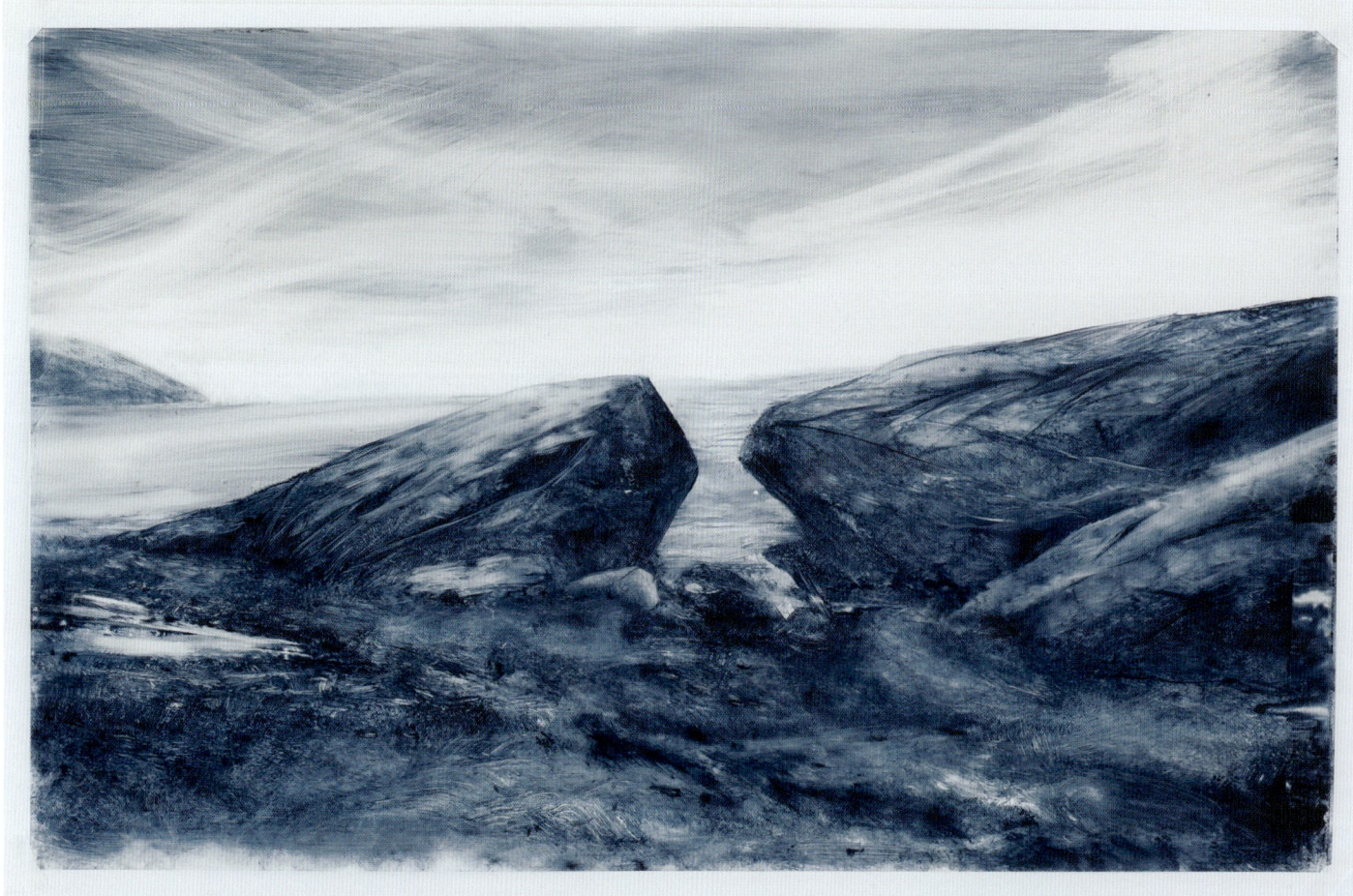

Brimstone Island is an uninhabited islet at the southern end of Vinalhaven Island. For the longest time Camden painter **Susan Williams** wanted to visit, having seen the black basalt stones that friends had collected there—"like trophies from a big adventure or touchstones from an island untouched," she writes. Getting there was impractical: a long haul by boat, often with fog and swells that made anchorage uncertain.

On September 10, 2019, while sailing with friends, Williams realized a bright fall sky and a flat sea made the trip possible. The resulting paintings have a somewhat foreboding look, befitting the island's name. Williams has noted at times her paintings "quietly hint at the anxiety of our times—the existential dread caused by climate change, the peril to democracies around the world, and the outsized irrationality and myriad absurdities of our everyday lives."

Susan Williams
Brimstone #4, 2019
Oil on acetate, 24 x 40 in.
Courtesy of Caldbeck Gallery, Rockland, Maine

Today

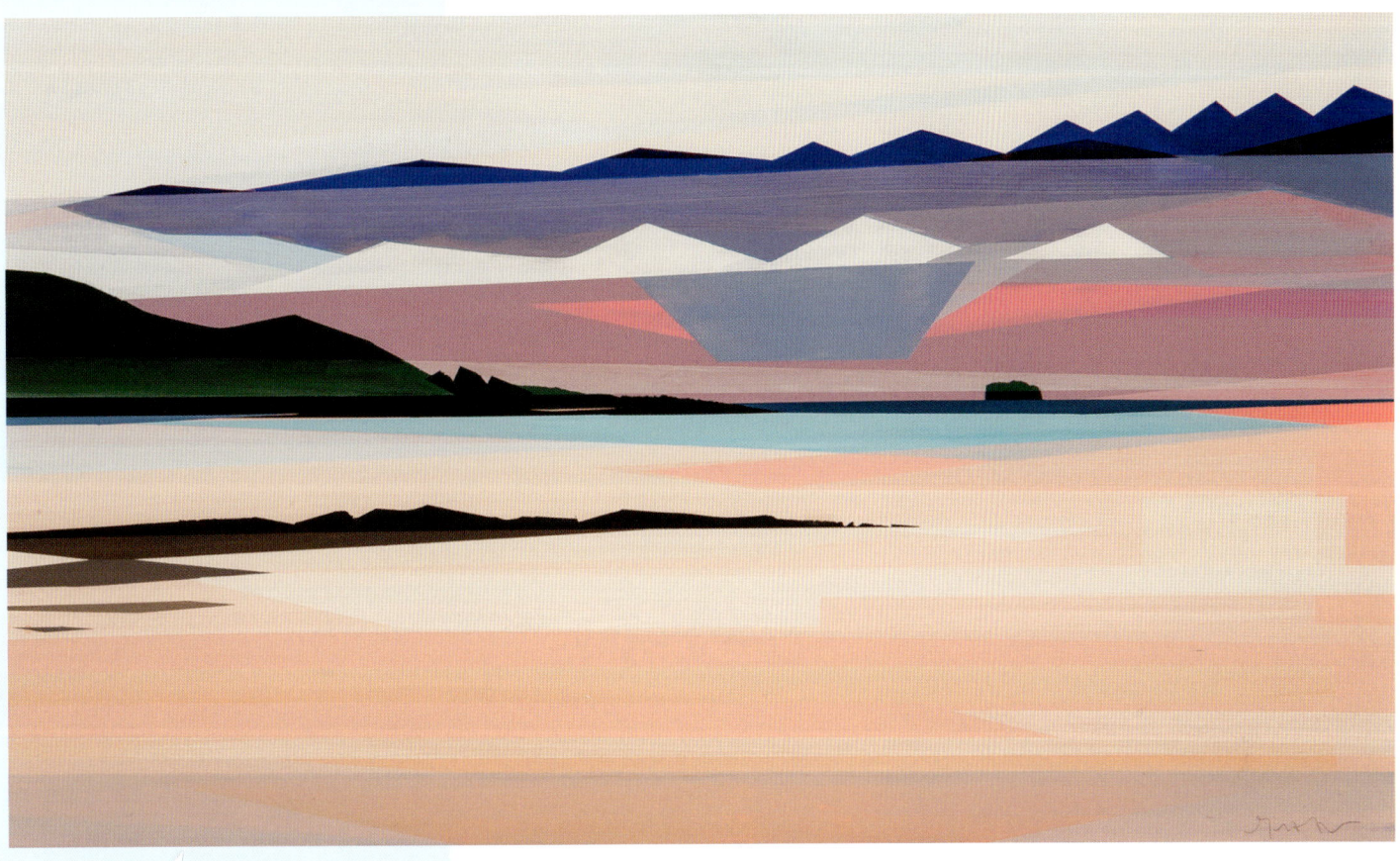

Greta Van Campen
Vinalhaven Day #3, 2020
Acrylic on panel
Courtesy Dowling Walsh Gallery, Rockland, Maine

A Thomaston resident from early in her life, **Greta Van Campen** practices a kind neo-precisionism in her acrylic paintings of Penobscot Bay, using clean definitive horizontal lines and vivid colors to represent and unify the chosen seascape. In *Vinalhaven Day #3*, she offers a wide-angle view of the bay and the Camden Hills translated into distinct geometric shapes and patterns. The painting started as watercolor studies the artist made while staying near Old Harbor with her family in August 2019.

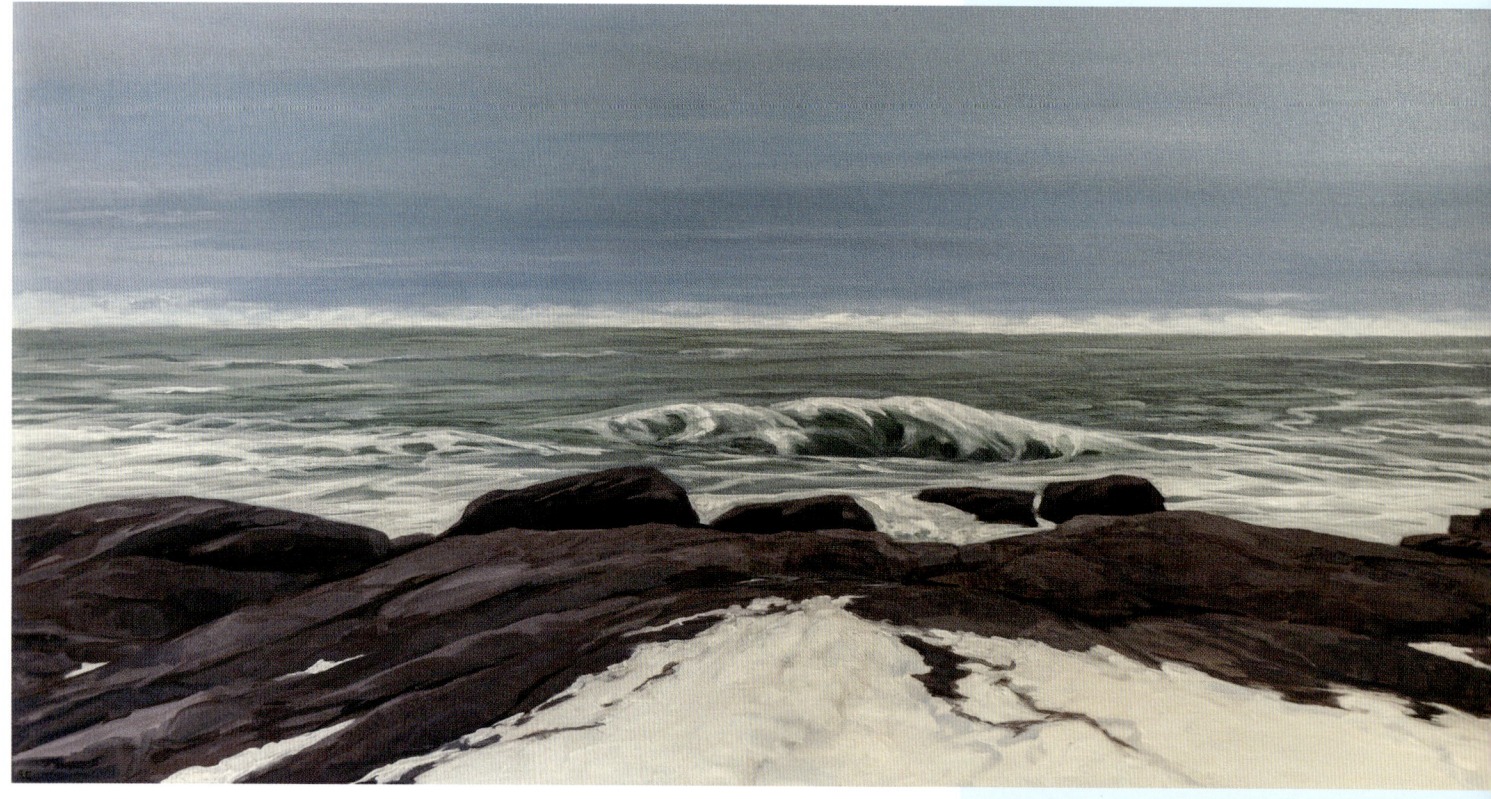

Elaine Crossman
Icy Ledges, 2021
Oil on canvas, 19 x 38 in.
Collection of Steve and Mary Karth
Courtesy of New Era Gallery,
Vinalhaven, Maine
Photo by William Trevaskis

    As a Vinalhaven year-rounder since 1976, **Elaine Crossman** knows winter. Regarding her painting *Icy Ledges* (2021), she notes her love of "the spare bony majesty of this rocky place in the middle of the enormous sea, especially in winter when the gale winds turn the waves translucent green." The day after a storm, she reports, "is always right for a hike out to a favorite ledge"—and a session at the easel.

    Philadelphia-based painter **Alexandra Tyng's** brother owns Indian Island at the entrance to Rockport Harbor and she has been able to paint the landscape and buildings from various angles over the years. "This island is one of those special places on which the buildings—lighthouse tower, keeper's house, barn, and shed—are grouped in a way that creates outdoor spaces with pleasing energy," Tyng relates. Warm early morning light produced the interesting shapes in her Hopper-esque painting *Peaked Shadow* (2012).

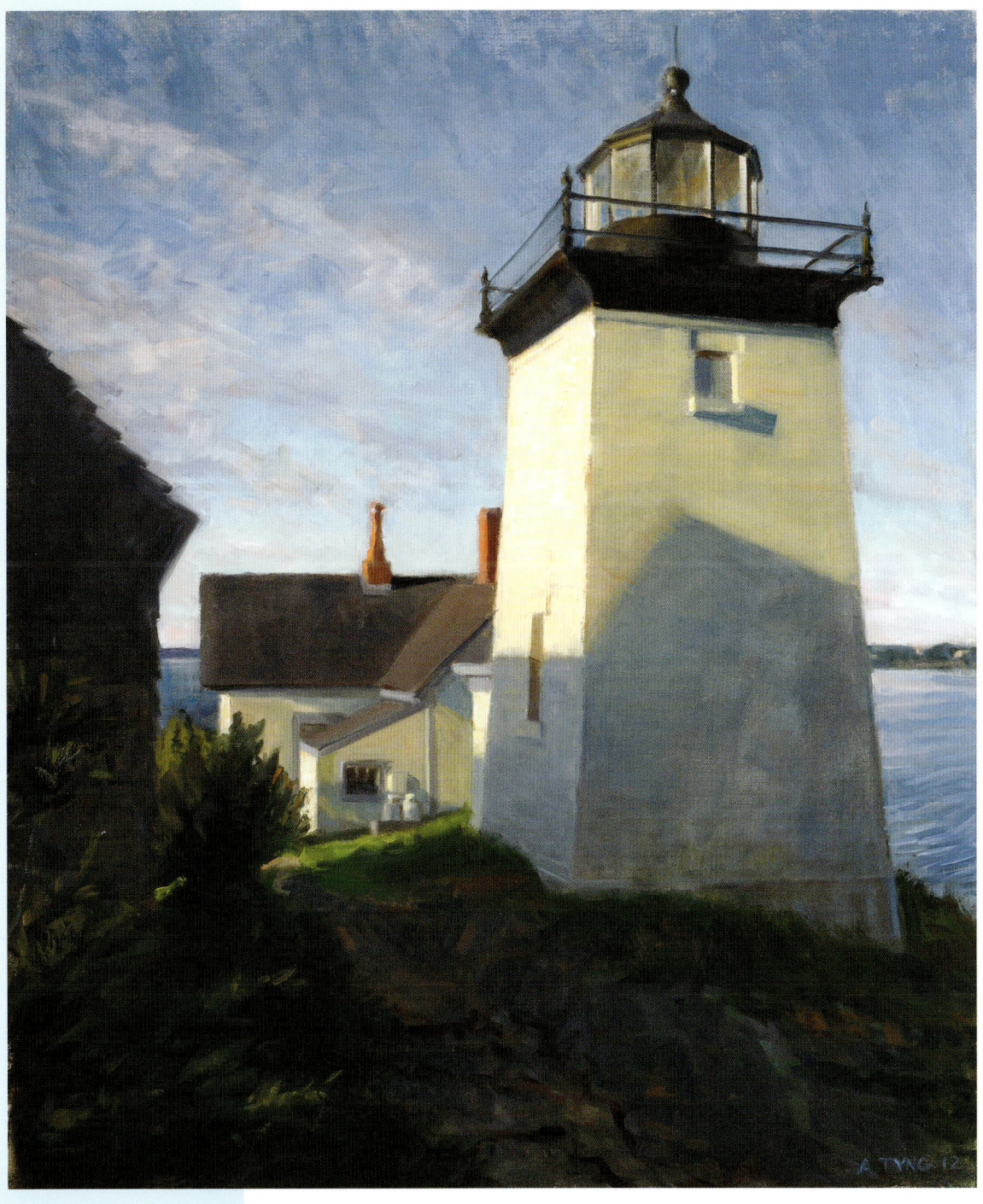

Alexandra Tyng
Peaked Shadow, 2012
Oil on canvas, 26 x 22 in.
Courtesy of Dowling Walsh Gallery,
Rockland, Maine
Photo by Karen Mauch

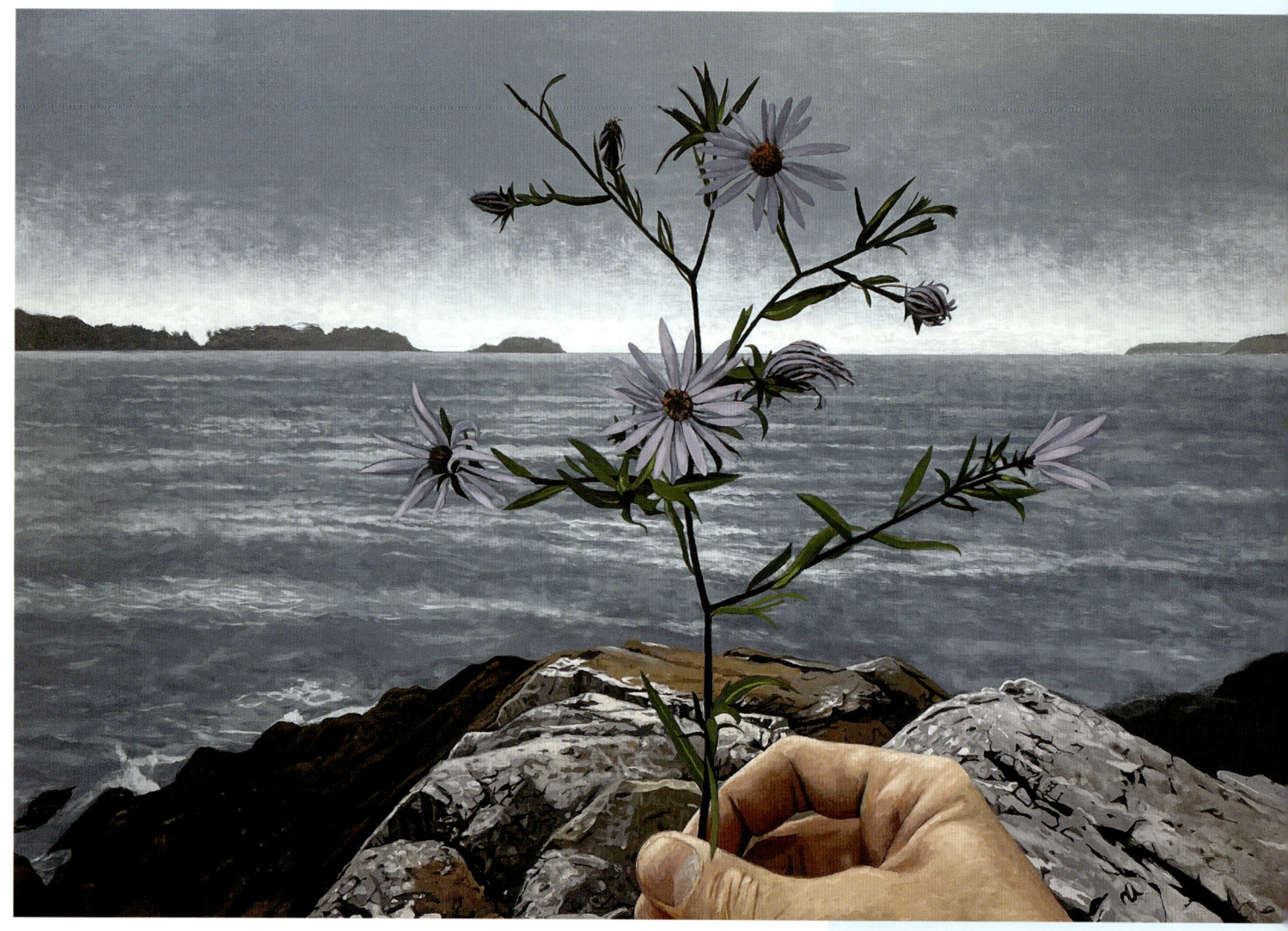

Christopher Mir
Crow Island Offering, 2021
Acrylic on canvas, 32 x 48 in.
Courtesy of Page Gallery, Camden, Maine

Christopher Mir's *Crow Island Offering* (2021) provides a view of outer Rockport Harbor and the end of Beauchamp Point as seen from the Harkness Preserve, which is managed by the Coastal Mountains Land Trust. The artist's hand holds a sprig of asters he found growing there. He sought to express in the painting "the power and poetry" of an extraordinarily beautiful place, "to give thanks for the magic of this reality."

Hawaiian-born Maine-based painter **Ian McKibbin White's** *Spite House Arriving at Deadman's Point* (2009) depicts an unusual incident in Maine history. In 1925 the Federal-period two-story manse traveled eighty-five miles on a barge from Phippsburg

Today

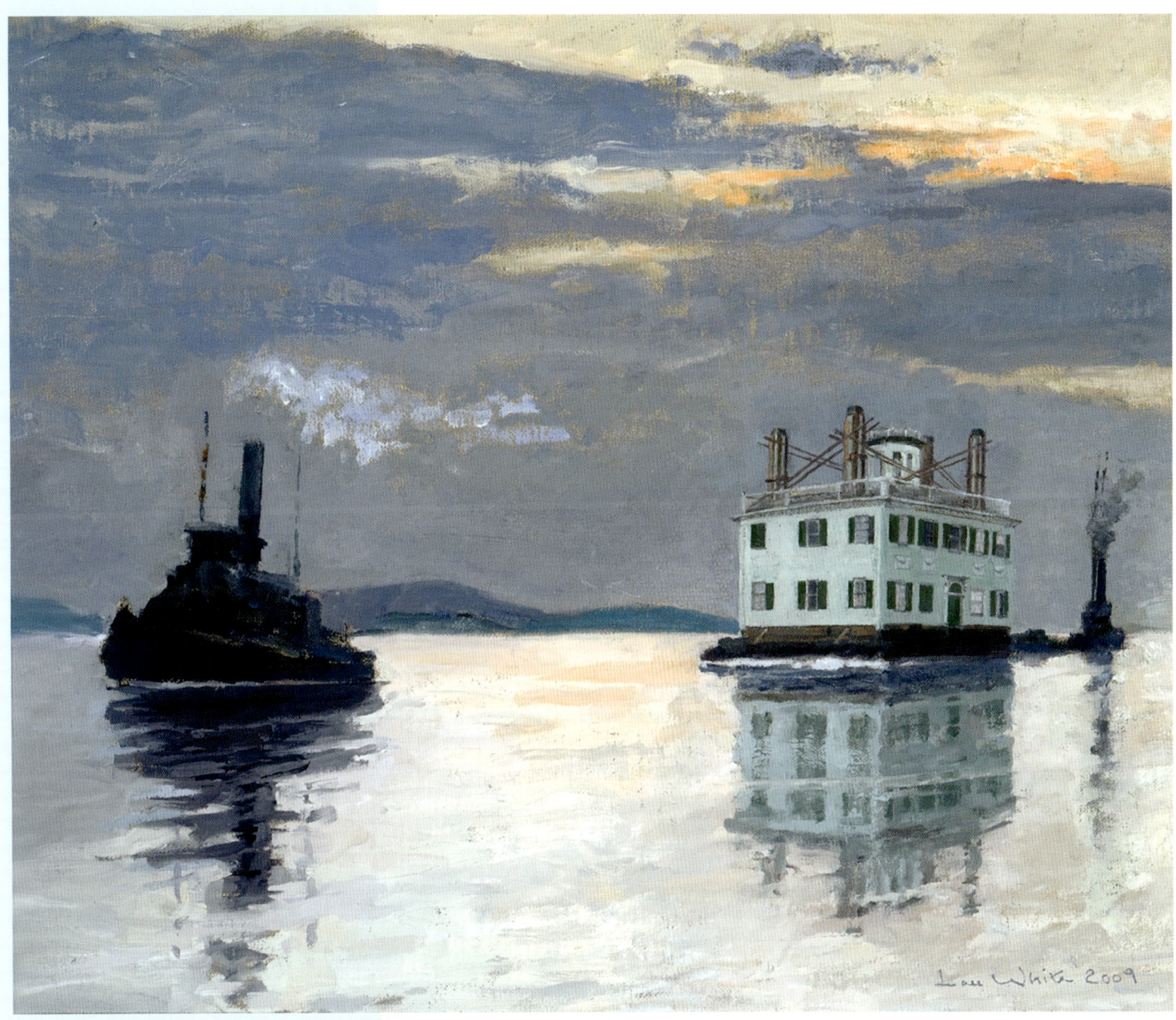

Ian McKibbin White
Spite House Arriving at Deadman's Point, 2009
Oil on canvas, 14 ⅝ x 17 ½ in.
Collection of Marylee and Charles W. H. Dodge

to Rockport, pulled and pushed by puffing tugboats. Listed on the National Register of Historic Places, the stately house is a surreal sight crossing the bay.

His paintings, White says, "unconsciously reflect change and the transitory aspects of life." The artist's creative impulse has extended to a distinguished museum career as director of the Fine Arts Museums of San Francisco and, in Maine, as the designer of the older Peary-MacMillan Arctic Museum at Bowdoin College.

The Penobscot name for what is now Camden is Megunticook, which can be translated as "great swells of the sea," thought to be a reference to the rolling hills that surround the town.

Watercolorist **Linda Norton** (1946–2018) spent her childhood summers in her grandparents' home in Camden. There she learned how to row, to read the tides, "where the fish were biting and where to pick mussels off the pilings," she recalled in a remembrance published in 2010. And there were art lessons: Her mother taught her how to paint and draw starting at age six.

When she returned to Camden as a professional painter later in life, Norton focused on the busy harbor, painting meticulous watercolors of various sailing vessels, drawn to their riggings, curves, and contours. *Roseway Reflections* (1999) pays homage to the "quiet and majesty" of the iconic schooner *Roseway*, which was built in 1925 as a racing vessel and now is home of the World Ocean School.

Moving to Camden from Brooklyn, New York, twenty or so years ago, **Colin Page** was introduced to the culture of boating, fishing, and exploring the coast by sailboat. As he settled in, Page painted the working waterfront and views of the harbor and bay from the Camden Hills. "The bay is a source of

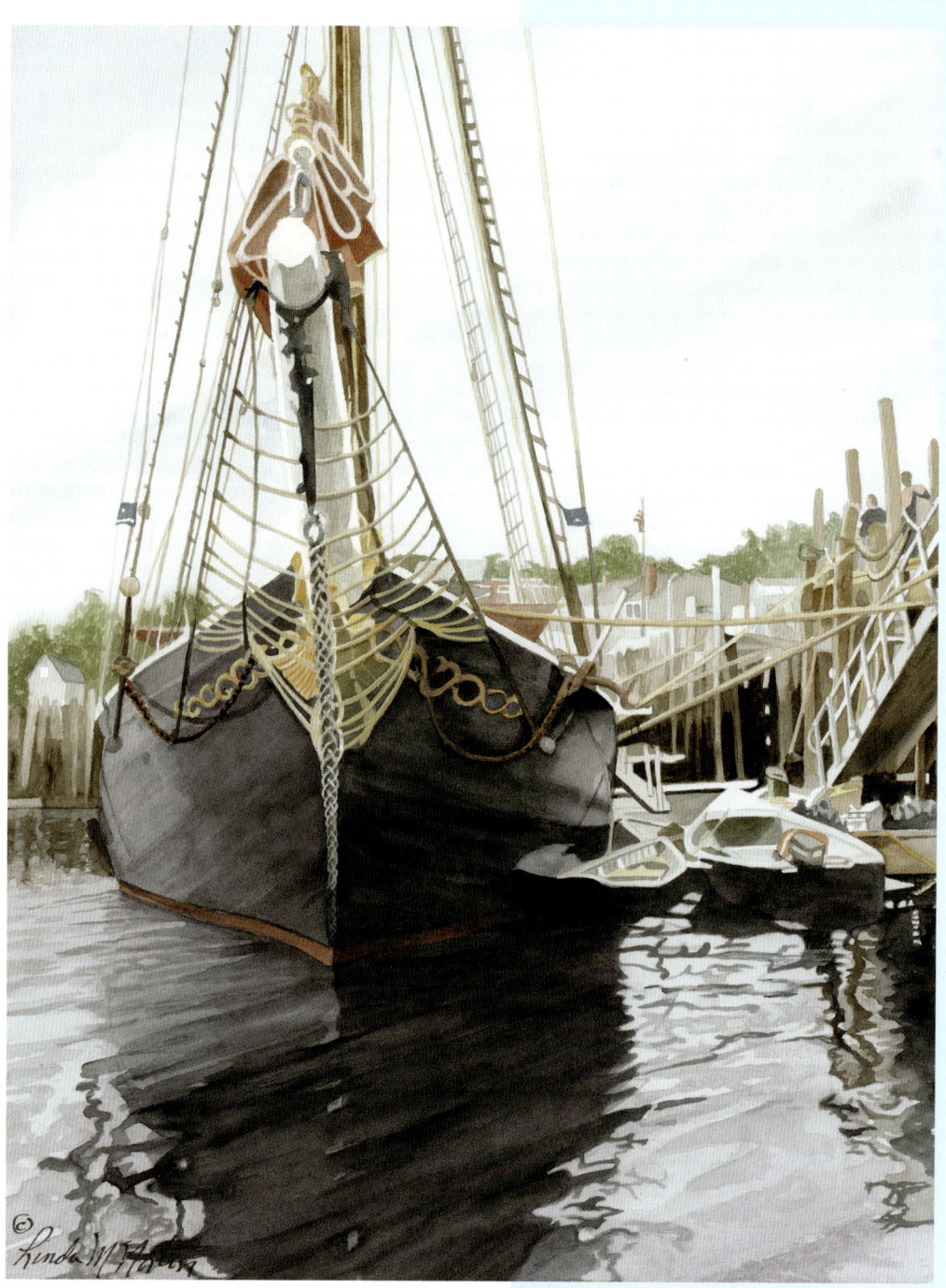

Linda Norton
Roseway Reflections, 1999
Watercolor on paper, 22 x 14 in.

Today

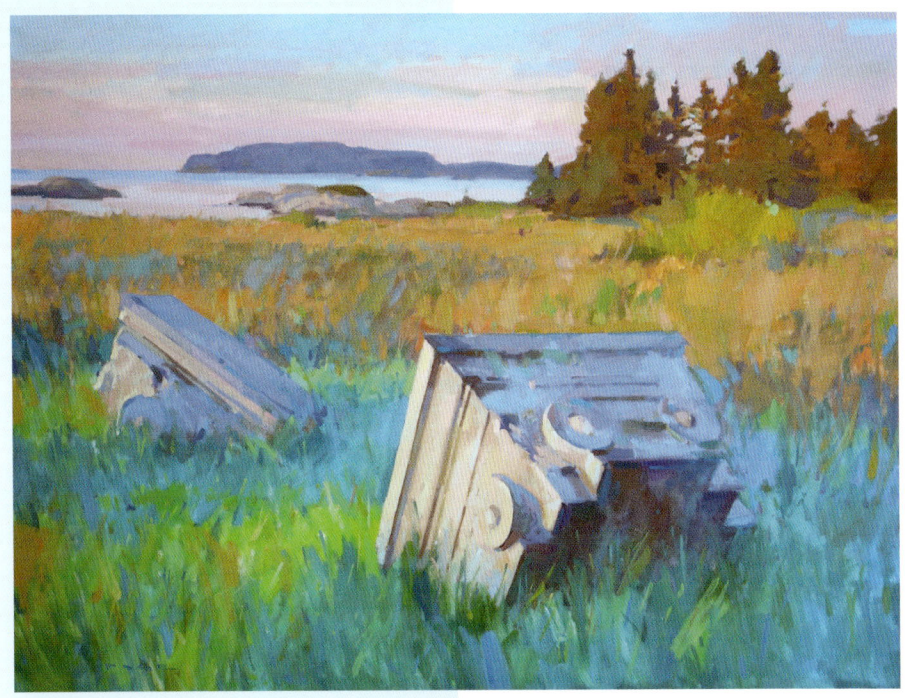

Colin Page
Columns, 2020
Oil on canvas, 36 x 48 in.

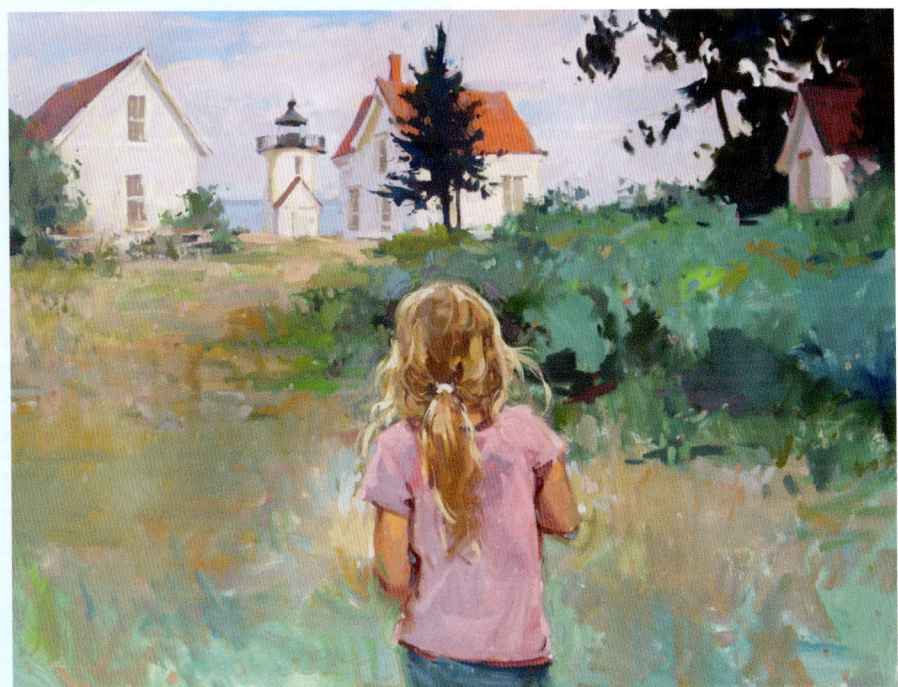

Colin Page
Island Explorer, 2021
Oil on canvas, 30 x 40 in.

adventure, a refuge at the end of a long day, an opportunity to learn, and a constantly deeper source of inspiration," Page noted. "Painting Penobscot Bay has been a big part of developing who I am as a painter."

When he took up sailing, Page discovered a fresh perspective—and new painting territory. *Columns* (2020) was prompted by a visit to Dix Island, which once boasted a thriving granite quarry and where remnants of the work of European stone workers can be found. "An idyllic landscape is broken up by reminders of the long history of human interaction with the bay," wrote Page.

In *Island Explorer* (2021), Page's daughter Hazel leads the way toward the lighthouse on Curtis Island, which friends of the artist take care of. "Our adventures on the bay always end up with windblown hair and shaggy clothes," he explains.

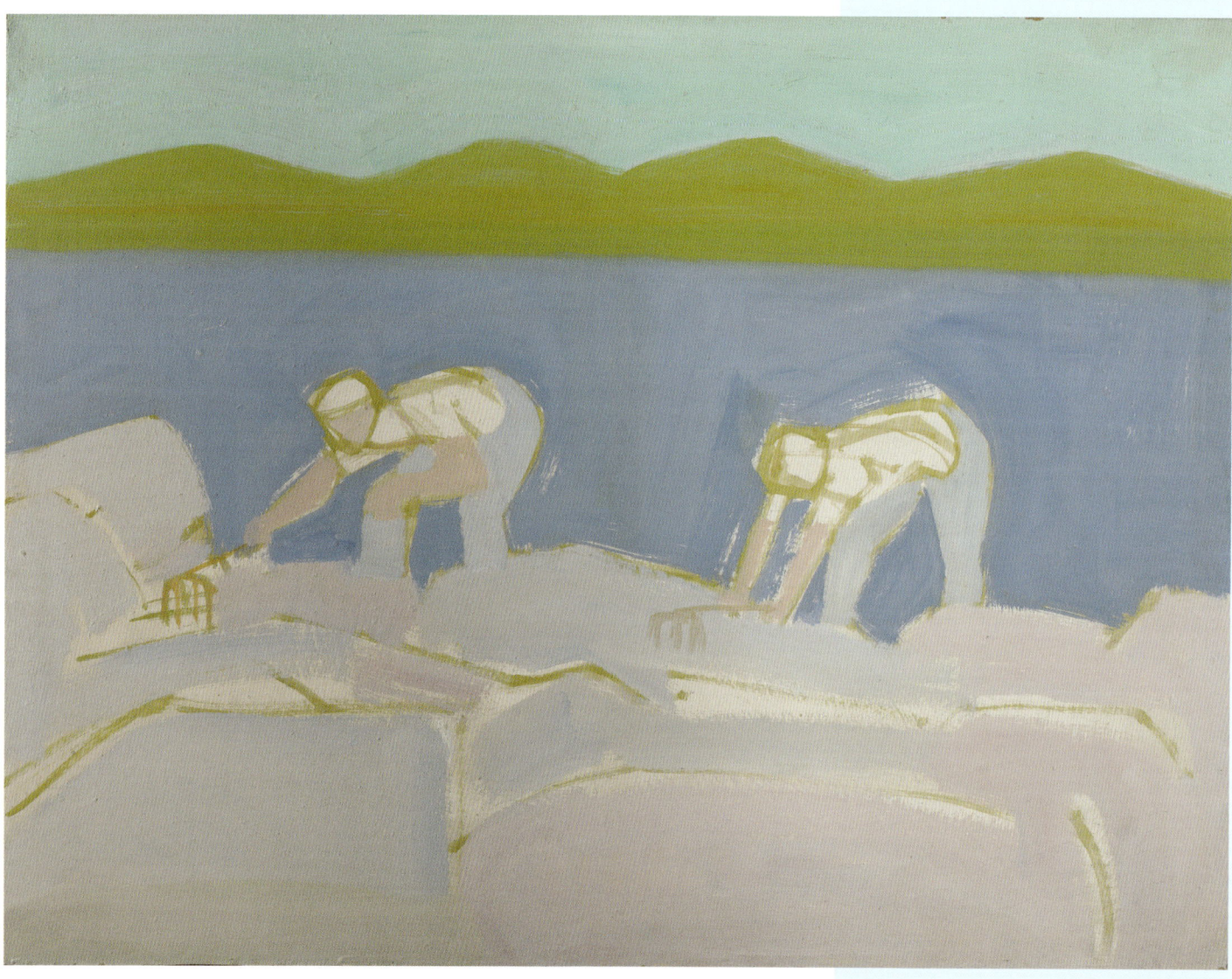

In his early years, the 1950s, in Lincolnville, **Alex Katz** often turned to the local scene for inspiration. On summer sojourns from New York City, the forerunner of Pop Art already practiced a simplified aesthetic, reducing elements of the landscape to their essence. In his *Clamdiggers at Ducktrap* (1956), two men rake the flats for surf clams, their motions seemingly choreographed against the bay and Camden Hills beyond. Katz once noted painting plein air at the Skowhegan School of Painting and Sculpture gave him "a reason to devote my life to painting."

Alex Katz
Clamdiggers at Ducktrap, 1956
Oil on Masonite, 30 x 40 in.
Colby College Museum of Art

Today

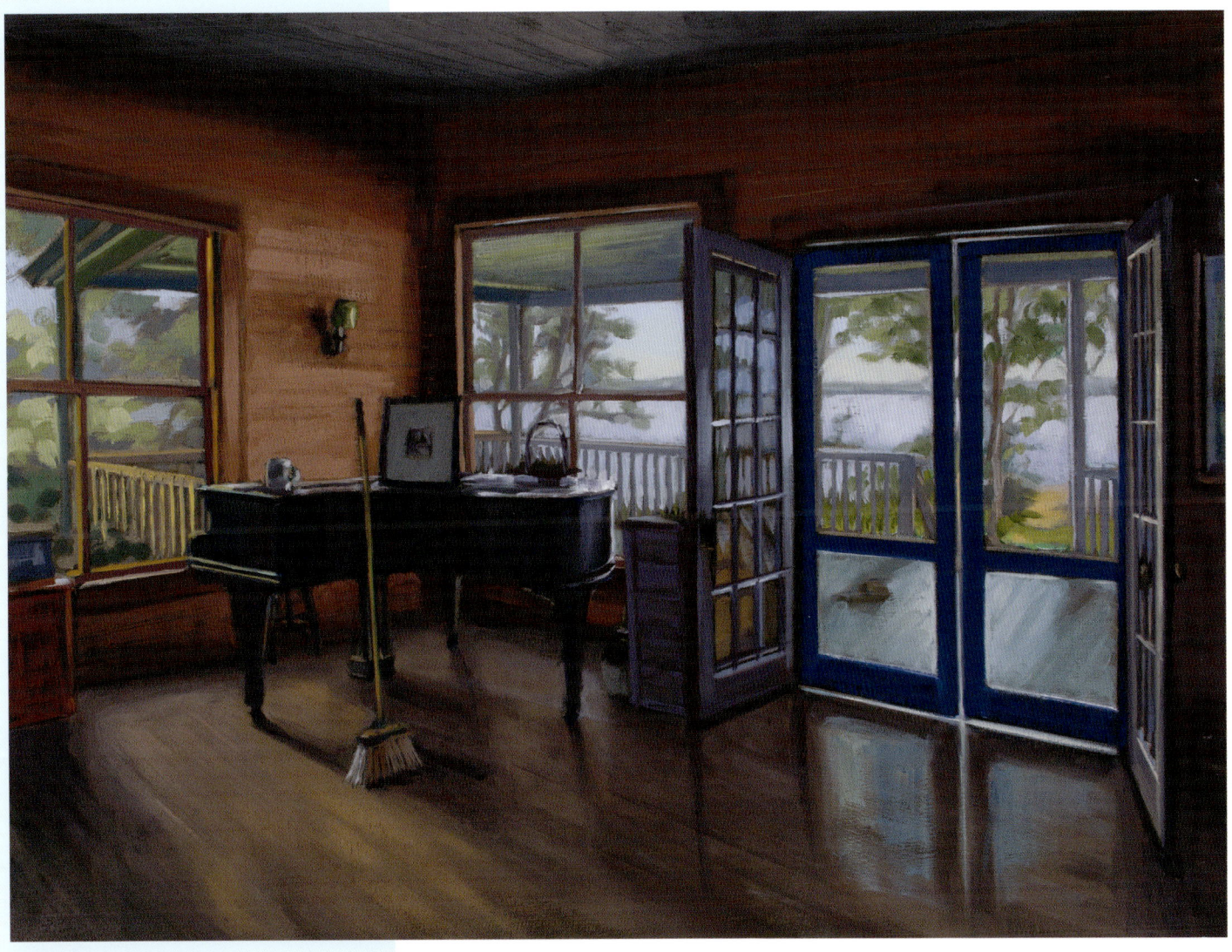

Alison Rector
Spring Sweeping, 2017
Oil on panel, 12 x 16 in.
Courtesy of Courthouse Gallery Fine Art, Ellsworth, Maine
Photo by Ken Woisard

Belfast-based painter **Alison Rector** specializes in interiors, "the light entering rooms and buildings," she writes. While working on paintings for an exhibition "How the Light Gets In"—the title references a line of a famous Leonard Cohen song—Rector visited a friend's cottage in the Bayside neighborhood of Northport to do some sketching. The view from inside caught her eye: the piano, the cool light falling from the wraparound porch, the blue of Penobscot Bay. "It was springtime," she writes, "a time for sweeping out the winter dust and readying for summer."

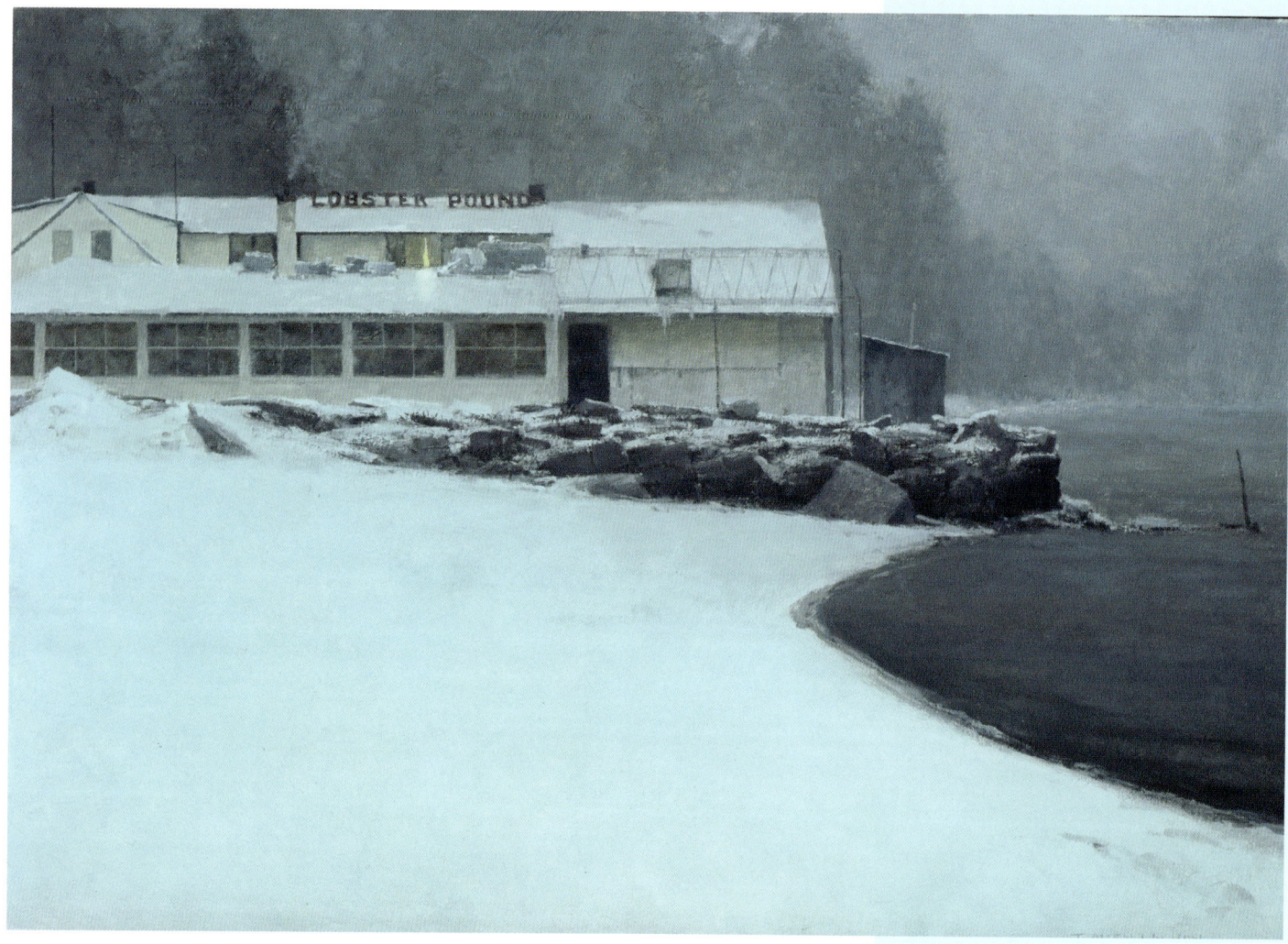

T. Allen Lawson
The Lobster Pound, 2006
Oil on linen, 24 x 34 in.
Courtesy of Page Gallery, Camden, Maine

Another season marks **T. Allen Lawson's** painting *The Lobster Pound* (2006)—*winter*. The Wyoming transplant who makes his home in Rockport rendered the well-known restaurant in Lincolnville in shades of white and gray, with a single flame-like light in a window lending a sense of occupation. Lawson once stated the transition from painter to artist happens "when you cross the line of painting what you see to painting what you feel about what you see." That line is crossed here: This image of winter coastal Maine resonates with a profound sense of place.

Lincolnville is the point of embarkation for Islesboro; the state ferry makes the round trip throughout the year, with fewer rides in the off season. The Penobscot people called Islesboro *Pitaubegwimenahanuk*, "the island that lies between two

Today

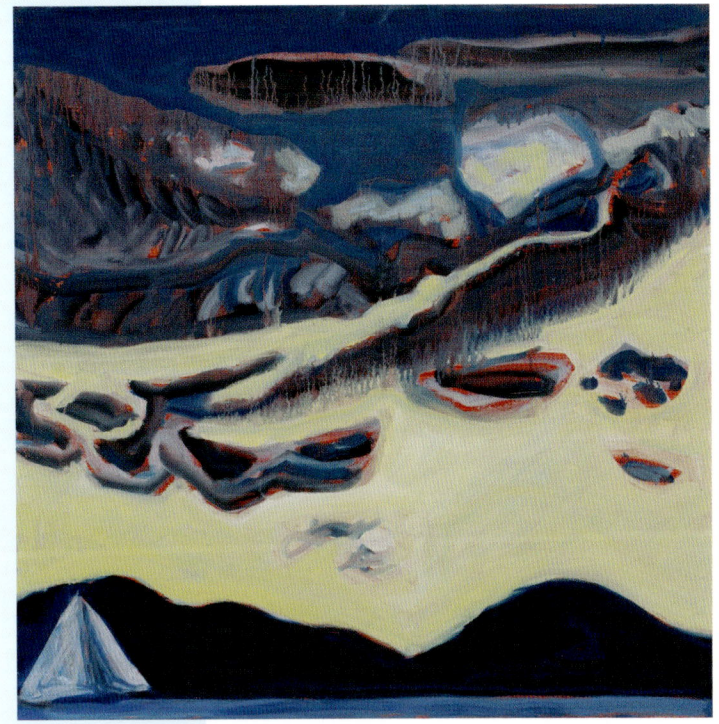

Brita Holmquist
Storm Passes,
2014
Oil on canvas,
24 x 24 in.

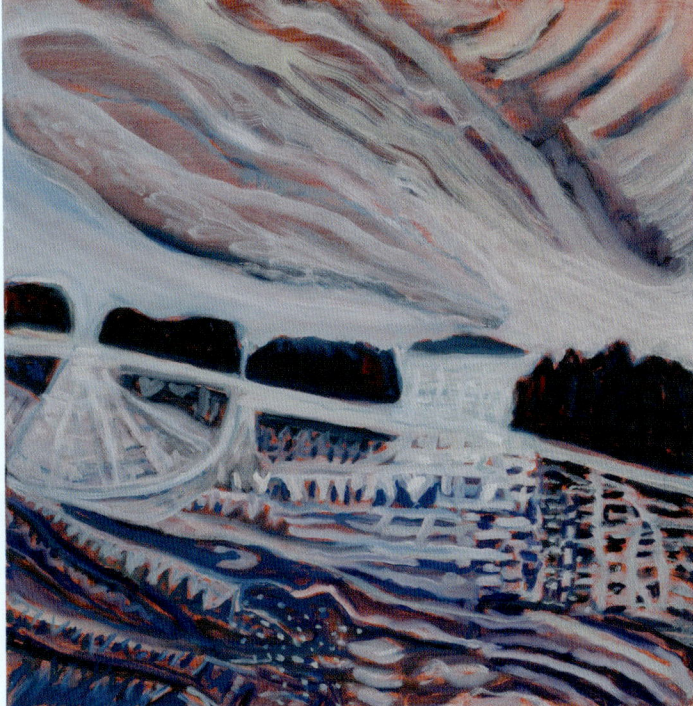

Brita Holmquist
Brackett's Channel from Maria's Porch,
2019
Oil on canvas,
24 x 24 in.

channels," the western and eastern waterways of Penobscot Bay.

Brita Holmquist has long made her seasonal home on Islesboro. Her vibrant, often semi-abstract landscapes of Penobscot Bay are marked by lively brushwork that convey the flux of weather and water and the tilt of the horizon. She especially likes the thunderstorms that come down the bay from the Camden Hills around Northport. From her house, she can watch them "throw themselves across the water." When the storm passes, she reports, there is often great clarity of light and wisps of the lingering black clouds. That is when she works rapidly, masterfully, "catching a precious moment in time."

Over the years Holmquist has painted the multitude of views from the island, including the prospect of Brackett's Cove from the porch of a friend's ancestral home. "In Maine," Holmquist once stated, "any turn in the road brings a possibility to encounter overwhelming beauty." Or any stretch of the bay: Her paintings of the archipelago consistently surprise.

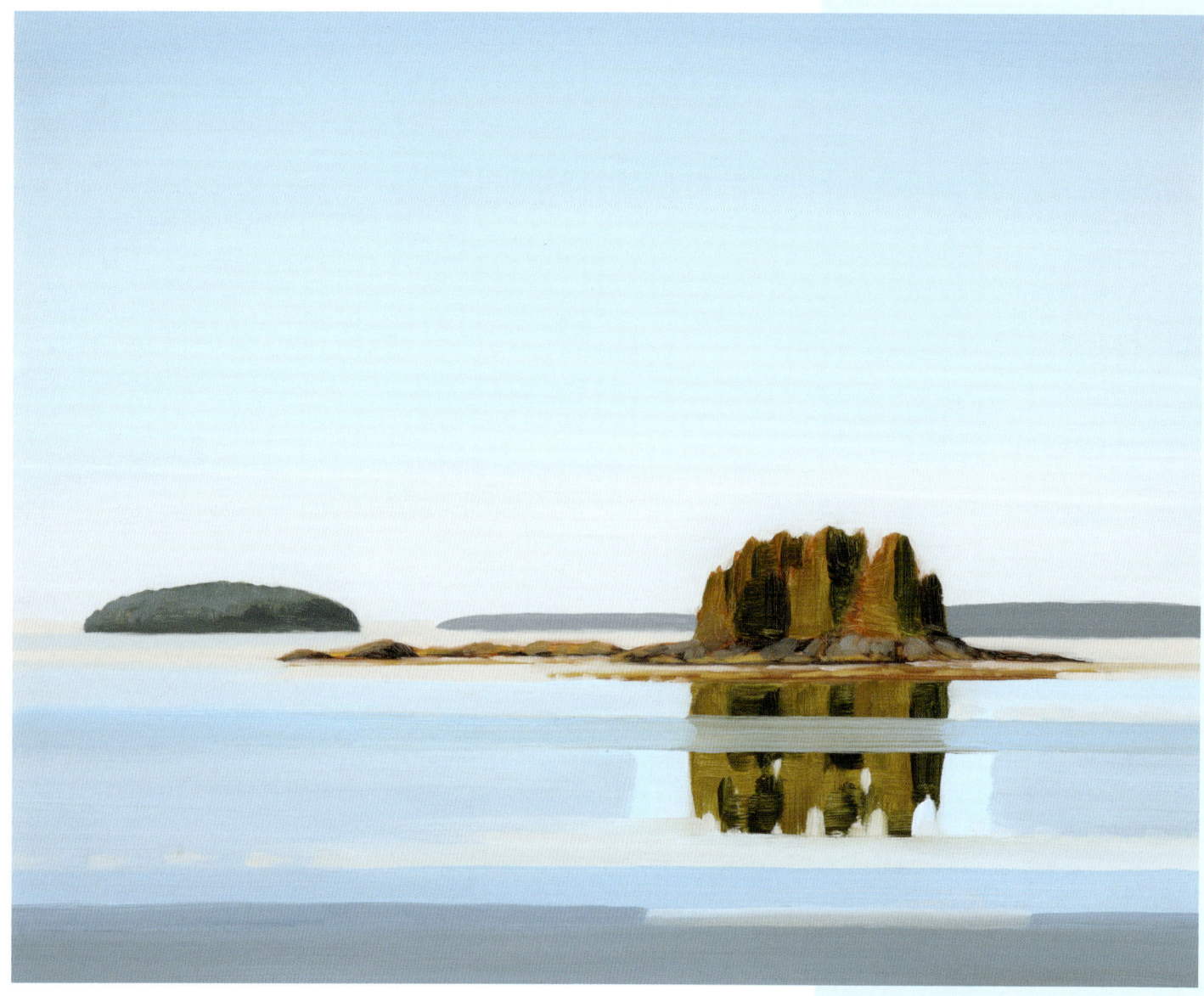

Nearly every year Holmquist shares her home and island with artist friends, among them, Stockton Springs painter **Sarah Faragher** who has been part of an annual Islesboro retreat for many years. Faragher, who was born in Bar Harbor, spent time on Vinalhaven when she was a child, so the landscapes and views are familiar and cherished.

In her painting of Thrumcap, a small island off Kissel Point on the eastern side of the island, Faragher captures the limpid still-morning light. "I see places as themselves, whole and complete, not belonging to anyone or anything," she writes. "And when I paint them," she adds, "I belong too."

Sarah Faragher
Morning Stillness, Thrumcap, Islesboro, Maine, 2017
Oil on panel, 8 x 10 in.
Collection of the artist
Photo by Ken Woisard

Today

Painter **Abe Goodale's** great-great-grandfather was Charles Dana Gibson. Today, he paints in his forebear's studio on Seven Hundred Acre Island off the southern end of Islesboro, but the subjects are vastly different: Where the Gibson Girls represented ideal women with perfectly coiffed hair, Goodale's portraits of fishermen, which he started painting in 2016, are true to life.

In the watercolor *Pause* (2018), the lobster boat captain stands at the starboard gunwale looking aft to his sternman while resting his gloved hands on traps to either side. In all his portraits, Goodale seeks to pay tribute to the stalwart individuals behind this "thriving yet fragile industry."

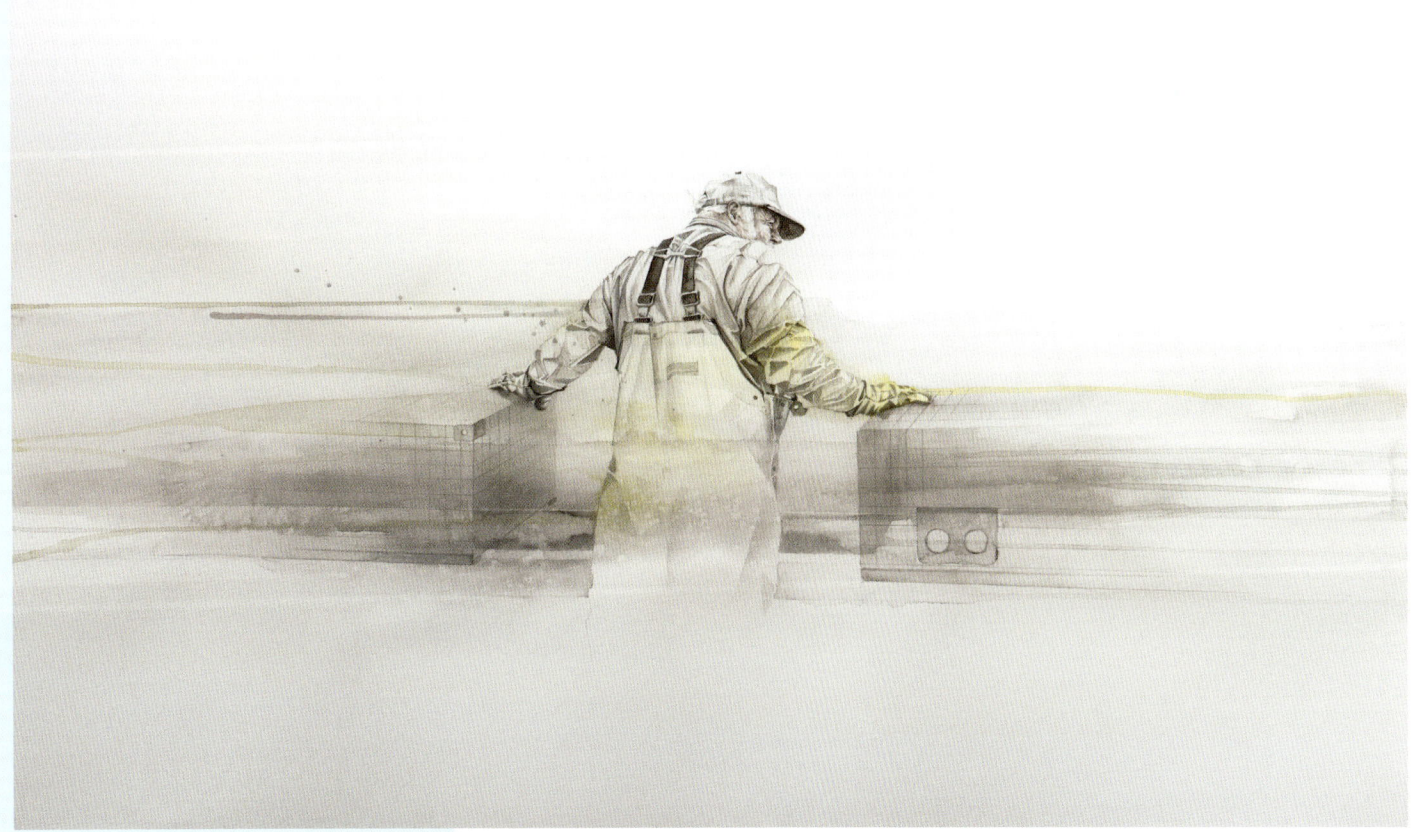

Abe Goodale
Pause, 2018
Watercolor on paper, 22 x 30 in.

Art of Penobscot Bay

"Belfast never was and isn't now a pretentious place. It just quietly and industriously minds its own business," wrote Louise Dickinson Rich about the town built at the mouth of the Passagassawakeag River where it flows into western Penobscot Bay.

The town's waterfront gazebo and boathouse provide the setting for **David Estey**'s *Belfast Summer Nights* (2006). The painter, who makes his home near the harbor, calls the painting "a narrative tribute" to the free Thursday-night music performances once held there. The painting was selected in a national competition for the 2010 AARP calendar, with a theme of "No place else I'd rather be." The figure in the lawn chair is the artist's father.

To fill out his artistic life in Belfast, Estey started an informal once-a-month "salon" of area artists. The artists check in via Zoom with a set agenda, which includes digital presentations of current work together with critiques, reports on museum

David Estey
Belfast Summer Nights, 2006
Oil on panel, 16 x 24 in.

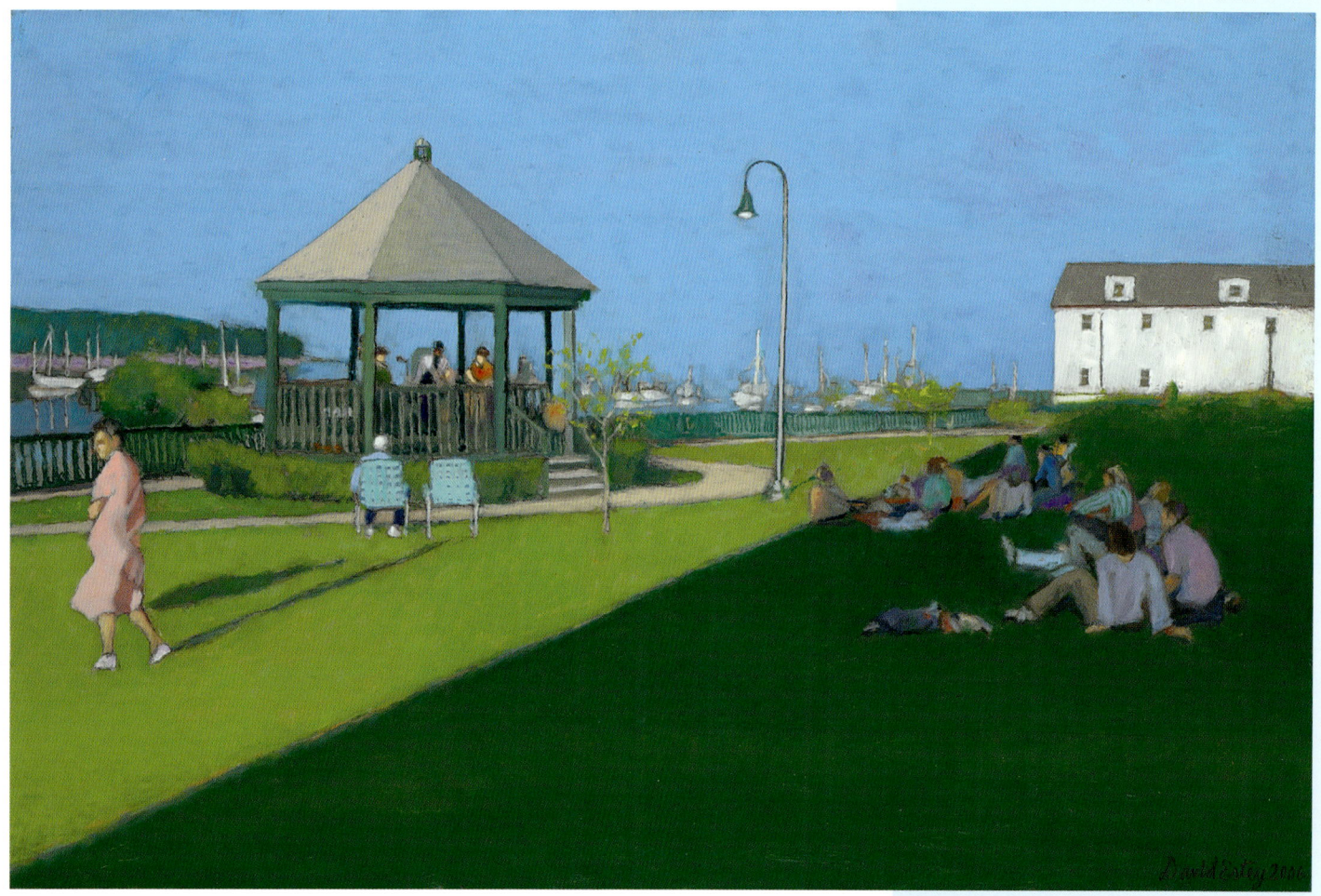

88

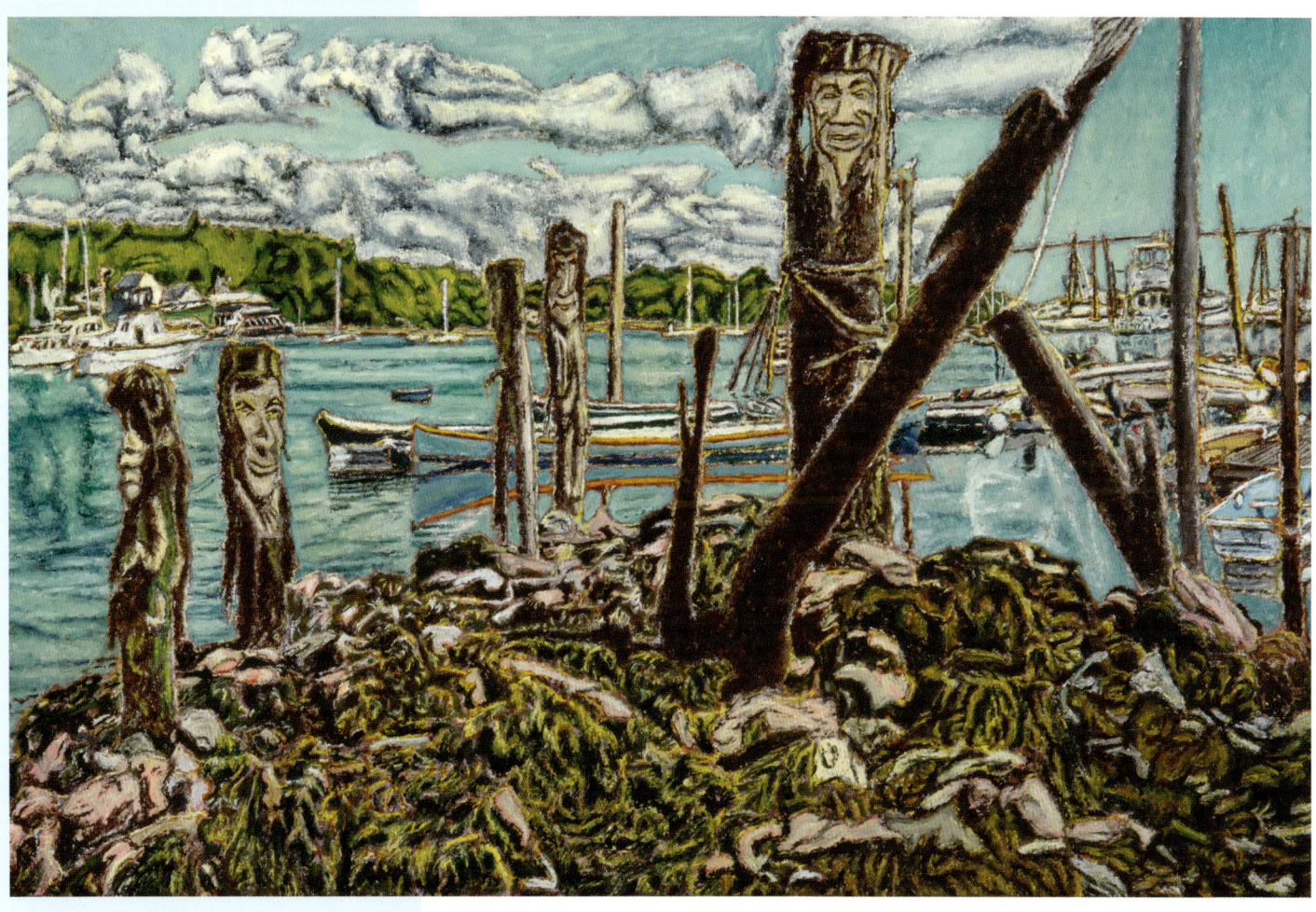

Jeff Loxterkamp
Guardians of Belfast, 2014
Oil on canvas, 24 x 26 in.
Photo by Ken Woisard

exhibitions, events to watch out for, and reviews worth reading—providing a supportive virtual community.

Wandering around Belfast one day, Bangor-based painter **Jeff Loxterkamp** encountered an unusual group of sculptures set in the old cribbing remains of a ship-building pier on the harbor. In the work of popular Belfast chainsaw sculptor Ron Cowan, elongated faces carved from wood emerge at low tide, hence their name, "The Long Breath."

Loxterkamp's *Guardians of Belfast* (2014) shows several of the figures, their gnarled visages staring this way and that. Painting them fulfills the painter's professed goal, "to draw the viewer into other worlds"—in this case, a real but fantastic site on the Maine coast.

Art of Penobscot Bay

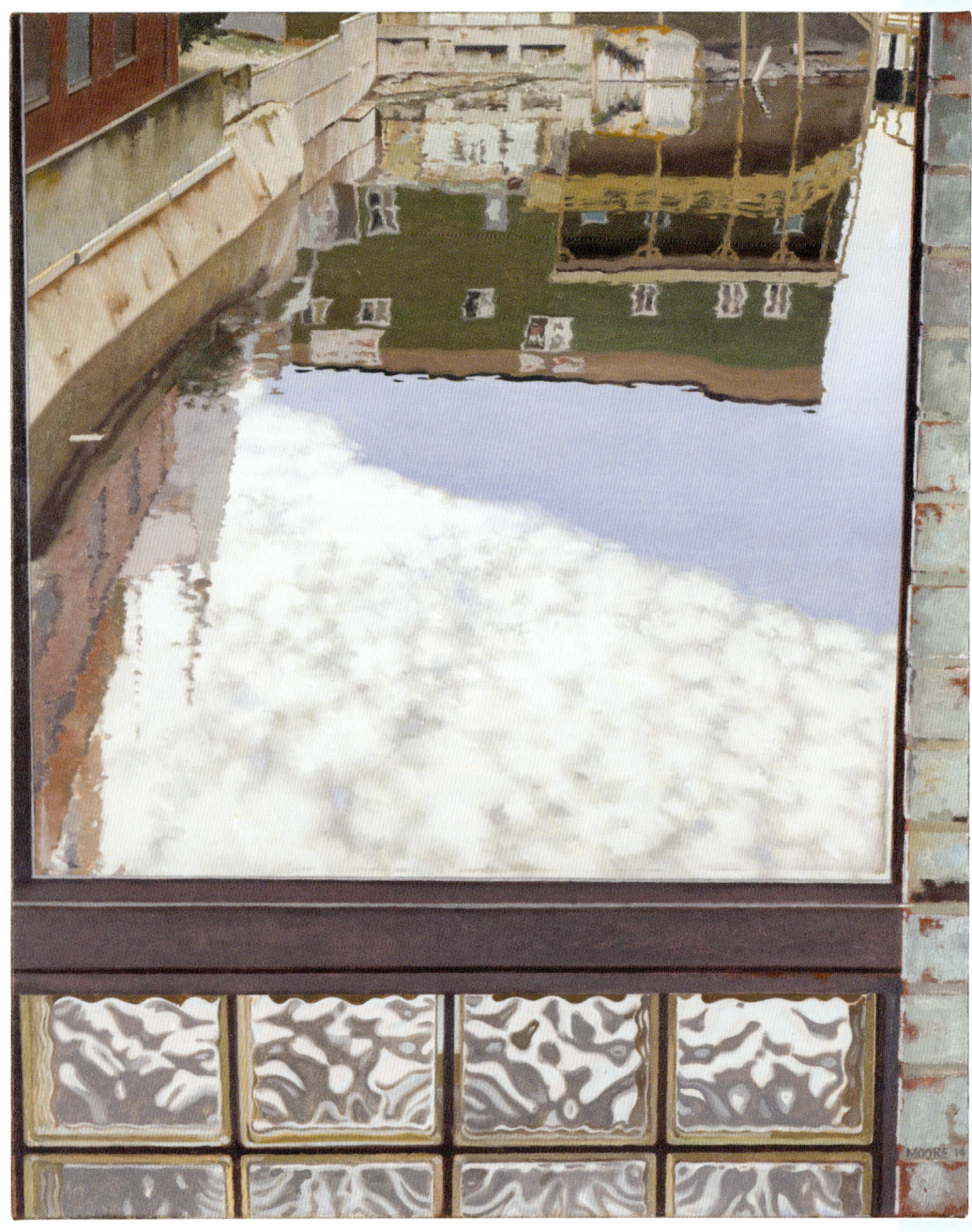

John Moore's painting *Wharf* (2014) also edges into another world. The composite view, he explains, is based on a public walkway that runs past the Front Street Shipyard in Belfast, while the framing window comes from his former studio at Globe Dye in Philadelphia. Moore noted how everything in his paintings "is real…, or should have been real, or could be real," adding, "That's the only rule: it could be real."

John Moore
Wharf, 2014
Oil on canvas, 44 x 36 in.

Today

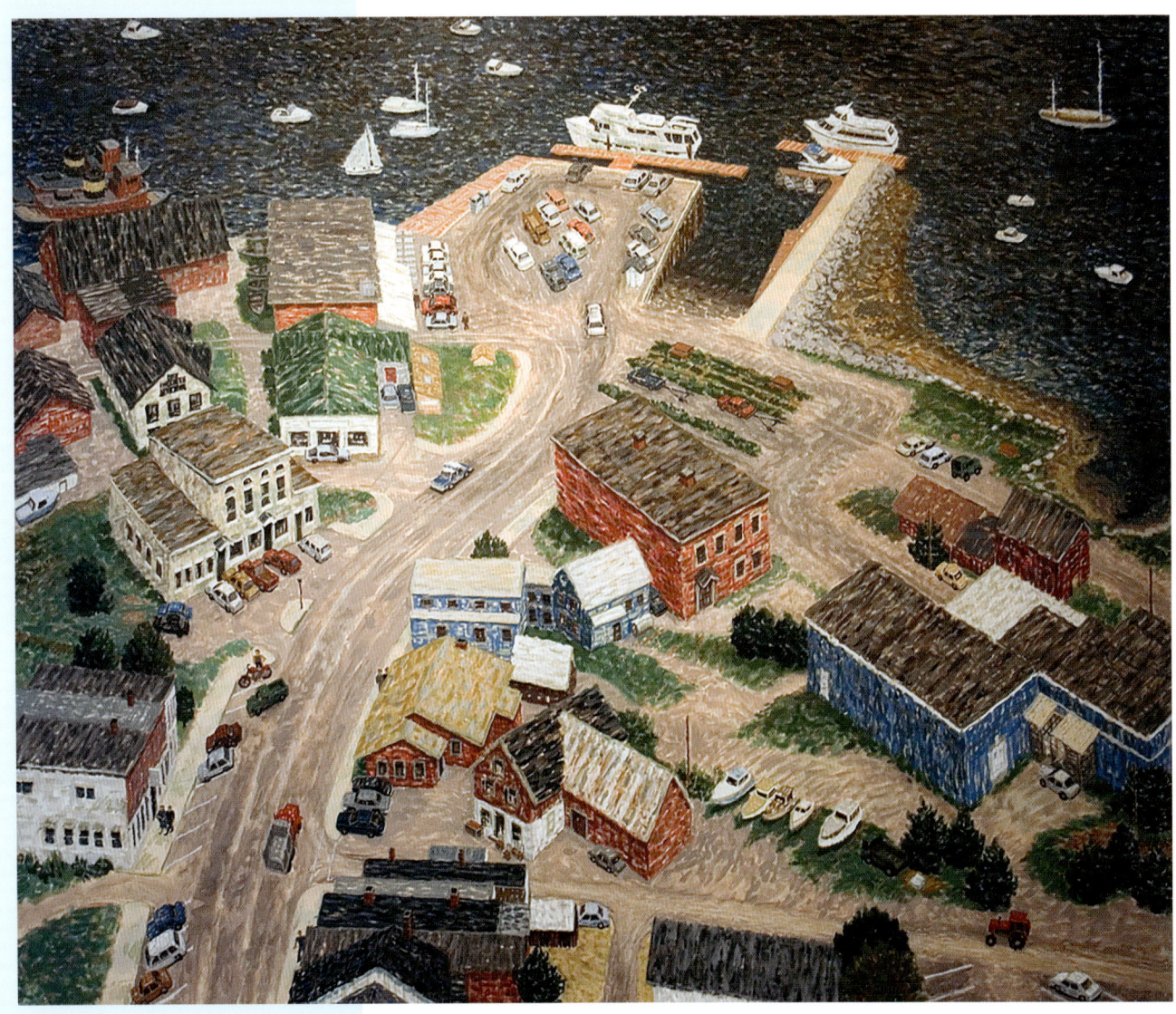

Yvonne Jacquette (1934-2023)
Waterfront of Belfast, Maine, 1990
Oil on canvas, 70 x 84 in.
Courtesy of the artist and DC Moore Gallery, New York City

Yvonne Jacquette's *Waterfront of Belfast, Maine* (1990), a bird's-eye view of the city's waterfront, is precise in its details, from the individual buildings that line Main Street to the various boats in the harbor. The painter, who divided her year between New York City and Searsmont, sometimes chartered planes and helicopters to fly her over chosen spots along the Maine coast. In a style that sometimes bears kinship to precisionist and pointillist art, she transforms the landscape below into shifting planes of paint strokes. Rooftops, roadways, water, and land display a dynamic energy that leads the eye across the landscape.

Art of Penobscot Bay

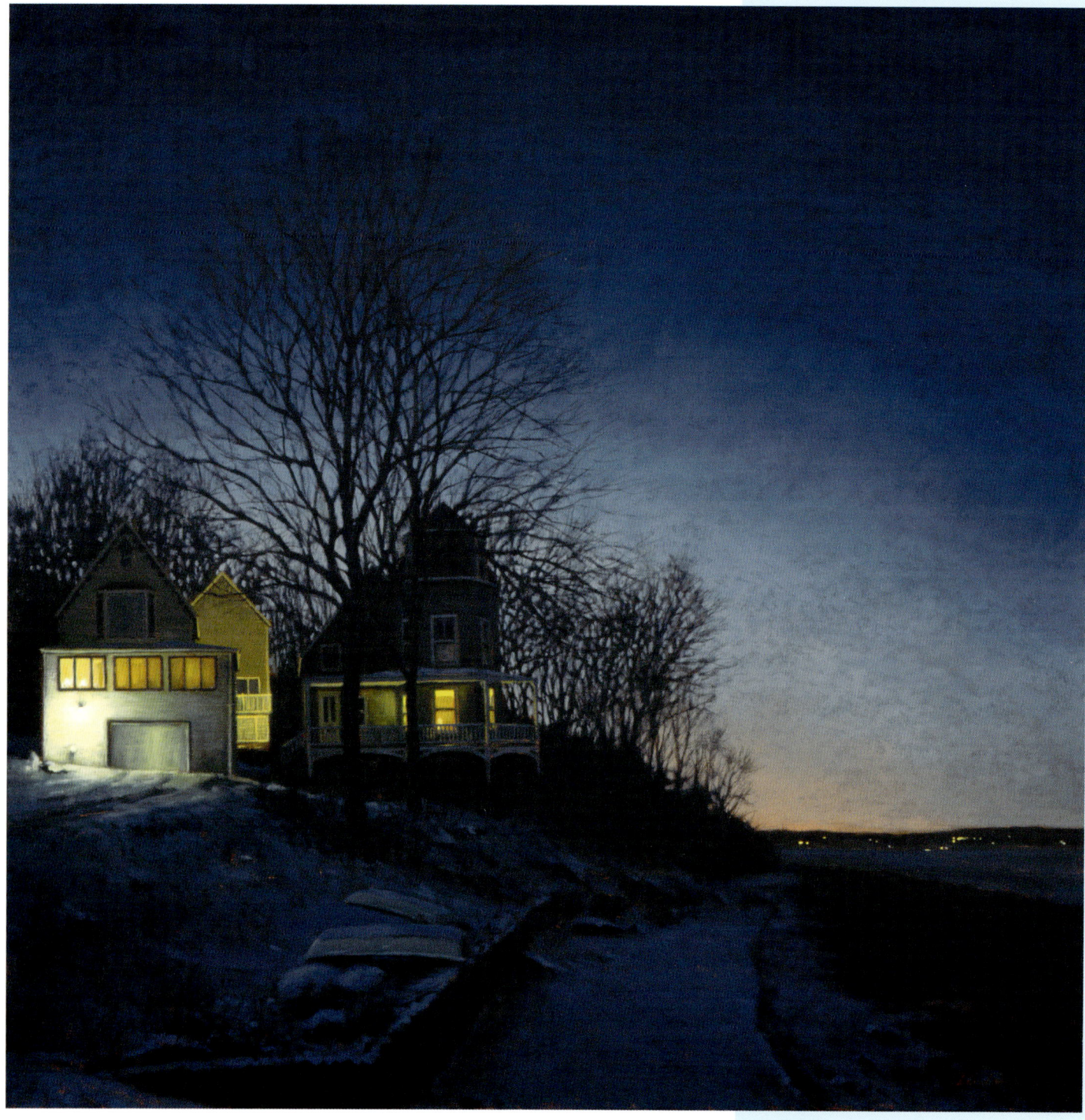

Bayside (1993) is one of the earliest paintings **Linden Frederick** made of Belfast after moving there in the early 1990s. "The area has so much history," the artist noted, "starting in 1848 as a camp meeting destination for a dozen Methodist congregations." Penobscot Bay appears in many of his paintings. "I can't think of a

Linden Frederick
Bayside, 1993
Oil on linen, 20 x 20 in.
Private collection
Photo by Jim Nickelson

Today

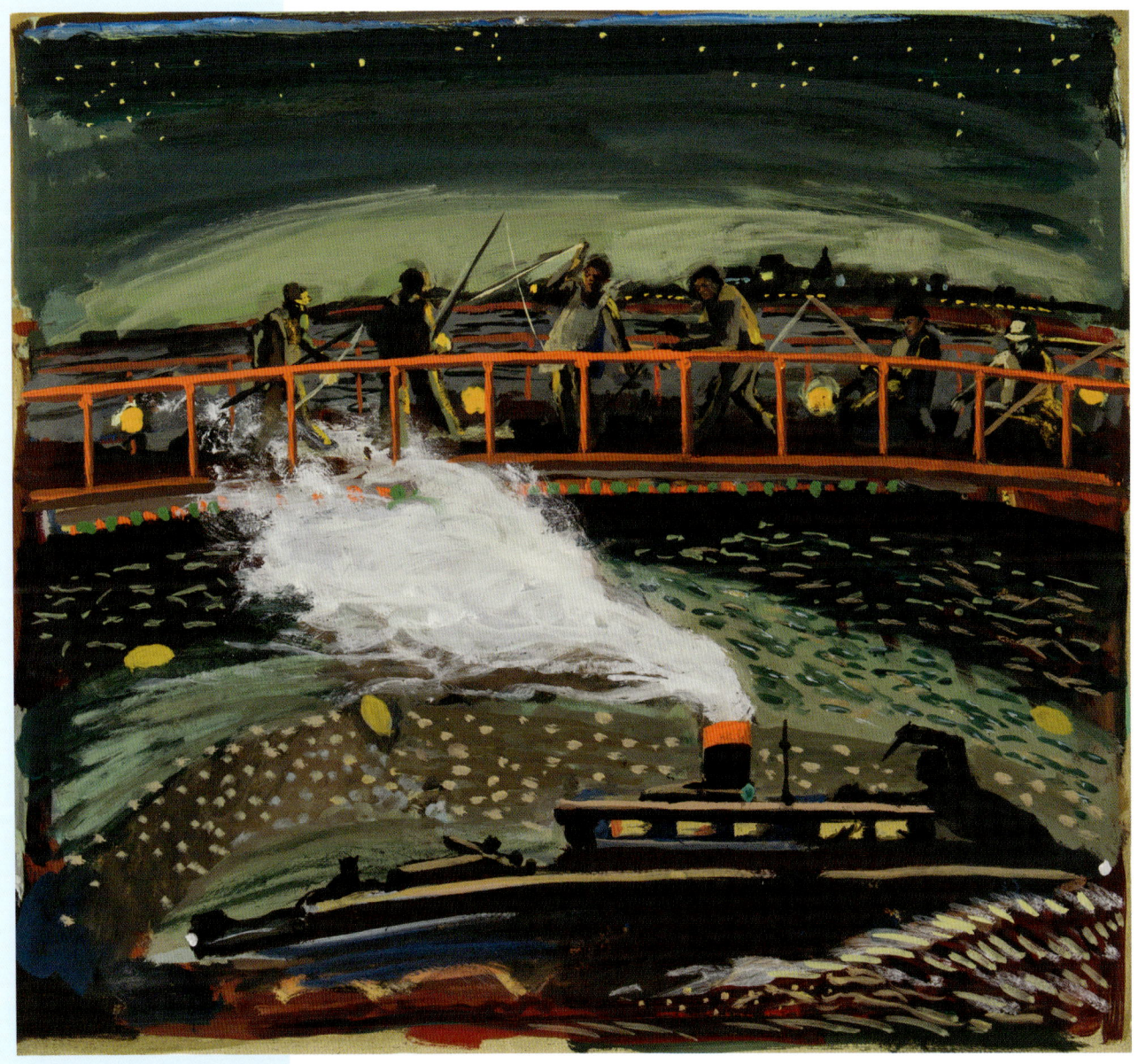

Robert Barnes
The Mackerel Run—Belfast Harbor,
2002
Casein on paper, 22 5/16 x 30 in.
Museum purchase with funds from the Elisabeth Myers Art Acquisition Endowment Fund, Eskenazi Museum of Art, Indiana University, Bloomington Indiana, 2002.27

more appealing backdrop to these Victorian cottages and the 1800s architecture in nearby Belfast."

A year after retiring as professor of art at Indiana University in Bloomington and settling in Searsport in 2001, **Robert Barnes** produced a series of caseins, "The Penobscot," consisting of enigmatic coastal scenes. One of them, *The Mackerel Run—Belfast Harbor* (2002), features a group of figures fishing from a bridge while a boat passes in front of them. The scene is almost frenetic in its energy.

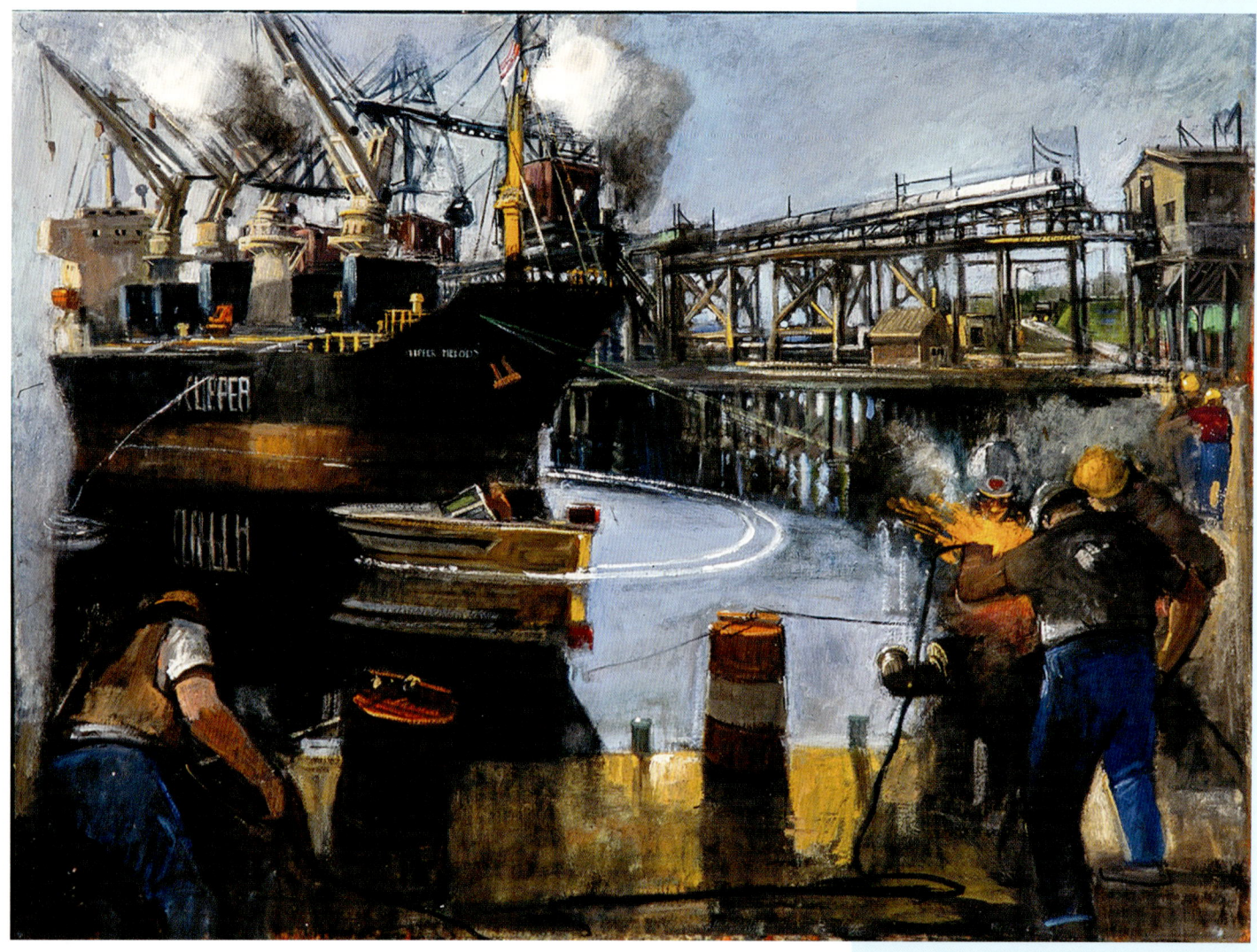

Nancy Morgan Barnes
Unloading the Clipper Melody, 2003
Oil on board, 24 x 32 in.

Barnes and his partner and fellow painter **Nancy Morgan Barnes** live in the historic Carver House in Searsport, former home of a well-known nineteenth-century shipmaster. Fittingly, Morgan Barnes has painted the town's Mack Point port where large container ships tie up. In *Unloading the Clipper Melody* (2003), the bulk carrier sits at the dock while workers in hardhats undertake shipyard tasks, including welding.

Today

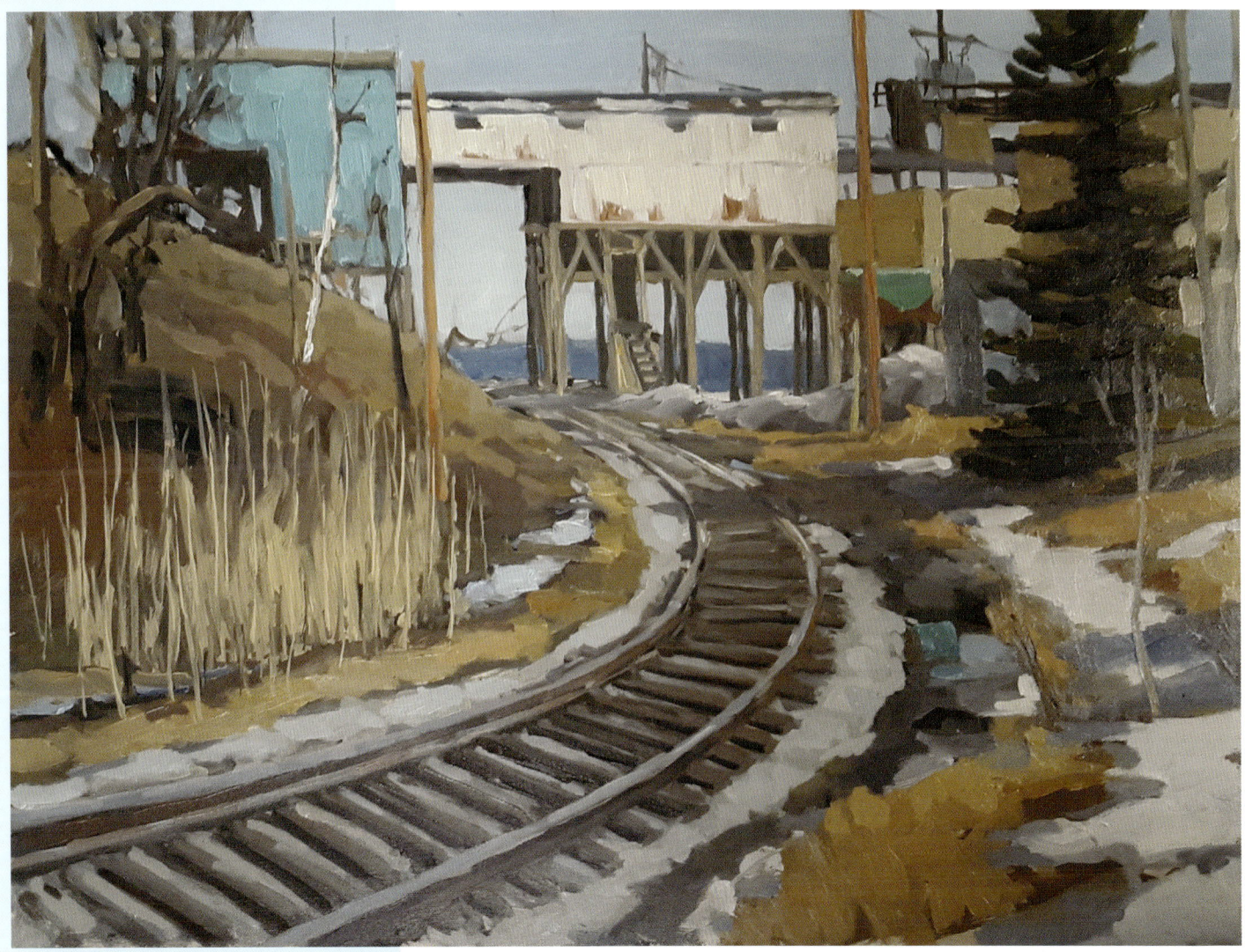

Stefan Pastuhov
Mack Point Rail, 2002
Oil on canvas, 18 x 24 in.

Stefan Pastuhov, a Mainer since 1984, has accompanied Morgan Barnes on plein air painting trips in the midcoast. Visiting the Mack Point facility in winter, he was struck by the design of the scene: the balance of the pine tree on the right and the hill on the left with the railroad tracks vanishing in the center. "The fact that I paint outside on location," he said, "makes each day new." Indeed, he feels that any day that goes by without dipping his brush in paint "is a disappointment if not a total loss."

Art of Penobscot Bay

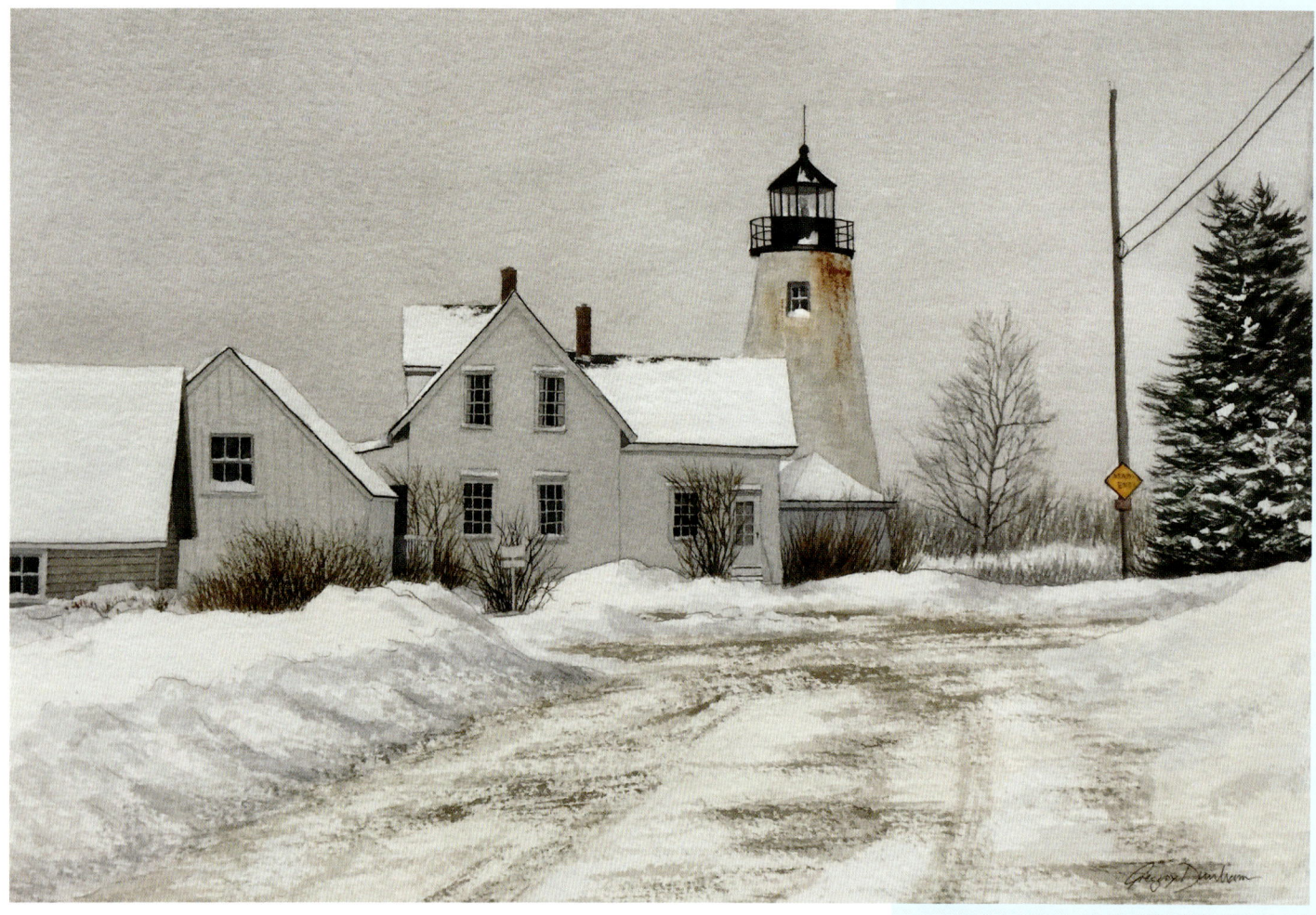

Gregory Dunham
After the Snow, Dyce Head Light, 2019
Watercolor, 9 ½ x 14 ½ in.
Private collection

"There is very little appearance of business about Castine. It is delightfully lethargic." Such was Samuel Adams Drake's take on the town on the eastern shore of Penobscot Bay as it appeared to him in the 1870s. Today, the place is bustling, from a busy Main Street and waterfront to the Maine Maritime Academy. And there are painters.

Long-time resident **Gregory Dunham's** inventory of watercolor views of Castine includes Dyce Head Light and Eaton's boatyard, both iconic landmarks. In *After the Snow, Dyce Head Light* (2019), the road and snowbanks lead the viewer to the conical rubblestone lighthouse. The painter sought to evoke the "quiet sense of stillness after the snow and the almost monochromatic colors of the sky, lighthouse, and keeper's house."

Today

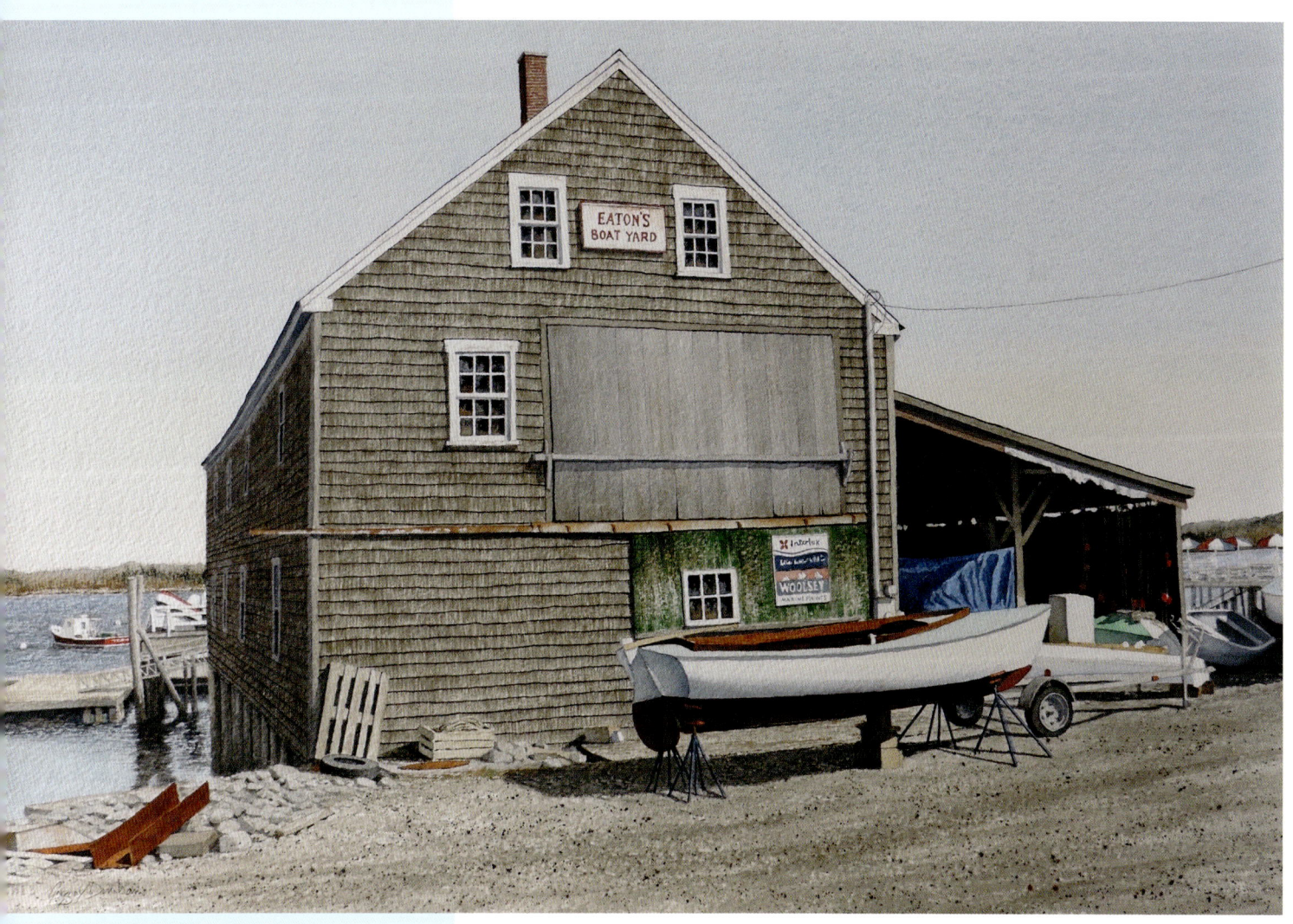

Gregory Dunham
Eaton's Boatyard, 2015
Watercolor, 15 x 22 ½ in.
Private collection

Even as he rues the loss of working waterfront buildings in Castine, Dunham notes how Eaton's boatyard, one of the last remaining structures of its kind, offers him "almost endless possibilities" for painting. In front of the building sits a Castine-class sailboat, designed and built by the Eaton family. A Castine-class sailboat race happens in the harbor every summer.

Art of Penobscot Bay

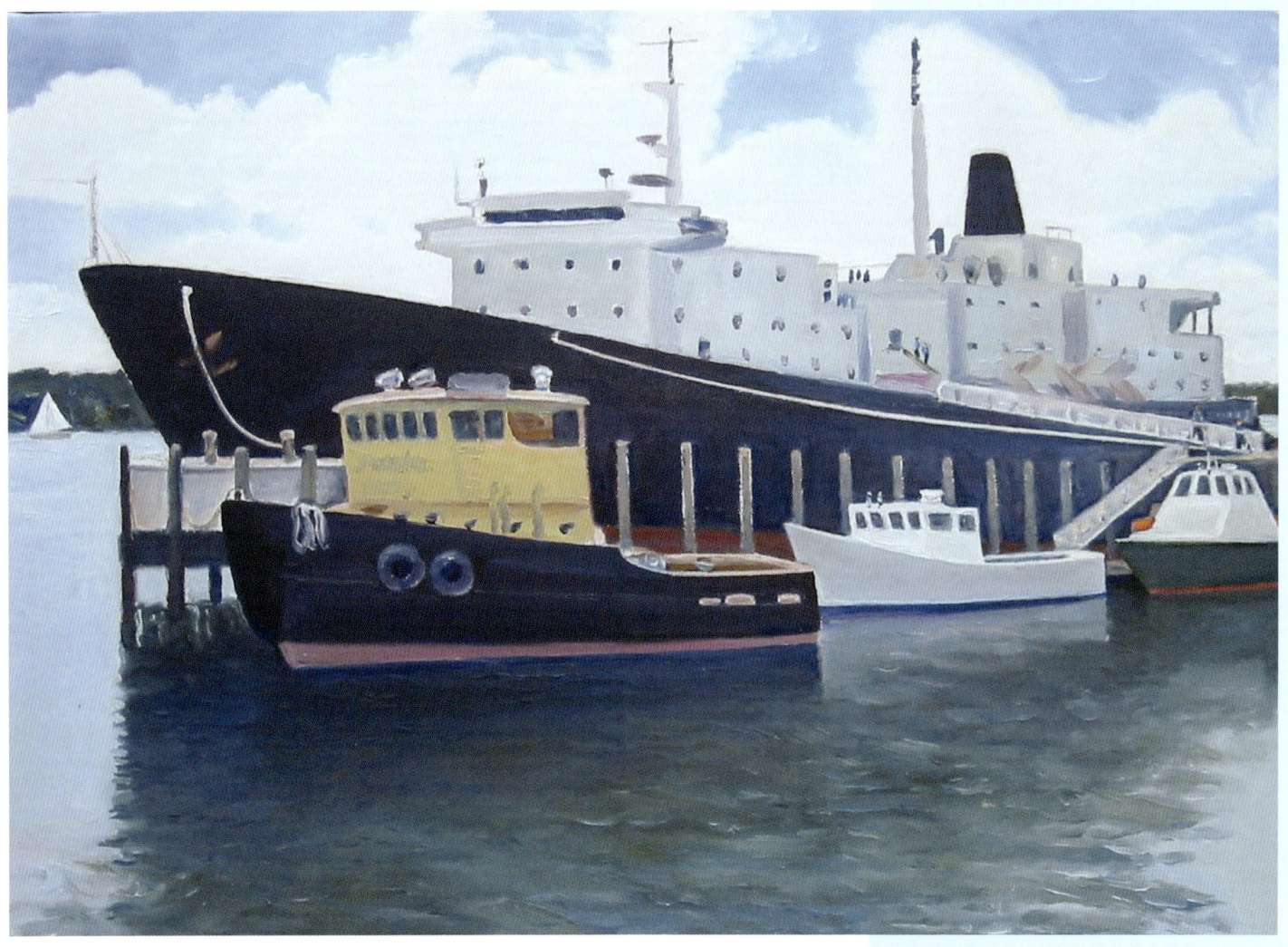

Sam Minot's *Castine Boats* (2010) depicts the Castine waterfront and includes the Training Ship *State of Maine*, the flagship of the Maine Maritime Academy fleet. Originally built for the Navy as a fast oceanographic research vessel, the ship was converted to a floating school in the 1990s, thereby offering an opportunity for midshipmen to get hands-on experience on the sea.

In describing how her painting *Main Street, Castine* (2020) came about, **Susan Parish Adam** recalled stopping her car in the middle of the street to take a photo of the view. "It was late September, so the streets were cleared of the seasonal traffic and tourists, the afternoon light was hitting the tops of the trees just right, and the Maine Maritime Academy sailing team was practicing in perfect alignment."

Sam Minot
Castine Boats, 2010
Oil on canvas, 17 x 21 in.

Today

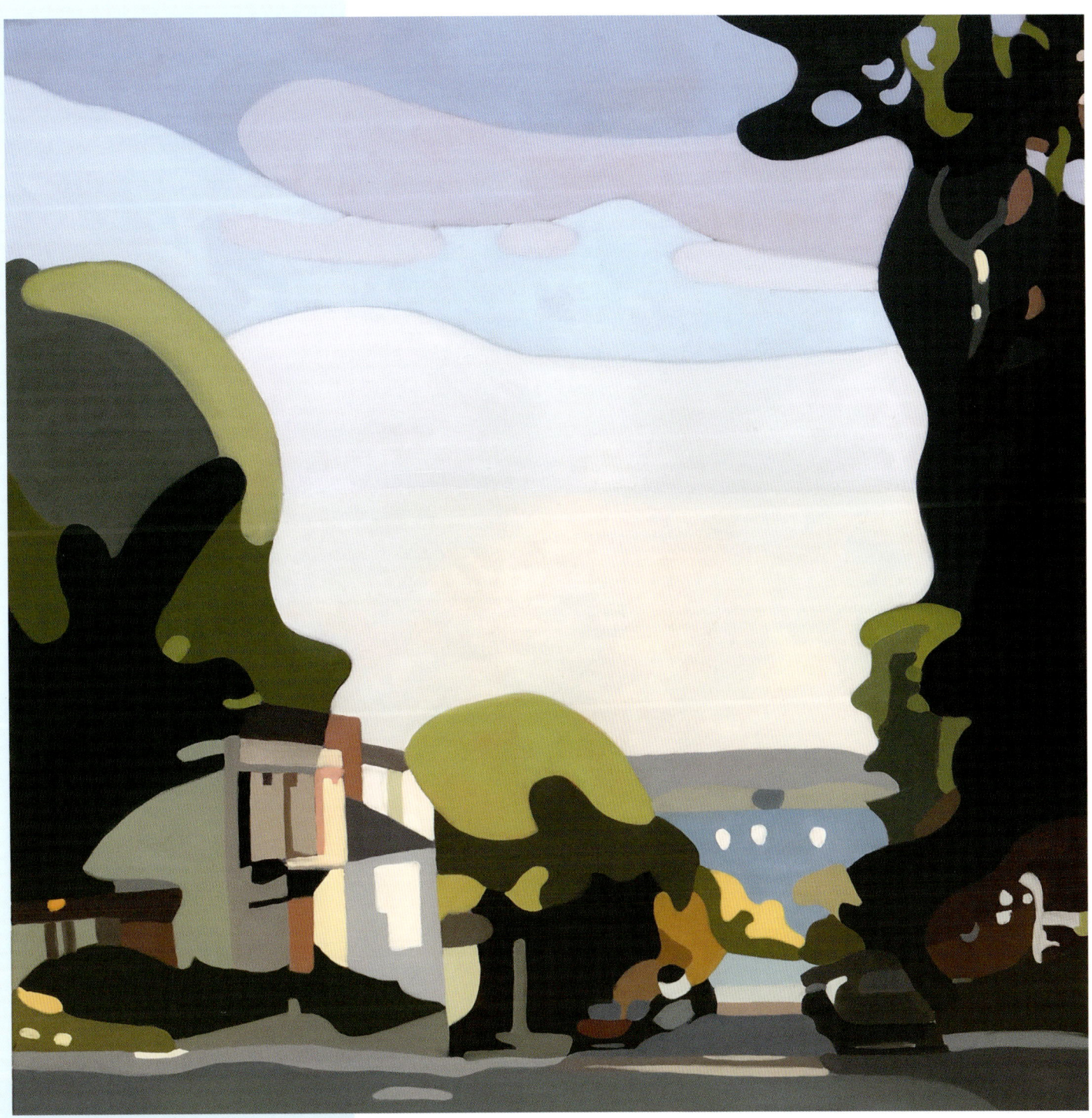

Susan Parish Adam
Main Street, Castine, 2020
Oil on canvas, 36 x 36 in.

Art of Penobscot Bay

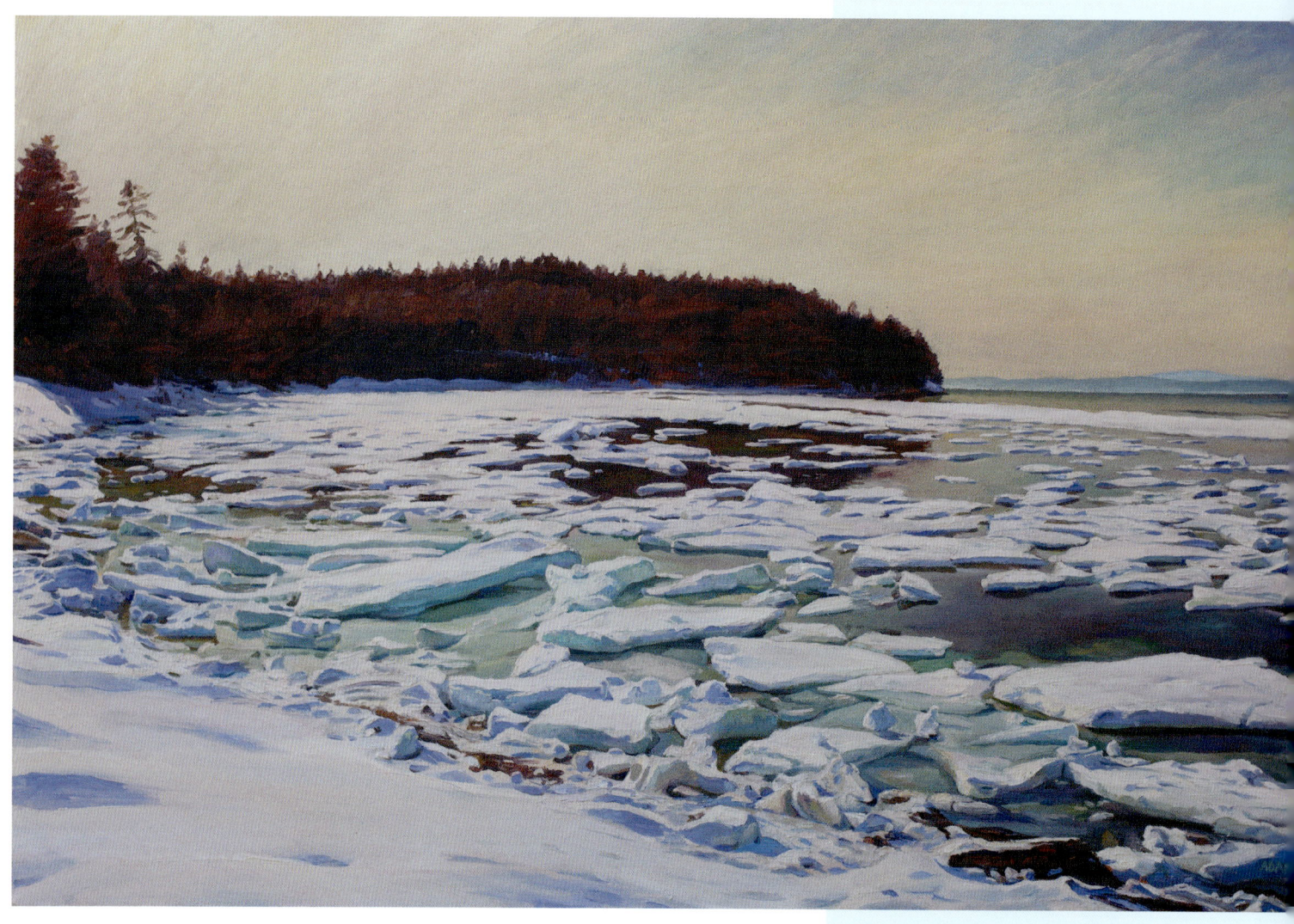

Adam and her husband Joshua moved to Castine twenty or so years ago. **Joshua Adam's** work has focused on "things marine," including an iced-in Wadsworth Cove. Since he painted this chilly scene in 2007, the painter reports winters have become less severe. "This 100 yards of ice seems like a lot," he wrote, but he saw a photograph from around 1915 showing people driving from Castine to Islesboro on the frozen sea.

Joshua Adam
Ice on Wadsworth Cove, 2007
Oil on canvas, 24 x 36 in.
Collection of Dr. Michael Mainen

Today

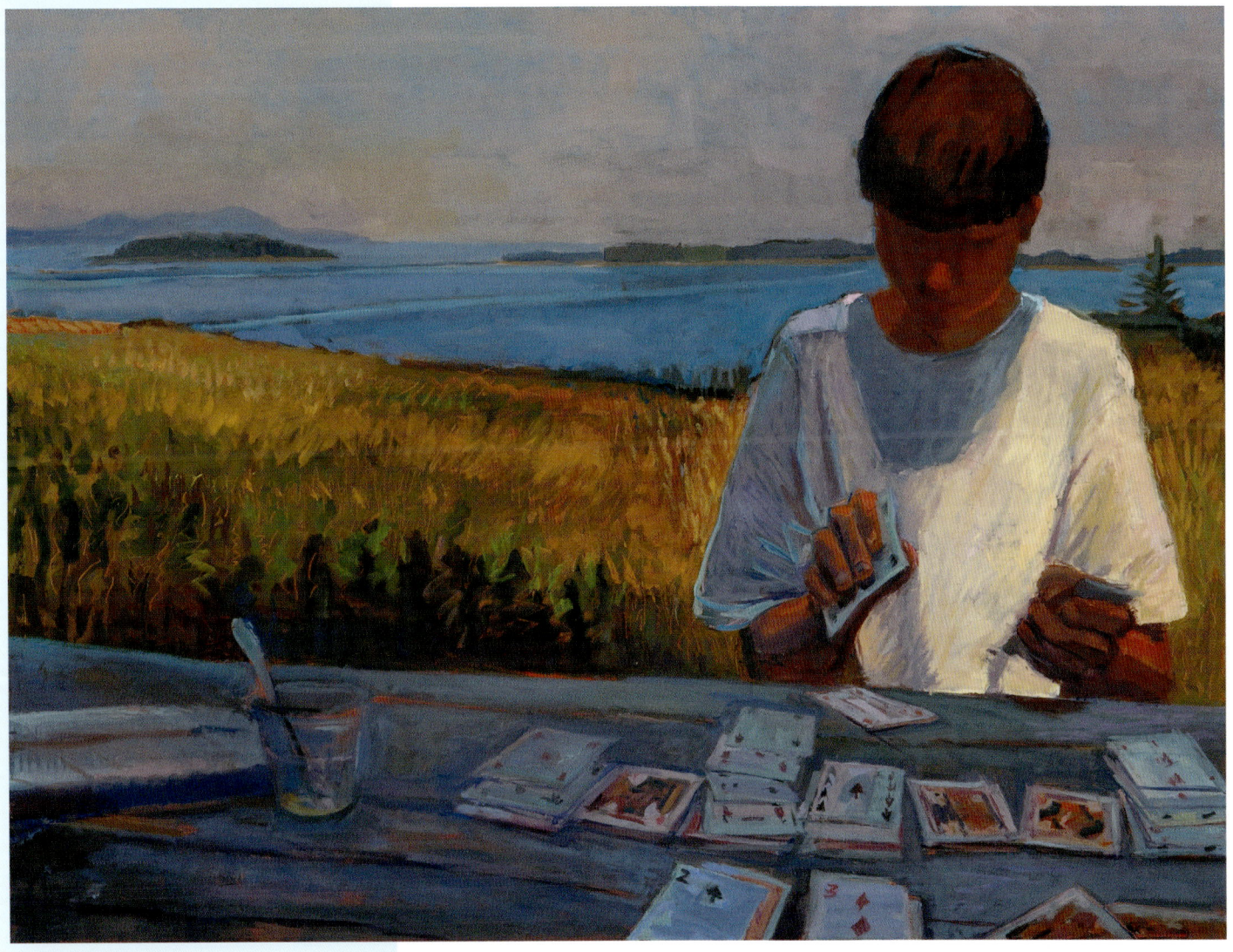

Louise Bourne
Island Solitaire, 2011
Oil on linen, 30 x 40 in.
Photo by Ken Woisard

"It seems that Old Man God when he made this part of the Earth just took a shovel full of islands and let them drop." Such was John Marin's impression of the archipelago he found off Stonington in 1919, his first summer in the area.

Sedgwick painter **Louise Bourne** has spent time on a number of those islands, taking in the "jaw-dropping splendor" of Penobscot Bay. Eagle Island between North Haven and Deer Isle is the setting for a painting of her son playing solitaire, his back to the view. Bourne did watercolors on site; later "set-ups" in her studio "provided vocabulary" for the painting.

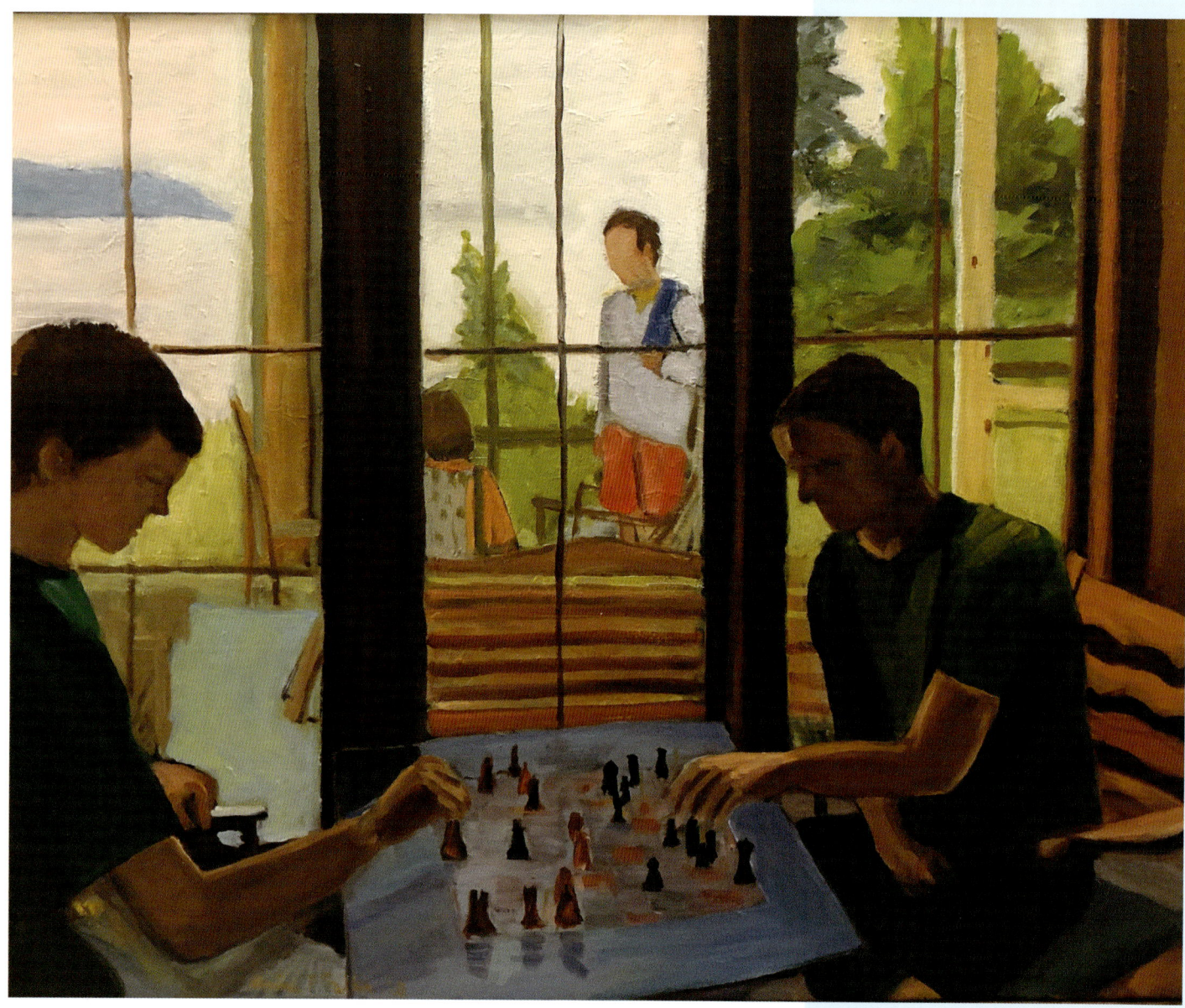

Bourne is one of a remarkable group of artists who have spent time on Great Spruce Head Island as part of the annual Art Week held in the former home of Fairfield Porter. Leading the program, **Anina Porter Fuller** carries on the artistic legacy of her uncle, painting on the island every summer.

Fuller's *Game of Chess* (2020) blends interior and exterior—and features family. Two figures—her grandsons—are focused on their contest while her son and daughter-in-law prepare to explore the island. Another painting features the island garden of the Porter family matriarch, Margaret Straus, tended to by her partner,

Anina Porter Fuller
Game of Chess, 2020
Oil on canvas, 24 x 30 in.

Today

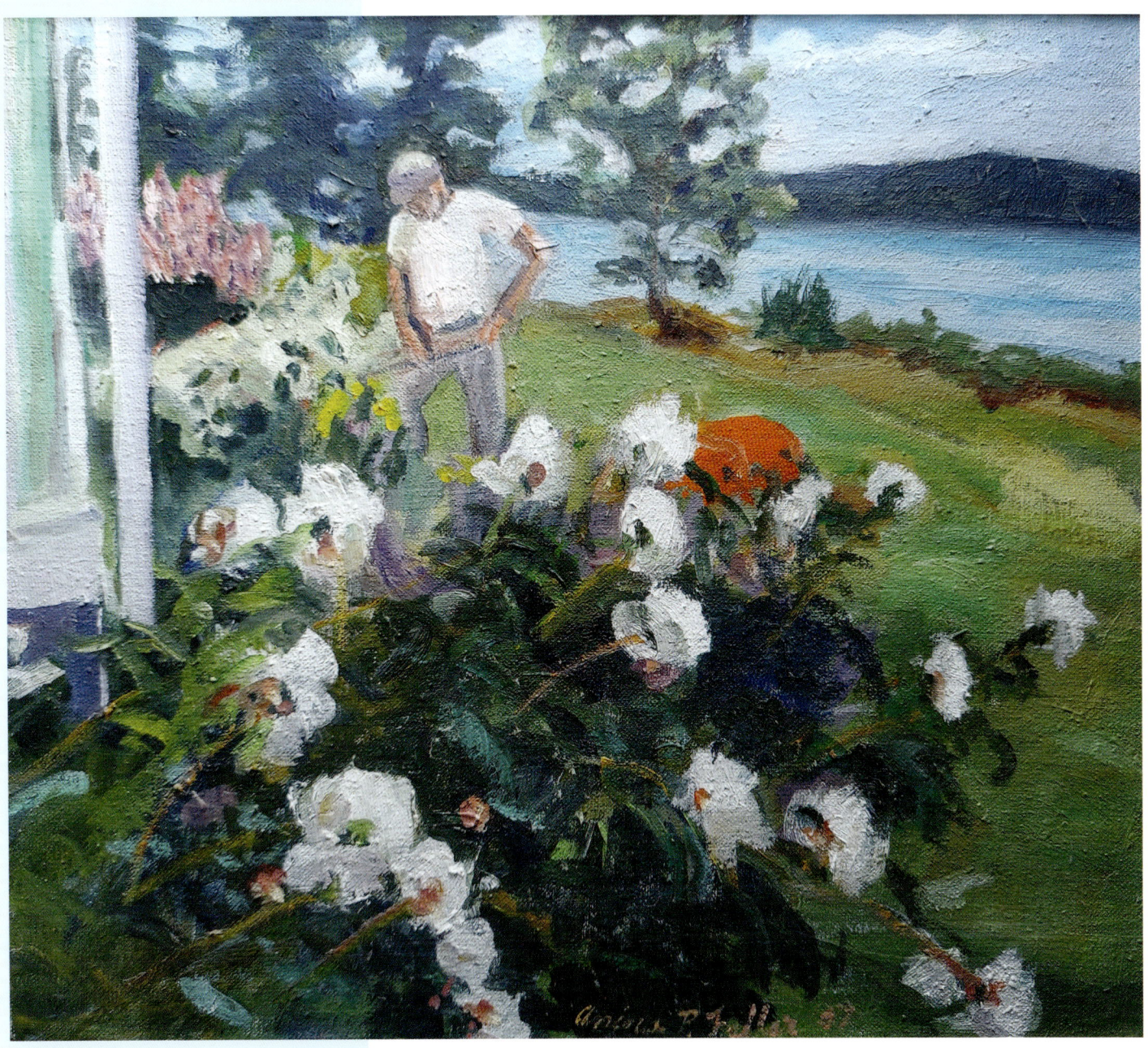

Anina Porter Fuller
Gardener, Great Spruce Head Island
Oil on linen, 14 x 16 in.
Collection of David Little and Mikki Jones-Little

Stanley Lorch. The execution here is freer, with the peonies bursting out across the foreground.

Fuller says she learned how to see in a different way from her two mentors, uncles Fairfield and Eliot Porter. About her passion for the colors on Great Spruce Head Island, she said, "It is thrilling to paint orange and alizarin hawkweed opening in the sun … dazzling morning light reflected on the table, or a vast, still expanse of greenish blue."

Art of Penobscot Bay

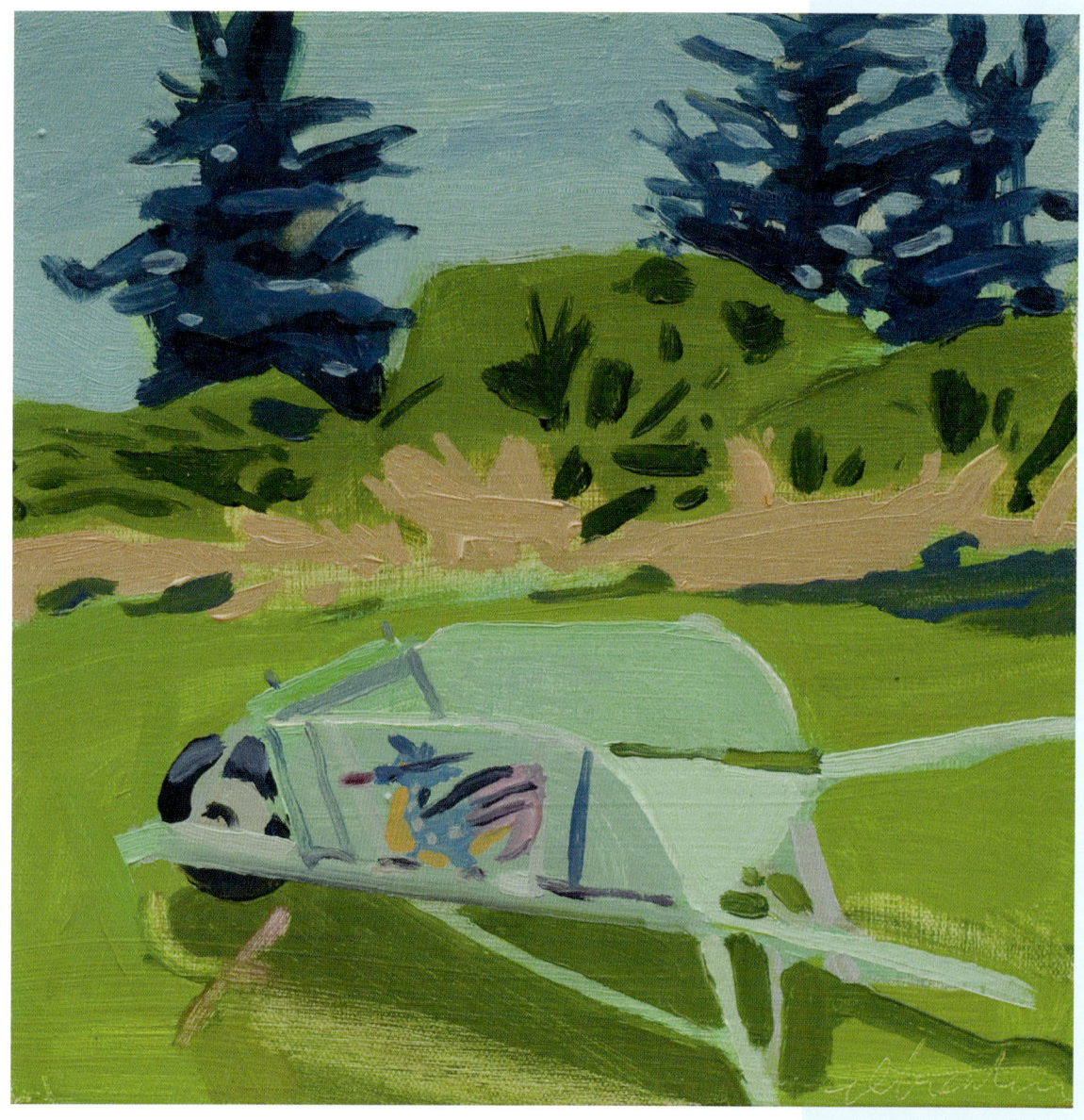

During her stay on Great Spruce Head, **Emily Trenholm** admired part of the island transportation system—wheelbarrows. And that inspired her *Great Spruce Head Wagon* (2012). Each wheelbarrow is marked to identify which cottage it belongs to, with the dragon associated with the "Big House." The painter, who lives in Brunswick, Maine, used the wheelbarrow, as Porter family artists have, to move her painting gear around the island each day and sometimes use the bottom board as a seat. She grew fond of it and painted its portrait parked on the grass one morning.

Emily Trenholm
Great Spruce Head Wagon, 2012
Oil on canvas, 10 x 10 in.
Courtesy Gallery Naga,
Boston, Mass.

Today

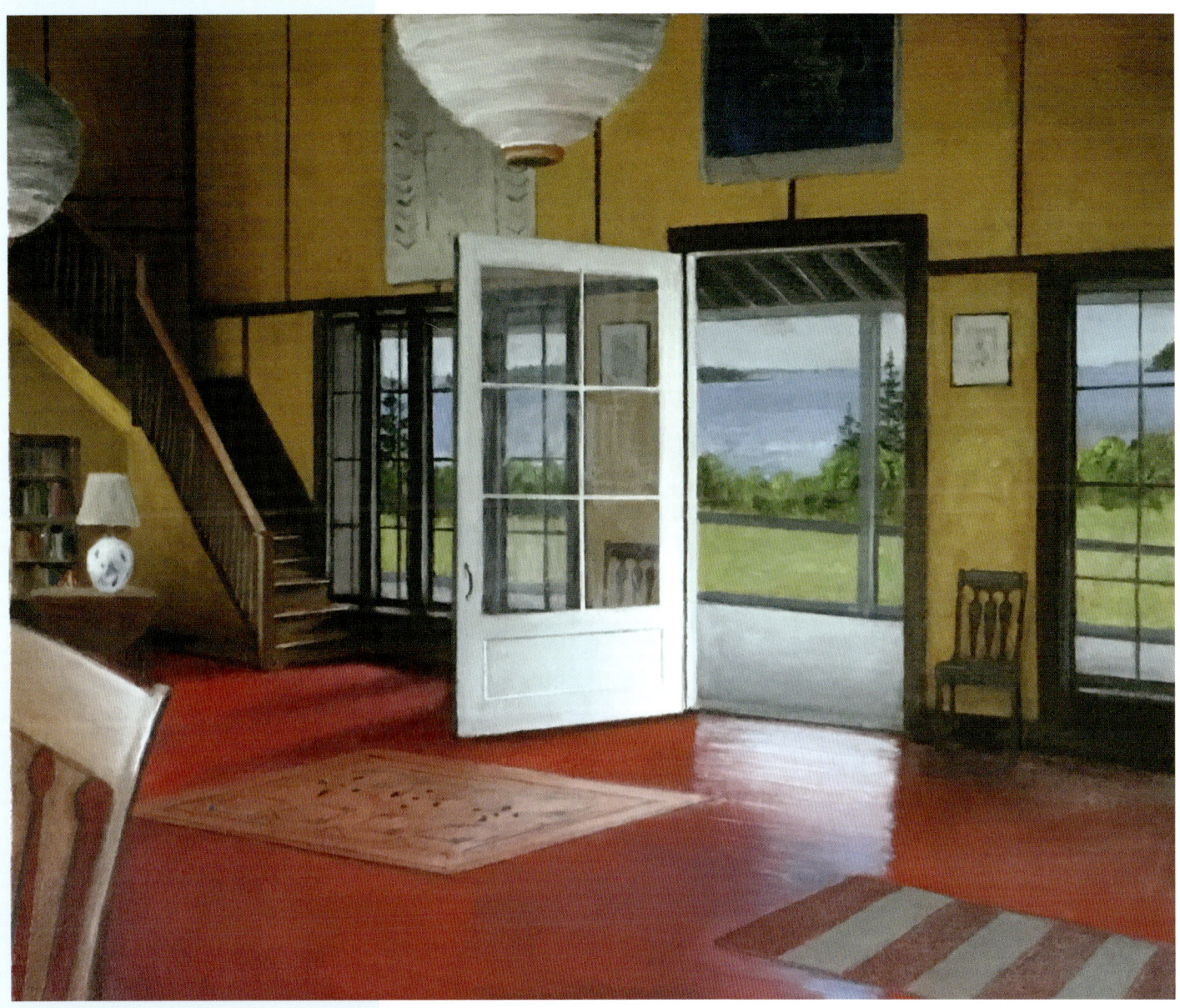

Joseph Keiffer
The Red Floor, 2019
Oil on canvas, 20 x 24 in.
Collection of Ellen Hope

Another guest, **Joseph Keiffer**, came to Great Spruce Head Island from New York City. He wrote, "with no specific intentions other than a vague expectation that this would be a landscape opportunity." Getting off the mailboat he immediately saw good views, but when he entered the Porter home, he found "a masterpiece of American summer house architecture" and painted it. He was struck by the red floors—"such a daring and playful stroke"—and the view of Penobscot Bay through the windows.

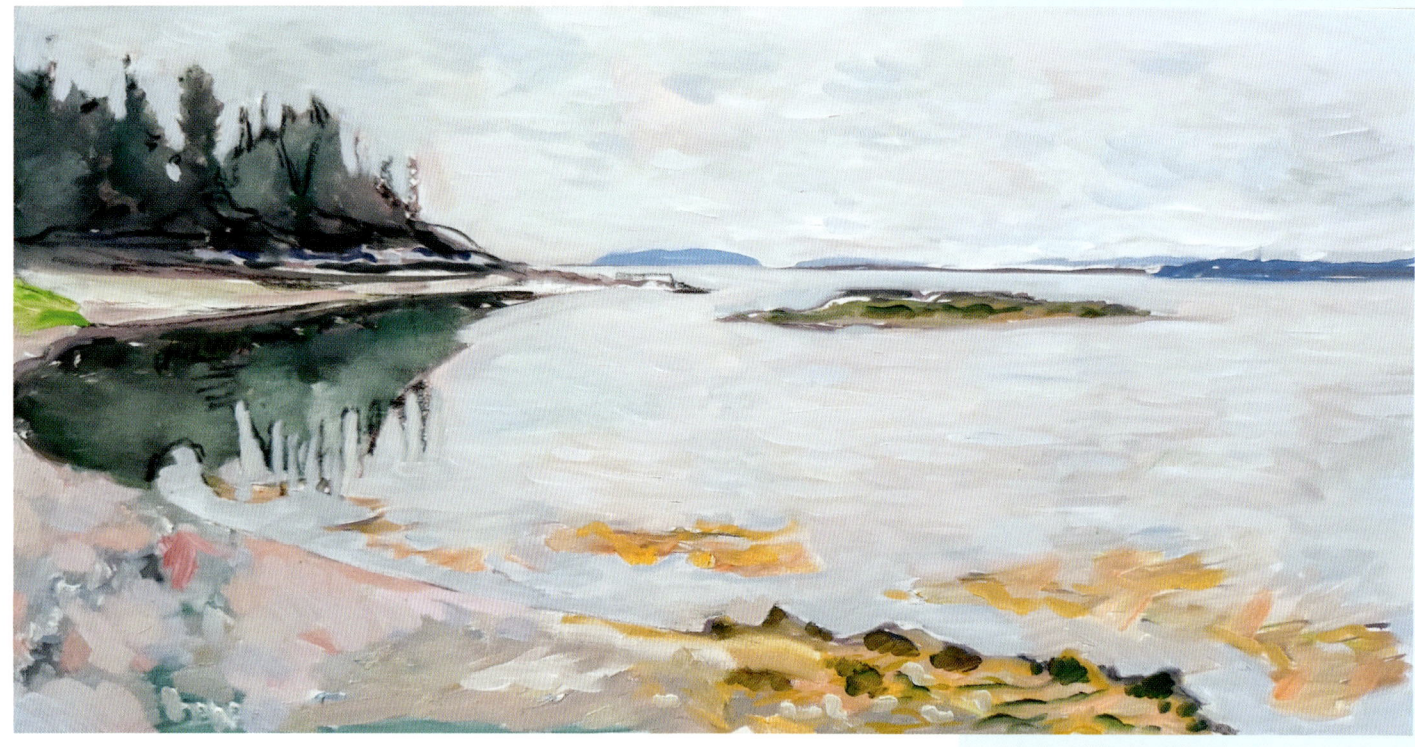

David Little
View from Double Beach, 2019
Oil on canvas, 18 x 36 in.

Portland-based painter **David Little** was on island at the same time as Keiffer. In his explorations, he discovered the double beaches, a well-known geographic element of Great Spruce Head, and set up his easel to paint the curving shoreline, the seaweed-stained water, and the reflection of island trees. "It was difficult not to be affected by the familiar scenes Fairfield Porter painted," he wrote. At the same time, "going outside to explore required letting go of the past, letting nature inspire and allowing one's own process for getting underway to kick into high gear."

During her stay on Great Spruce Head Island, **Krisanne Baker** snorkeled the intertidal areas, swimming among the flowing rockweed. As an artist and educator, Baker, who fittingly lives in Waterford, Maine, studies marine ecology and advocates for the ocean's stewardship. Her paintings sometimes feature phosphorescent pigments that highlight the natural bioluminescence of her underwater subjects. Among her favorite sayings: "Water is life."

Today

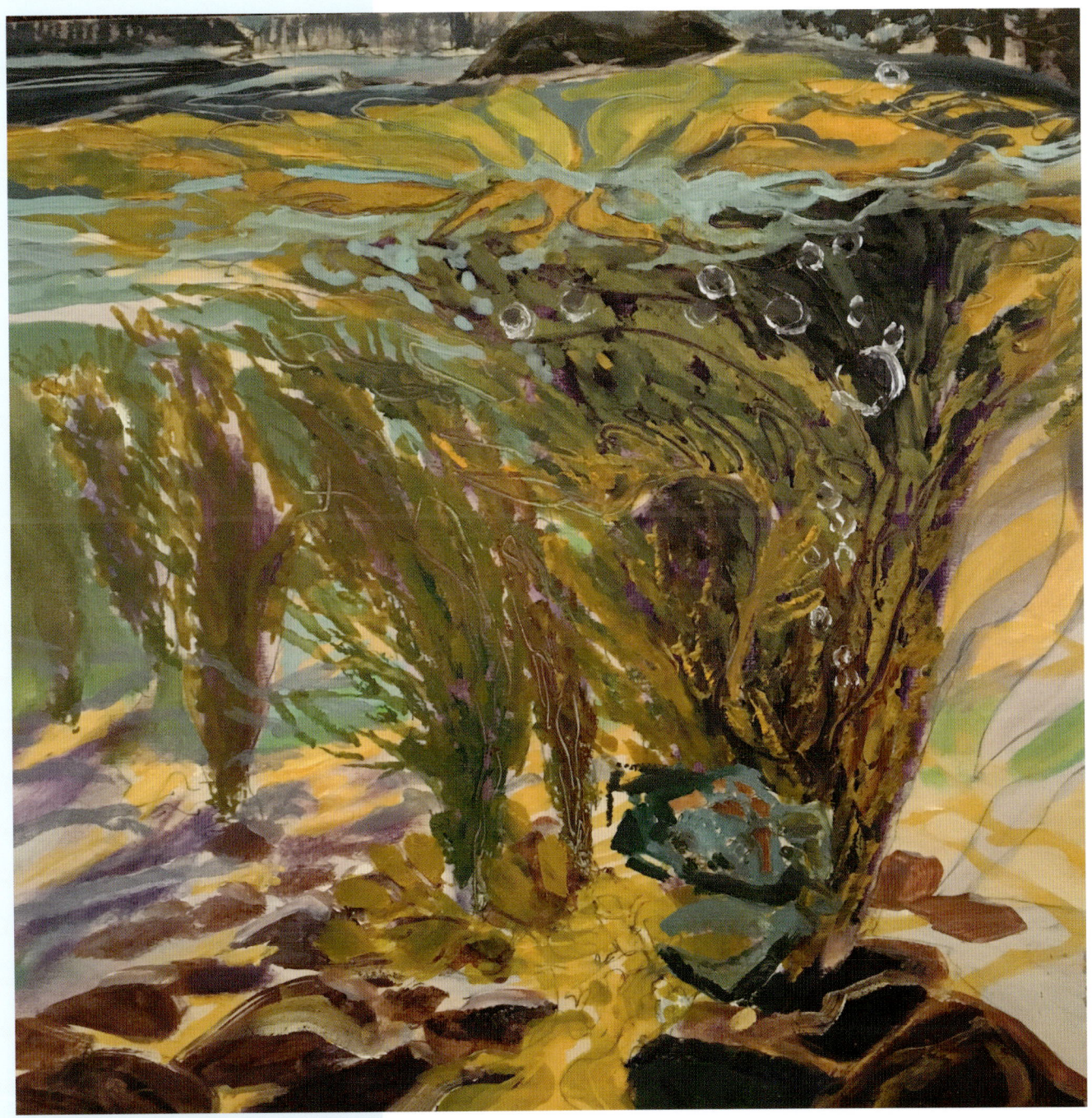

Krisanne Baker
*Ascophyllum nodosum (Rockweed),
High Tide GSHI*, 2018
Oil on wood panel, 12 x 12 in.

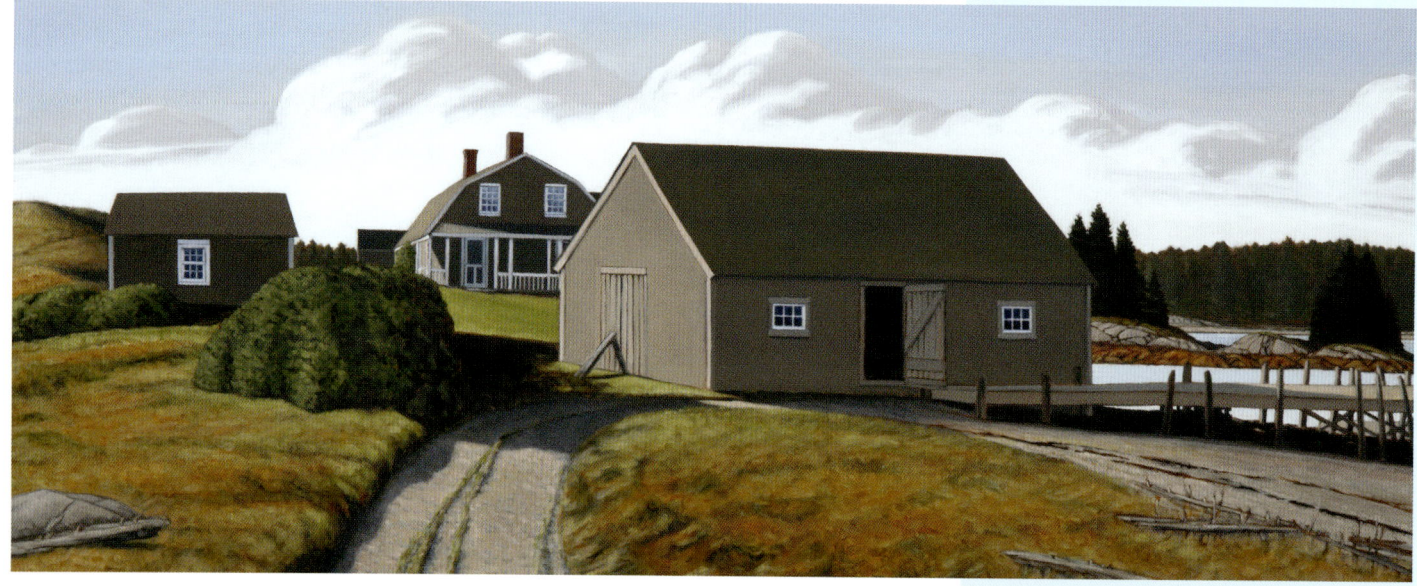

Sarah Faragher
Afternoon Shadows, Bear Island, Maine, 2010
Oil on canvas, 24 x 60 in.
Collection of the artist
Photo by Ken Woisard

In 2004, while visiting Great Spruce Head Island, **Sarah Faragher** explored nearby Bear Island. Conversing with an islander, she learned of Birch Lodge, a humble dwelling that could be rented in June. Invited to consider this option, Faragher soon found herself taking up annual summer residence in the middle of Penobscot Bay, her painting supplies at the ready—and her soul as well, brimming with the possibilities of retreat and reflection.

In *Autobiography of an Island: A Memoir,* 2022, Faragher shares her experiences painting on Bear. In the book she describes a number of specific paintings, including *Afternoon Shadows, Bear Island, Maine,* a broad horizontal canvas that features the harbor and several buildings. Certain elements of the view—the dark open door of the boathouse, the clouds building up, a bank of rugosas casting a shadow over the island road—lend mystery to the scene. "The painting feels like a stage set," Faragher wrote, "and something is about to happen."

On summer sojourns from their home in Michigan in the 1970s, painter **Mary Aro** and her family rented a cottage on Cape Rosier in Brooksville, across the Bagaduce River from Castine. "We experienced a different way of life there," Aro recalls. She saw a "radical love and concern for nature" in the people there, including back-to-the-land icons Scott and Helen Nearing. Aro began to paint, with a focus on watercolor.

Today

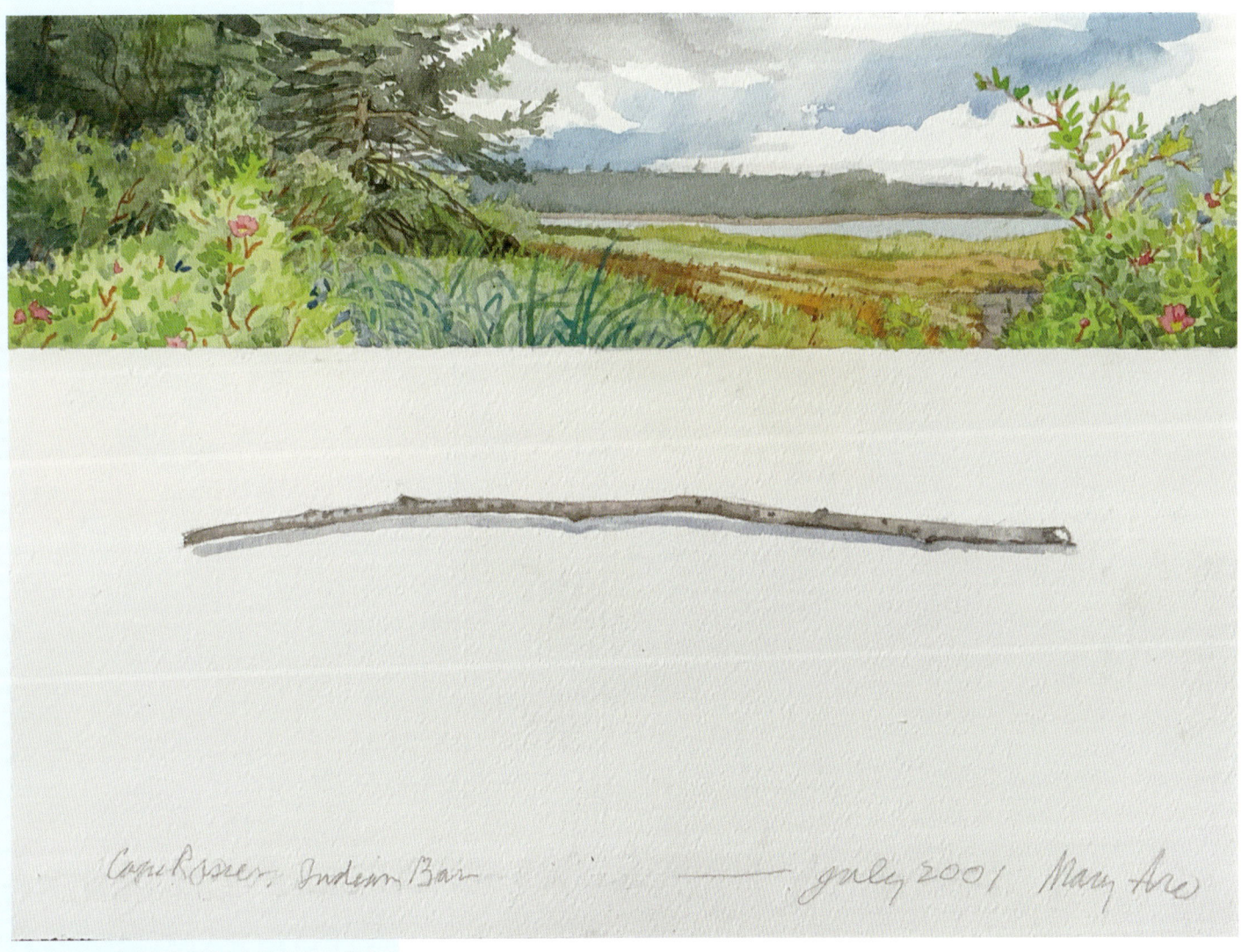

Mary Aro
Cape Rosier, Indian Bar, 2001
Watercolor on paper, 12 x 9 in.
Photo by Kris McLeod

Aro renders the landscape as she sees it: "a narrow band of life." Below it, she intentionally leaves an empty white space to which she later adds a memento from her time spent immersed in a special place. In *Cape Rosier, Indian Bar* (2001), she combines a plein air view of a summer meadow with a careful rendering of a single stick, emphasizing, "the horizontal and ephemeral nature of the landscape" and the loss she feels when she is no longer there.

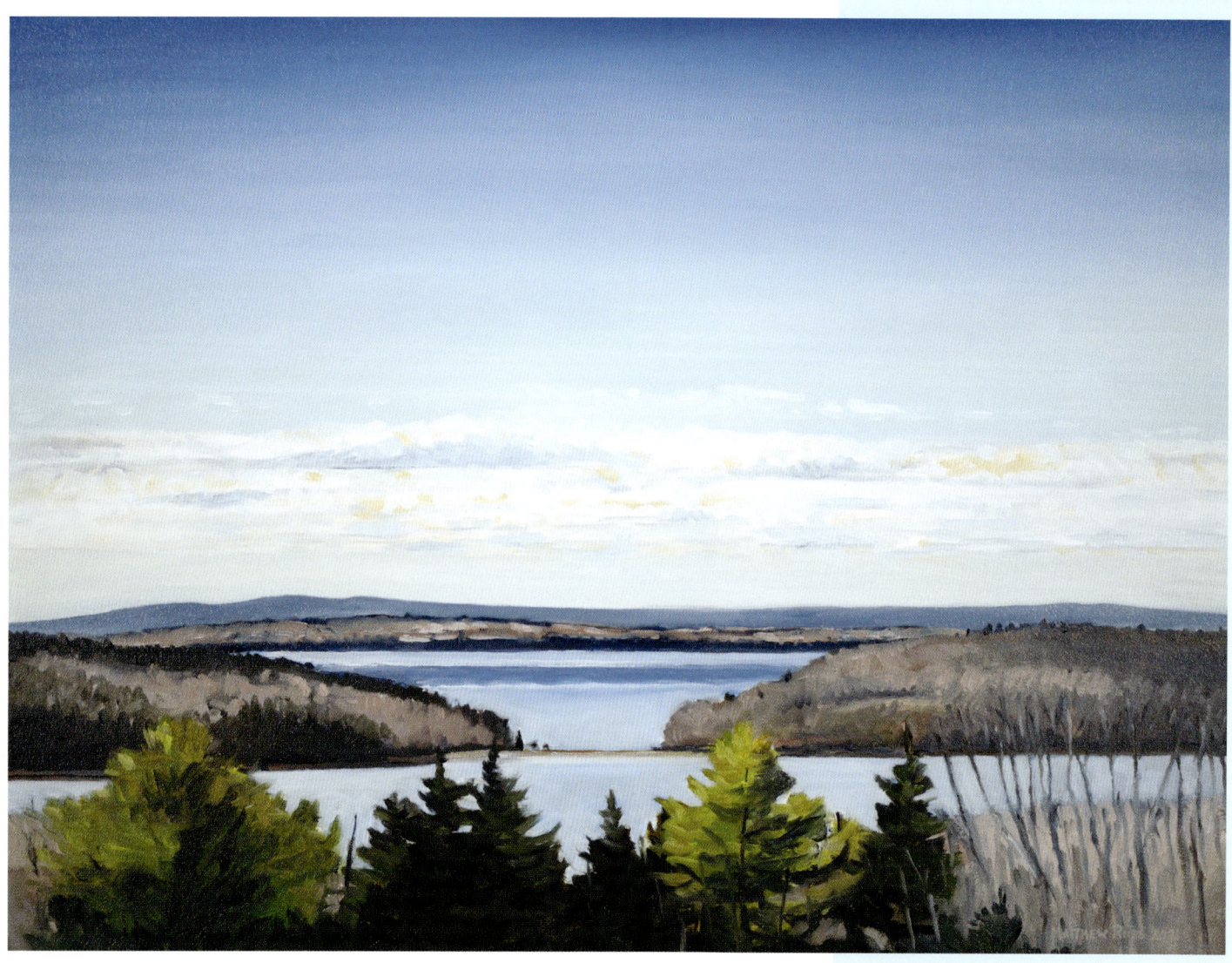

The Cape Rosier area also inspired Waterville painter **Matthew Russ**. In his *Indian Bar #3* (2021), he provides an elevated perspective of the narrow crossing that divides Ram and Smith coves. According to the painter, the bar was part of the larger *Minnewo'kun*, or "many directions route" the Penobscots used to move from the interior to the far reaches of the bay. Russ often backpacks painting gear into remote locations. In 2020, he visited and painted twenty sites on the Maine Island Trail, which connects more than two hundred islands along the Maine coast.

Matthew Russ
Indian Bar #3, 2021
Oil on canvas, 18 x 24 in.
Private collection

Today

Adele Ursone
Bucks Harbor, Gray Day, 2016
Oil on board, 19 x 15 in.

Bucks Harbor in South Brooksville lies east of Cape Rosier and north of Little Deer Isle and was one of the settings in Robert McCloskey's children's book, *One Morning in Maine*. In *Bucks Harbor, Gray Day*, **Adele Ursone**, who divides her time between Deer Isle and New York City, offers a view of a spruce-topped corner of land barely visible in the fog. In her chosen setting, she wrote, "edges become so blurred reality dissolves into abstraction."

Art of Penobscot Bay

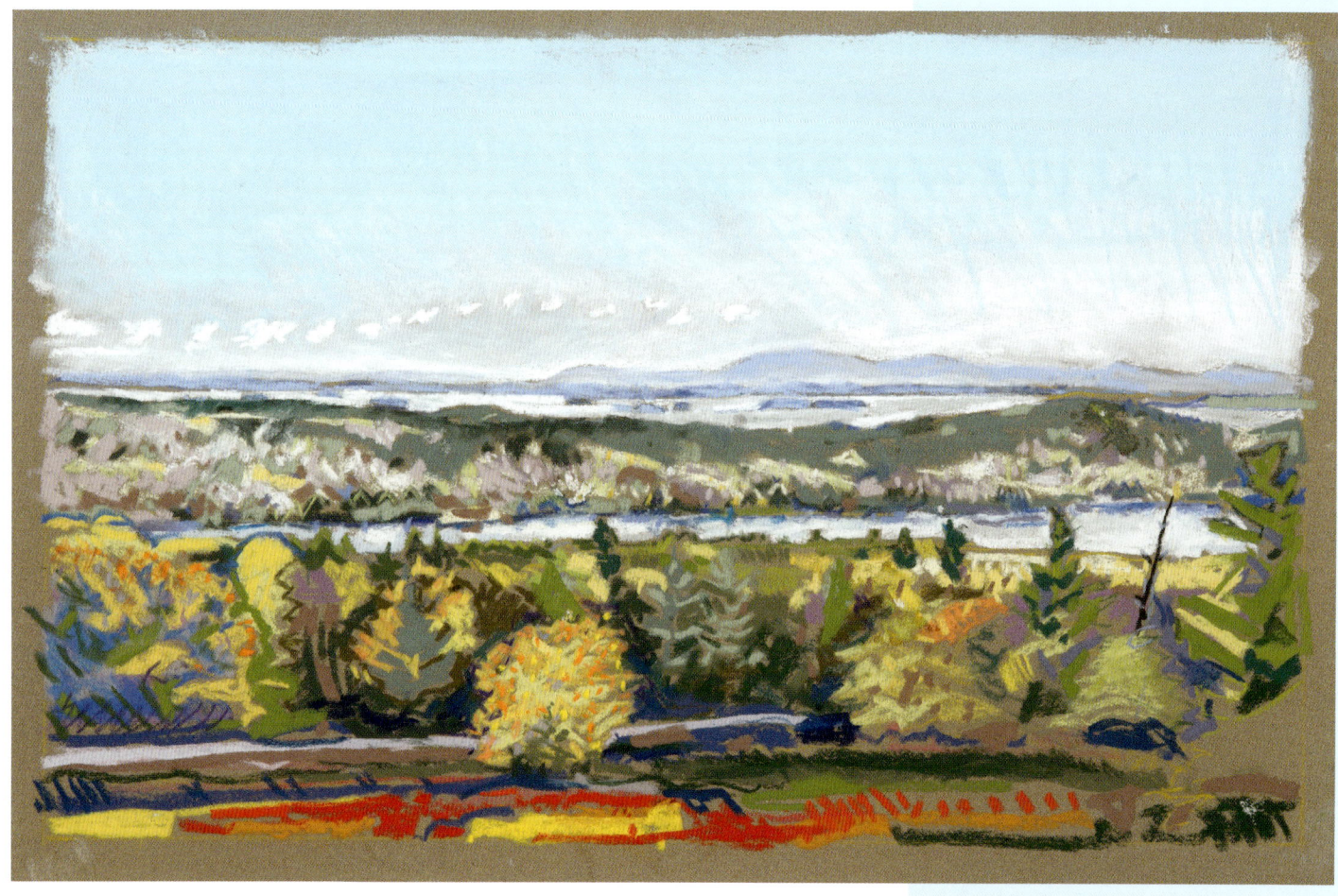

Among the most painted views on the coast of Maine, Caterpillar Hill in Sedgwick offers a panoramic view of Penobscot Bay. **Lawrence Moffet** heads there every fall from his long-time home in Deer Isle, "looking for the intense reds of wild blueberry plants." His pastel *Caterpillar Hill Color* (2021) includes glimpses of Walker's Pond, Eggemoggin Reach, Penobscot Bay islands, and the Camden Hills.

Lawrence Moffet
Caterpillar Hill Color, 2021
Soft pastel on sanded paper
12 ¾ x 19 ½ in.
Photo by Ken Woisard

Today

John Neville's *Regatta, Eggemoggin Reach* (2018) came about while the painter was sailing a 27-foot Albin Vega sloop from East Blue Hill to his home on the Damariscotta River. As the sailboat passed the Pumpkin Island lighthouse to enter Eggemoggin Reach, the painter was in the galley making a cup of tea when the crew called him to take over the helm. "It appeared every boat in Penobscot Bay was heading our way," Neville recounted. They managed to maneuver past the regatta and the artist was able to turn this vision into a painting.

John Neville
Regatta, Eggemoggin Reach, 2018
Oil on canvas, 36 x 60 in.
Courtesy Courthouse Gallery Fine Art, Ellsworth, Maine

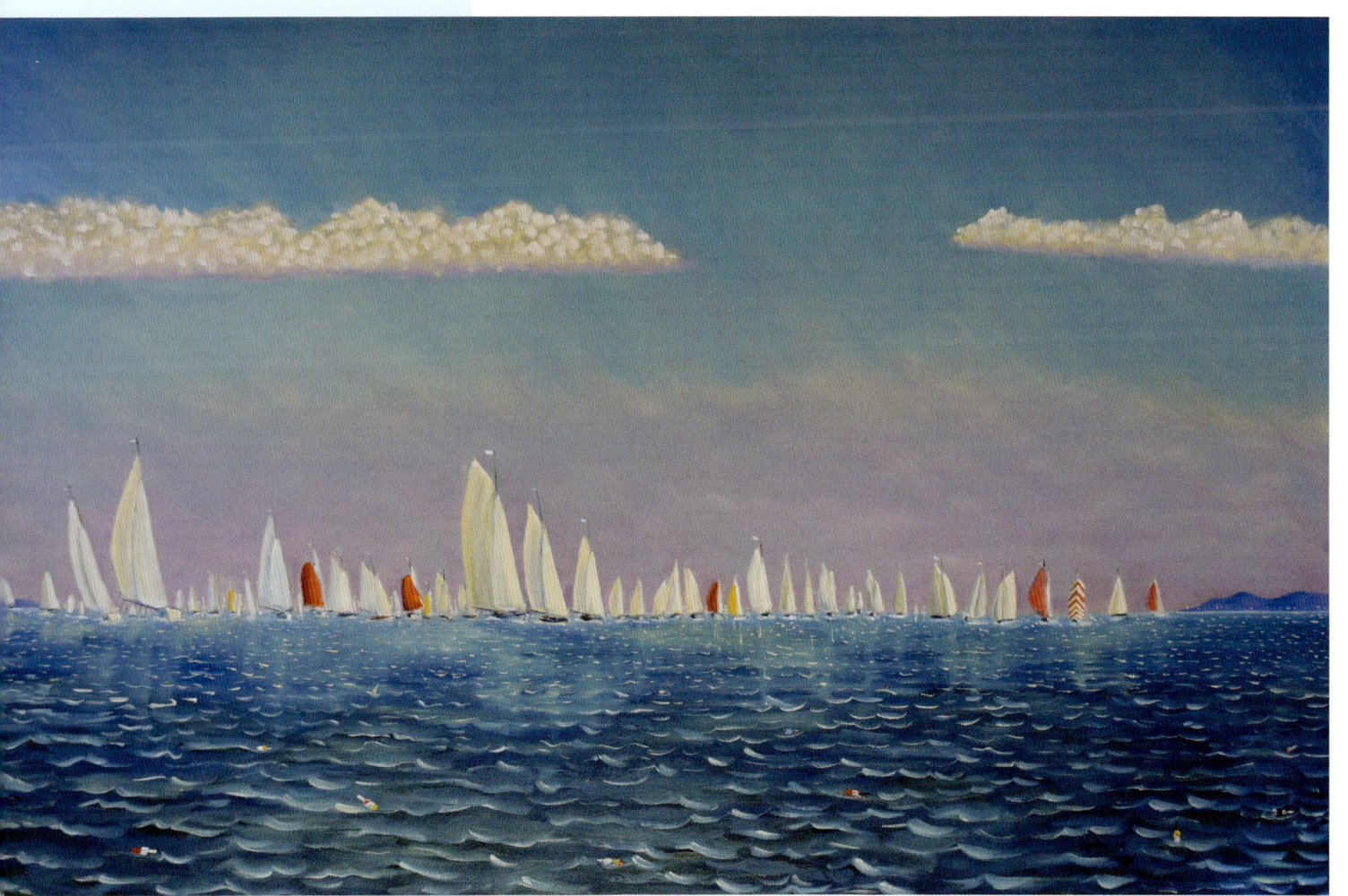

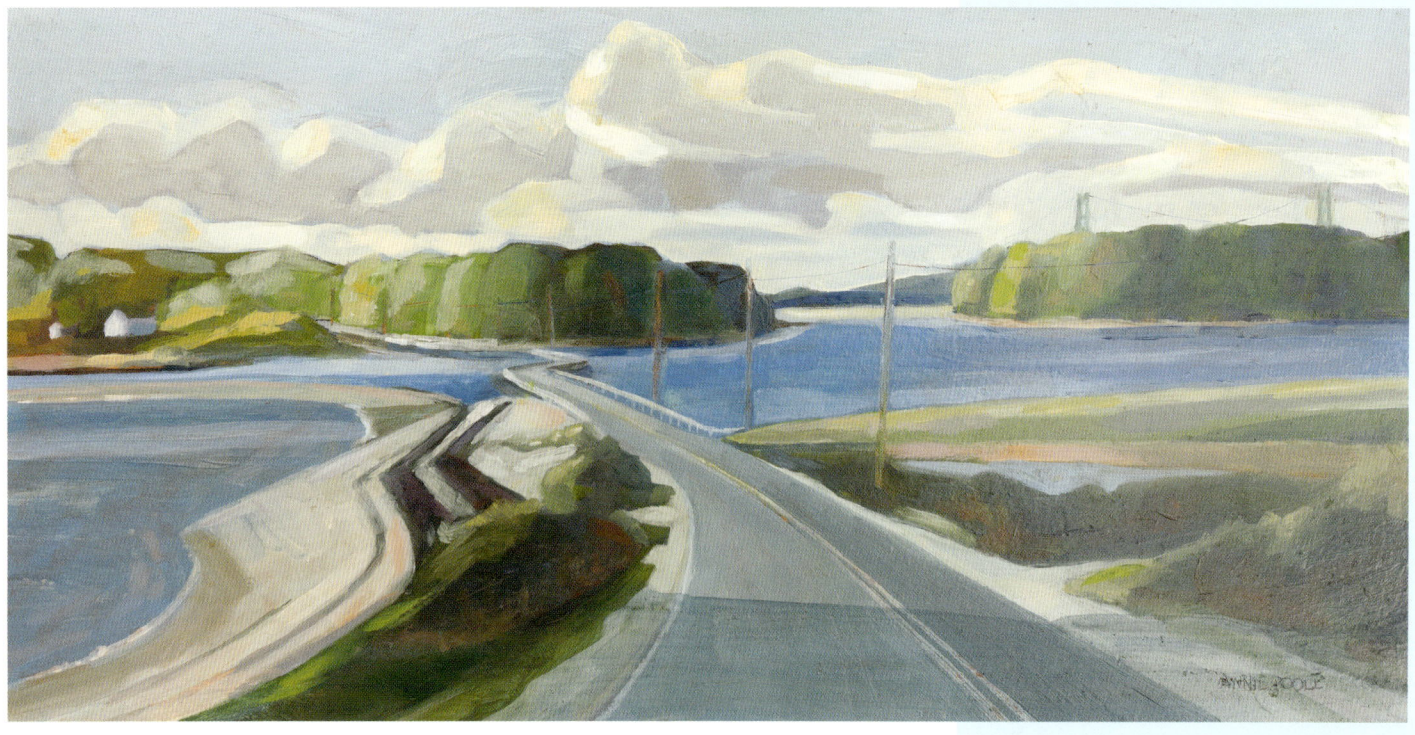

To get to Deer Isle by car you drive over a winding causeway that requires your absolute attention. In her painting of this curving road, **Annie Poole** looks back at Eggemoggin Reach and the Deer Isle bridge on what might be a fall day of light and clouds. A Brooksville resident since 1980, she seeks to highlight the "deep relationships and connections" she has with everyday things and nearby places.

Annie Poole
Deer Isle Causeway, 2018
Oil on panel, 6 x 12 in.

Today

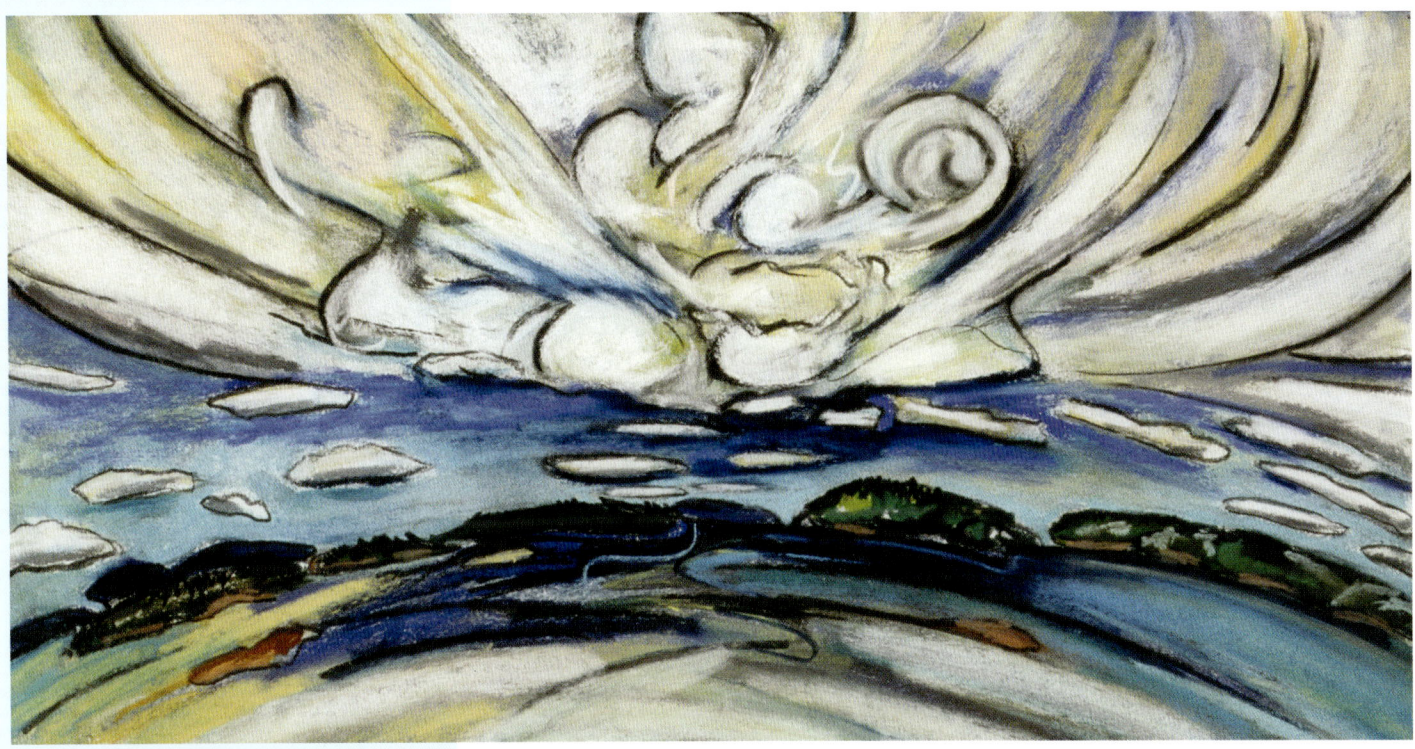

Susan Webster
View from Sheephead Island, Deer Isle, Maine, 2008
Pastel, 10 x 18 in.
Photo by Ken Woisard

Susan Webster knows about connecting to place. For many years, she and her husband and their two sons spent weekends during the fall on Sheephead Island, just off Sylvester Cove and the village of Sunset in Deer Isle. "In the daytime," she recalled, "we harvested mussels, walked trails, explored beaches, and napped on the deck and porch. At night we cooked, ate by candlelight, played board games, read by the gaslight lamps, and slept with windows open to the lulling sound of the ocean's constant movement. Time stood still."

Webster's favorite beach faced northwest where the view spans Vinalhaven, North Haven, the Porcupines, and Eagle and Butter islands. Encircled overhead by cumulus clouds and surrounded by "scattering light" of the yellow, blue, and green sea, she endeavored to document the breadth of it, "the experience of the wind and sun in my eyes, the smell of the seaweed, the desire to become a part of this island life and to record the sweetness of being alive."

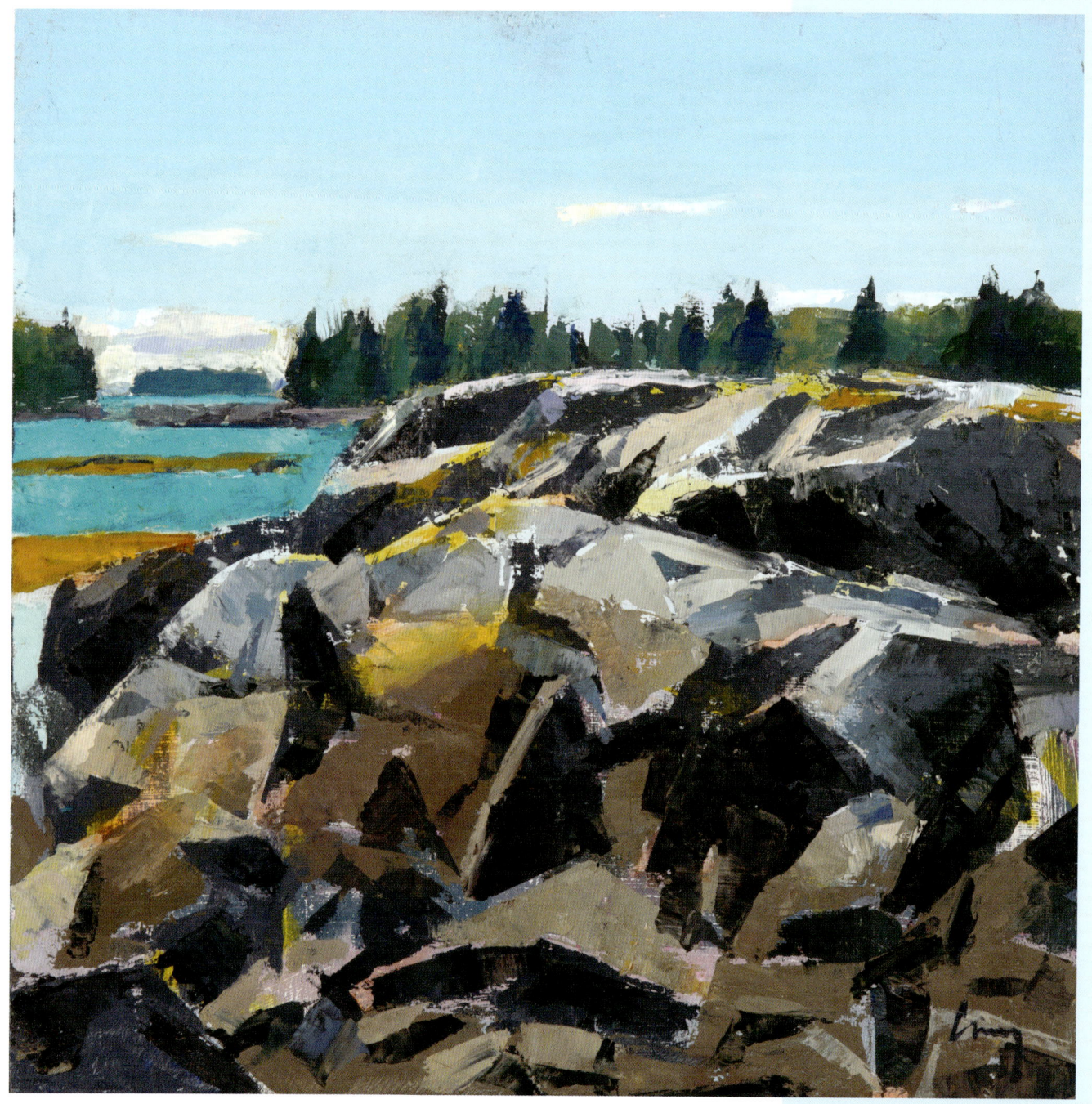

Tom Curry
Sheephead Island, 2007
Oil on birch panel, 12 x 12 in.
Courtesy Courthouse Gallery Fine Art, Ellsworth, Maine
Photo by Ken Woisard

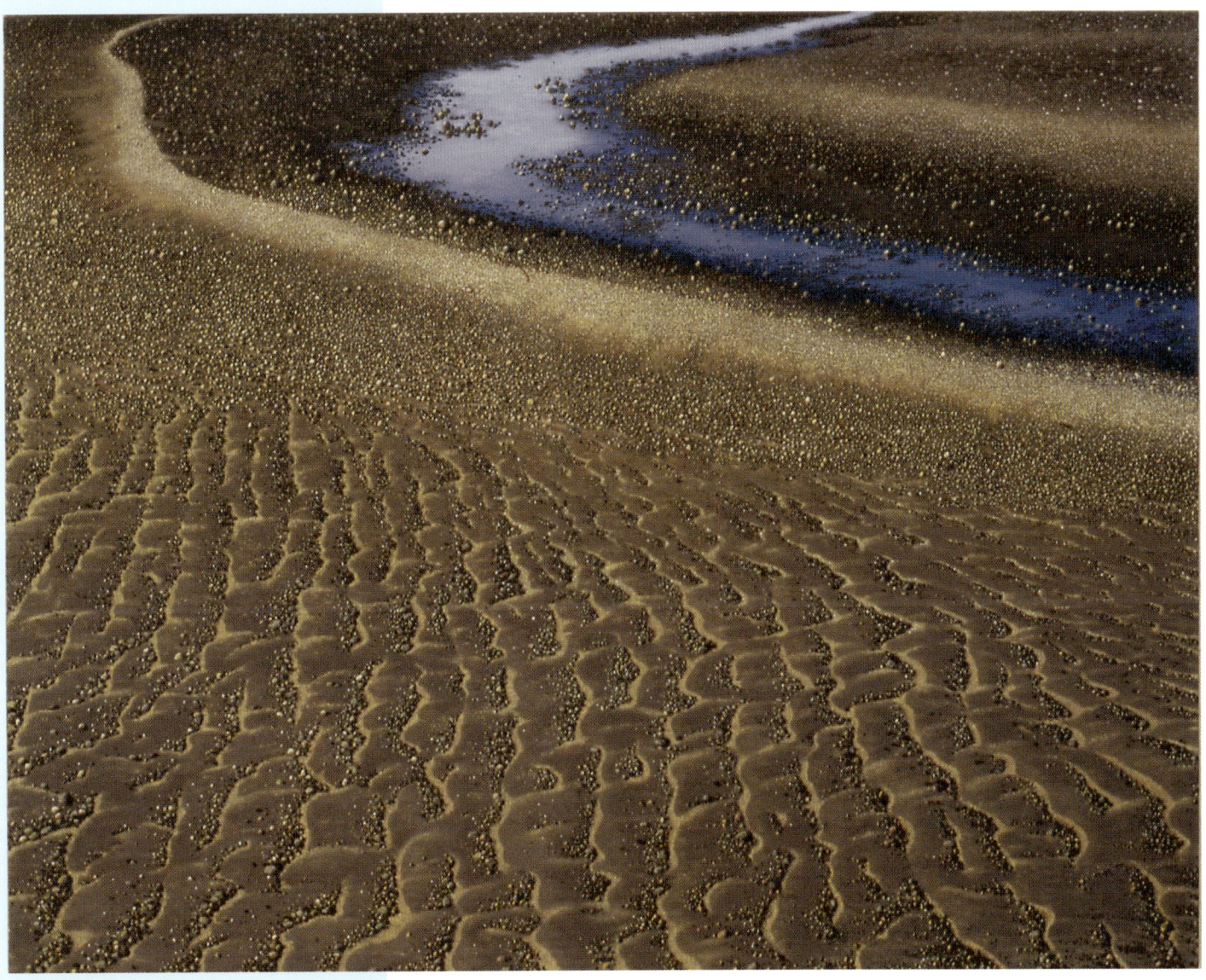

Vaino Kola
Causeway Tidal Flats, 2006
Oil on canvas, 44 x 56 in.
Courtesy Turtle Gallery,
Deer Isle, Maine
Photo by Ken Woisard

Sheephead Island is connected to the mainland at low tide. On painting trips from his home in Brooklin, Maine, **Tom Curry** has explored the island, drawn to its rocky shore and distant prospects. On one visit he set up his easel on a precarious perch, a pile of rocks, which he rendered using a palette knife. He remembers how Clark "Chip" Moseley, a birder and beloved veterinarian, was nearby studying an eagle nest with a scope as he painted.

Finnish-born painter **Vaino Kola** moved to Deer Isle in 1995 upon retiring from his longtime teaching position at Wheaton College. His landscapes have a cool quality, the palette tuned to northern hues. "In an often chaotic, violent, troubling world, there's a clear need for art," he told critic Kristen Andresen in a 2006 interview, adding, "It touches our soul, reminds us who we are, and helps us regain our center." Kola's paintings testify to the truth of these words.

Art of Penobscot Bay

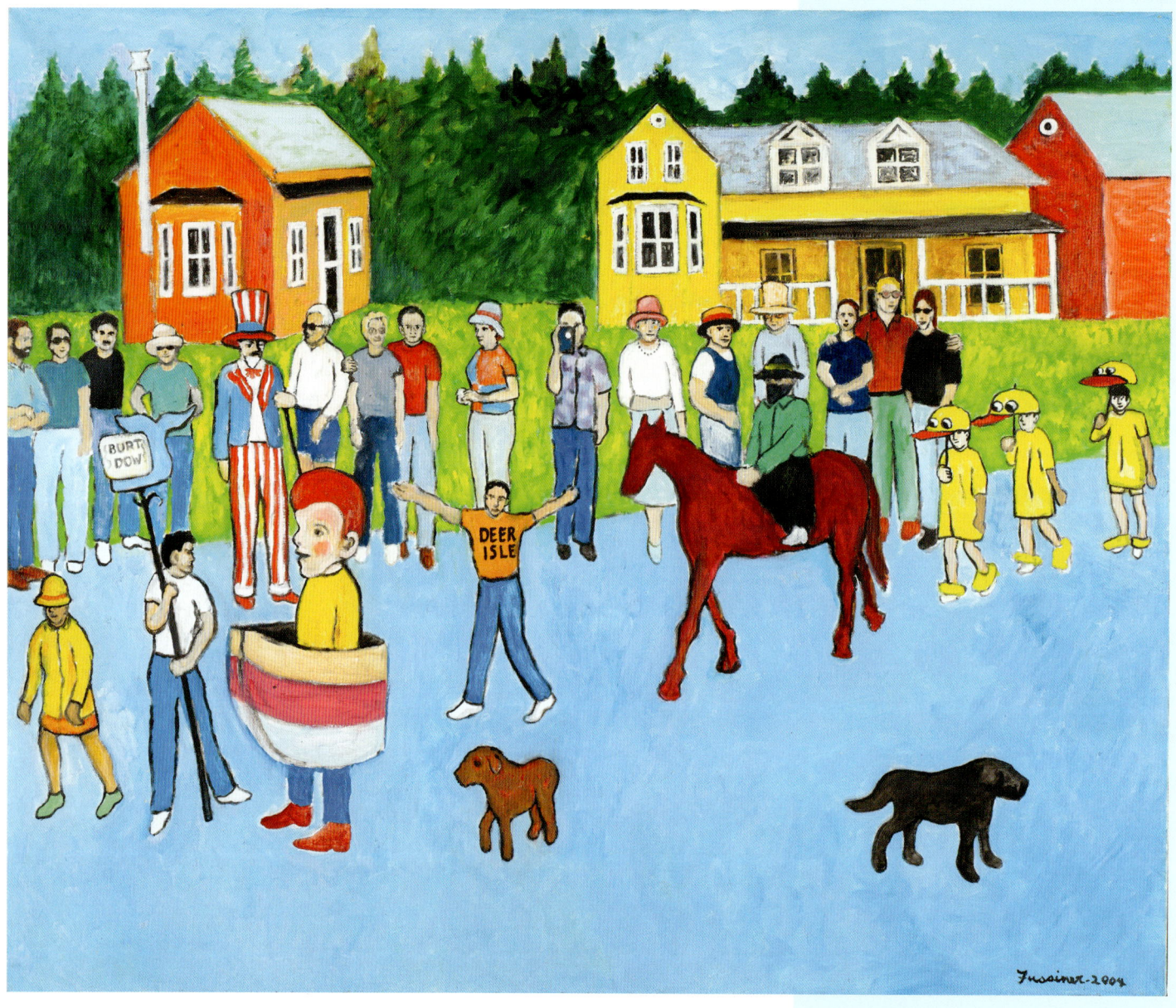

In his years summering in Deer Isle, **Howard Fussiner** (1923–2006) often painted the Fourth of July parade, drawn to the colorful spectacle of neighbors filling the streets. In 2004, the town honored famed Maine children's book author Robert McCloskey (1914–2003) with a special procession. According to the artist's son, Saul Fussiner, the floats referenced McCloskey's various books, including *Make Way for Ducklings, One Morning in Main*e, and *Burt Dow, Deep Water Man.* The painter captured a part of the revelry in his colorful canvas.

Howard Fussiner
Parade for Robert McCloskey, 2004
Oil on canvas, 40 x 48 in.
Photo by Kevin Van Aelst

Today

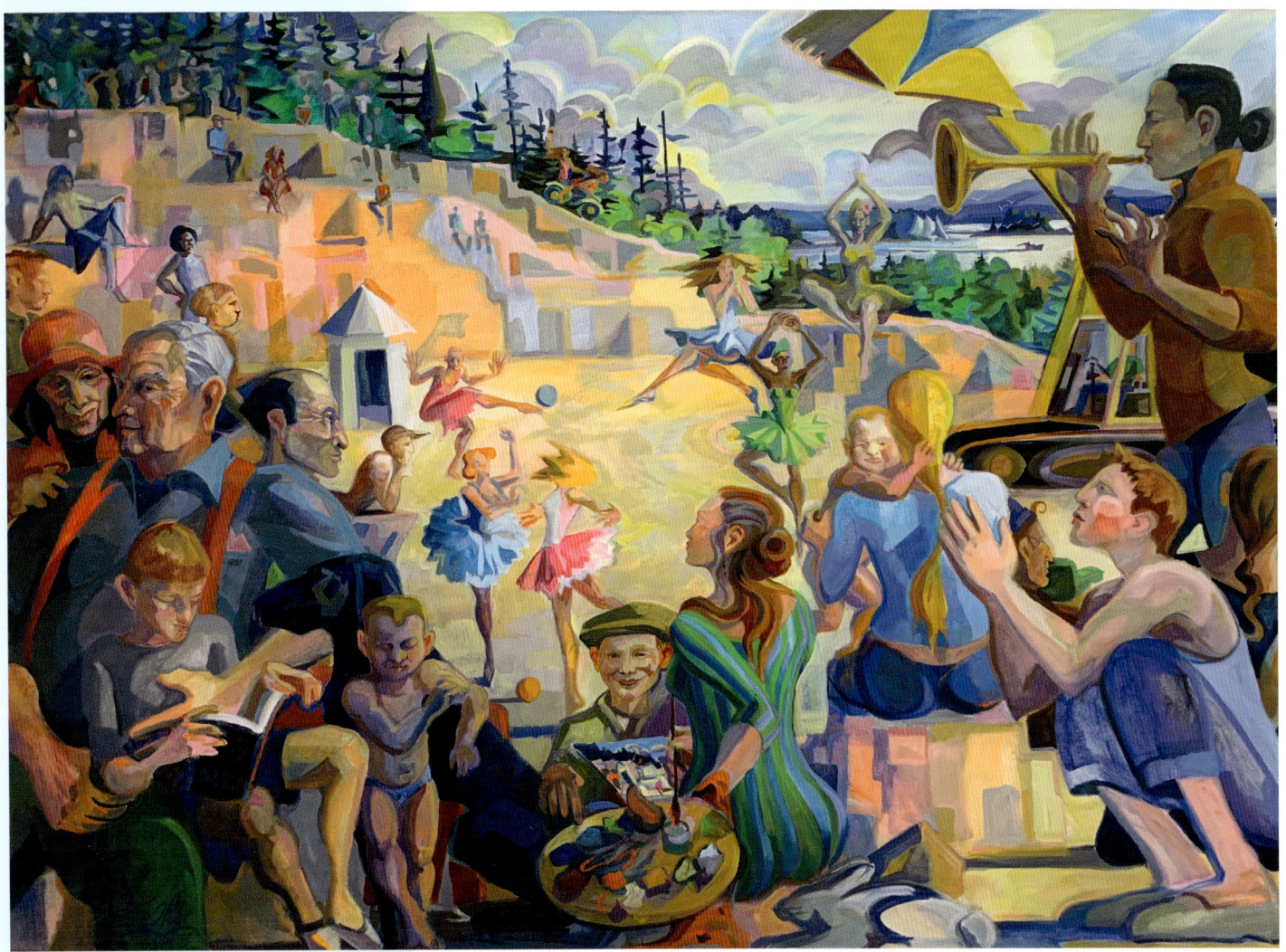

Jill Hoy
Quarryography, 2009
Oil on canvas, 46 x 64 in.

Jill Hoy grew up in Deer Isle in the 1960s and has lived part of the year in Stonington for many years. *Quarryography* (2009) responds to a performance directed by Allison Chase, one of the founders of the Pilobolus Dance Company, held in the Oceanville quarry, which looks out on Isle au Haut. Commissioned by the Stonington Opera House, the piece featured all manner of equipment for suspending dancers over the granite landscape. Hoy populated the crowd with island friends and family. "It was," she stated, "a once-in-a-lifetime commemoration of pure human magic and the power of creation."

Another Hoy painting, *Viola and the Peapod* (2020-2021), straddles "documentation and the personal." The double-ended rowboat, known as a peapod, reminds the artist of her father who suspended his boat by ropes in the family barn on King Row in Deer Isle. The one in the painting, a gift from a local backhoe operator, serves as "an excellent form for a still life painting" in Hoy's yard as well as a perching place for her black cat. She added colorful lobster buoys, a few mackerel, and, taking some artistic license, Stonington's west side vantage point on Penobscot Bay.

Hoy shared her home and life with **Jon Imber** (1950–2014), who approached coastal subjects with a lyric sense of subject grounded in the legacies of Marsden Hartley, Willem de Kooning, and his teacher Philip Guston. The still life/landscape *Shells and Island* is built from broad and vigorous brushstrokes, bridging representation and abstraction. The painter's valiant battle to overcome ALS is documented in the film *Imber's Left Hand*.

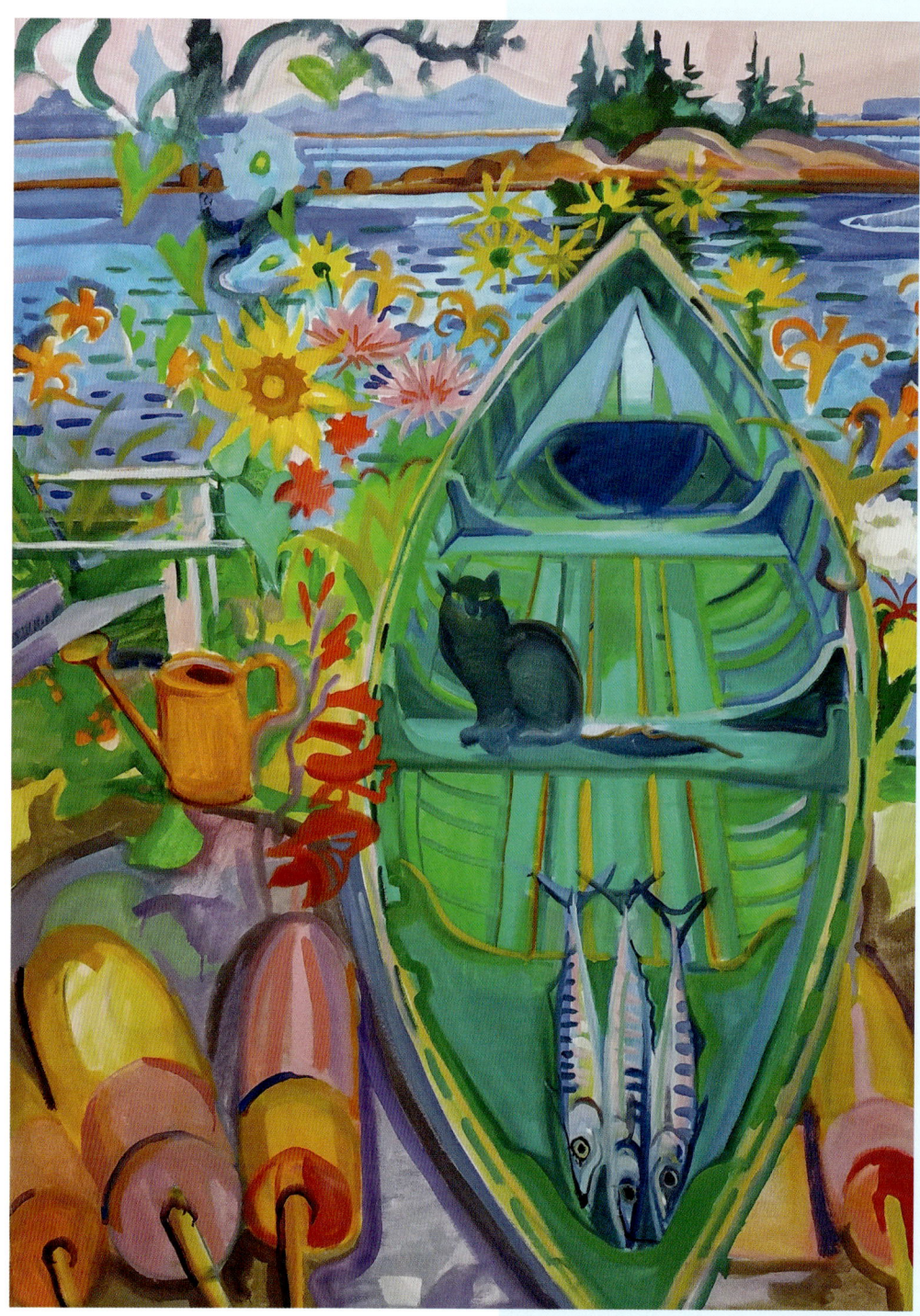

Jill Hoy
Viola and the Peapod, 2020–2021
Oil on canvas, 46 x 34 in.
Private collection

Today

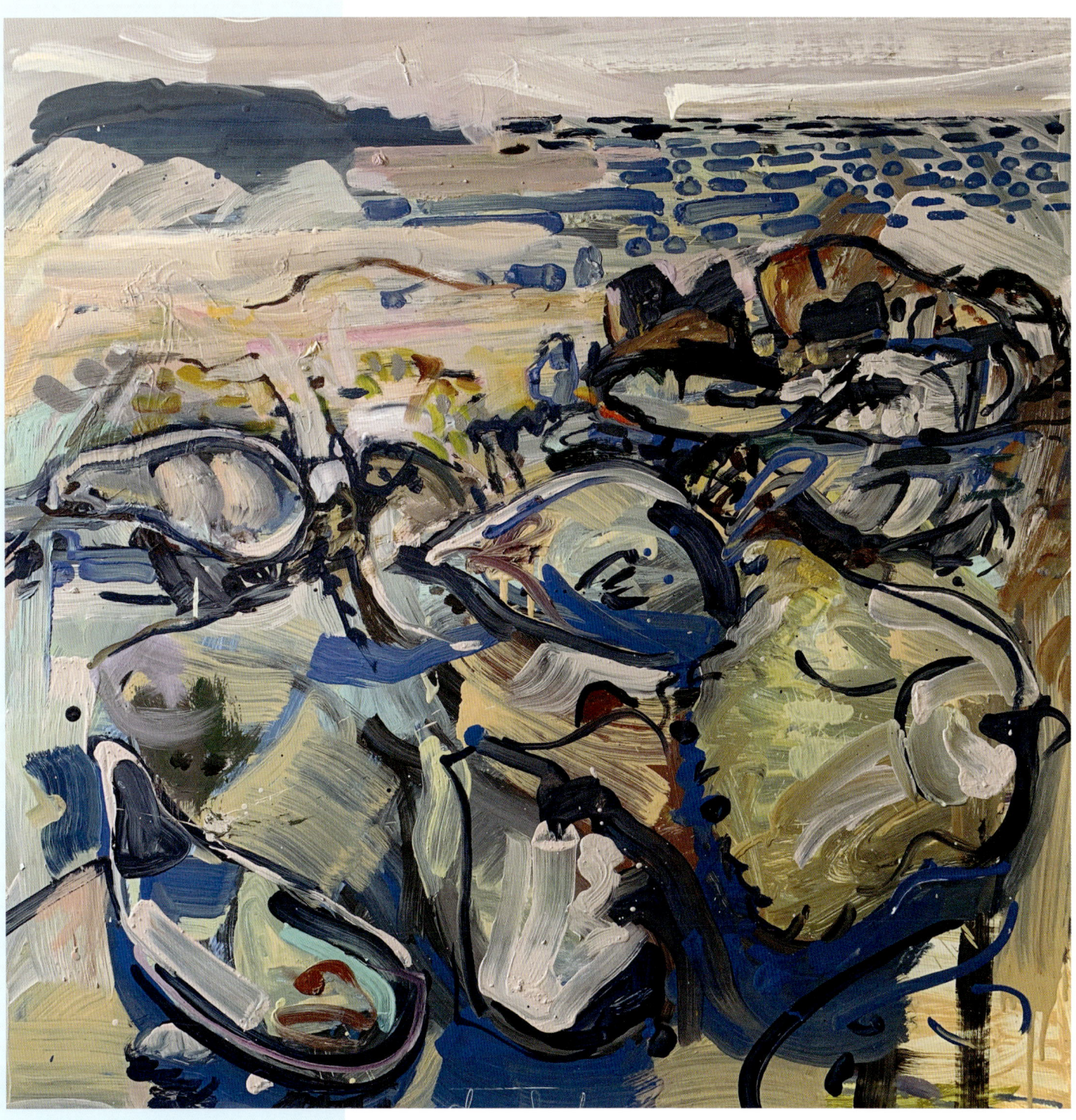

Jon Imber
Shells and Island, 2001
Oil on birch panel, 36 x 36 in.
Estate of Jon Imber

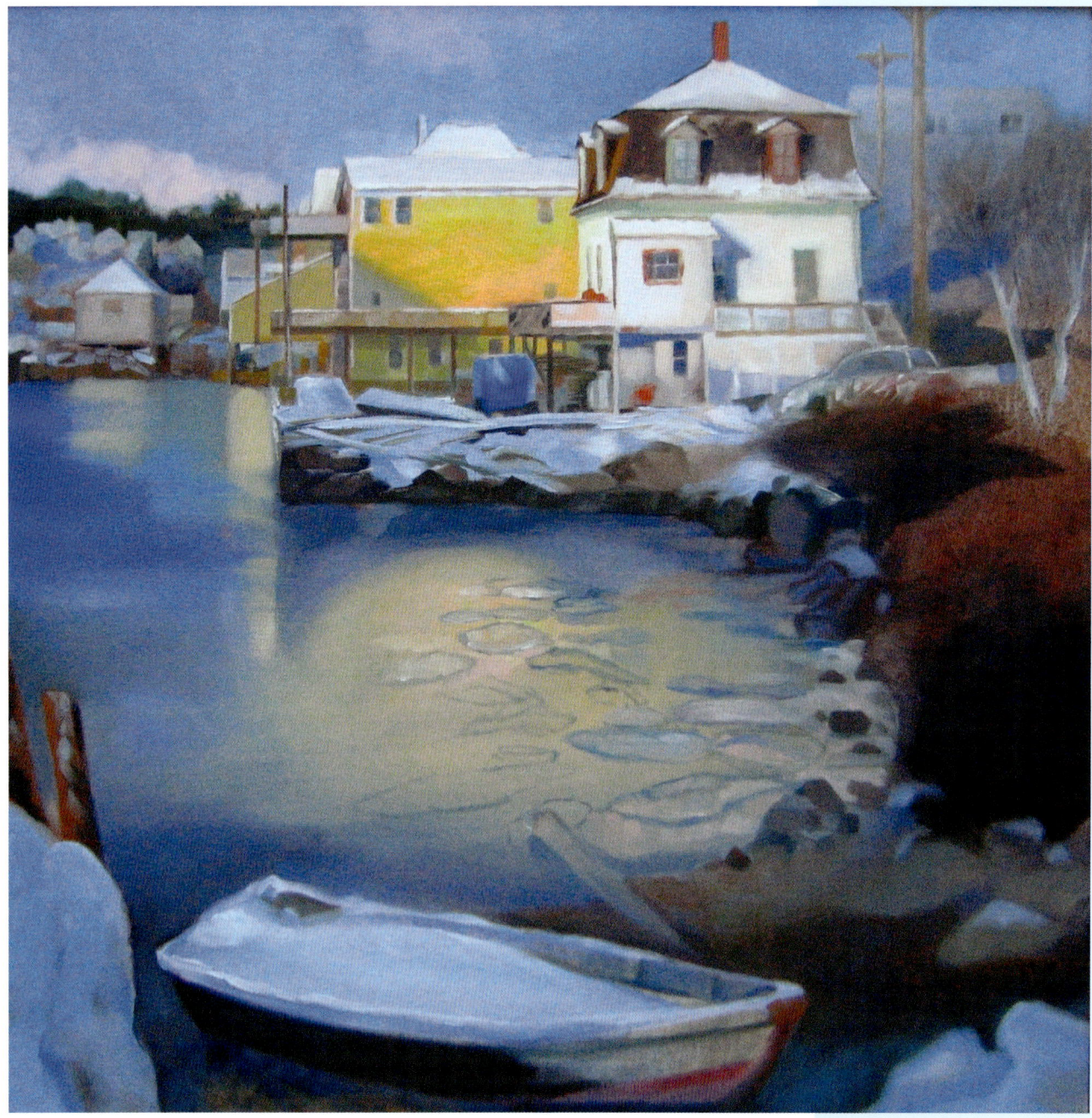

"For me there is no town more beautiful than Stonington," said **Siri Beckman**, a Chicagoan who moved there in the 1970s (she now lives in Bath). One winter morning while walking to the post office Beckman caught sight of sunlit buildings along Stonington's waterfront. "I knew I had to put down this very familiar scene in paint"—not an unusual response from an artist, but a little surprising knowing that Beckman is one of Maine's foremost printmakers.

Siri Beckman
Morning Light, 2011
Oil on canvas, 18 x 18 in.
Private collection

Today

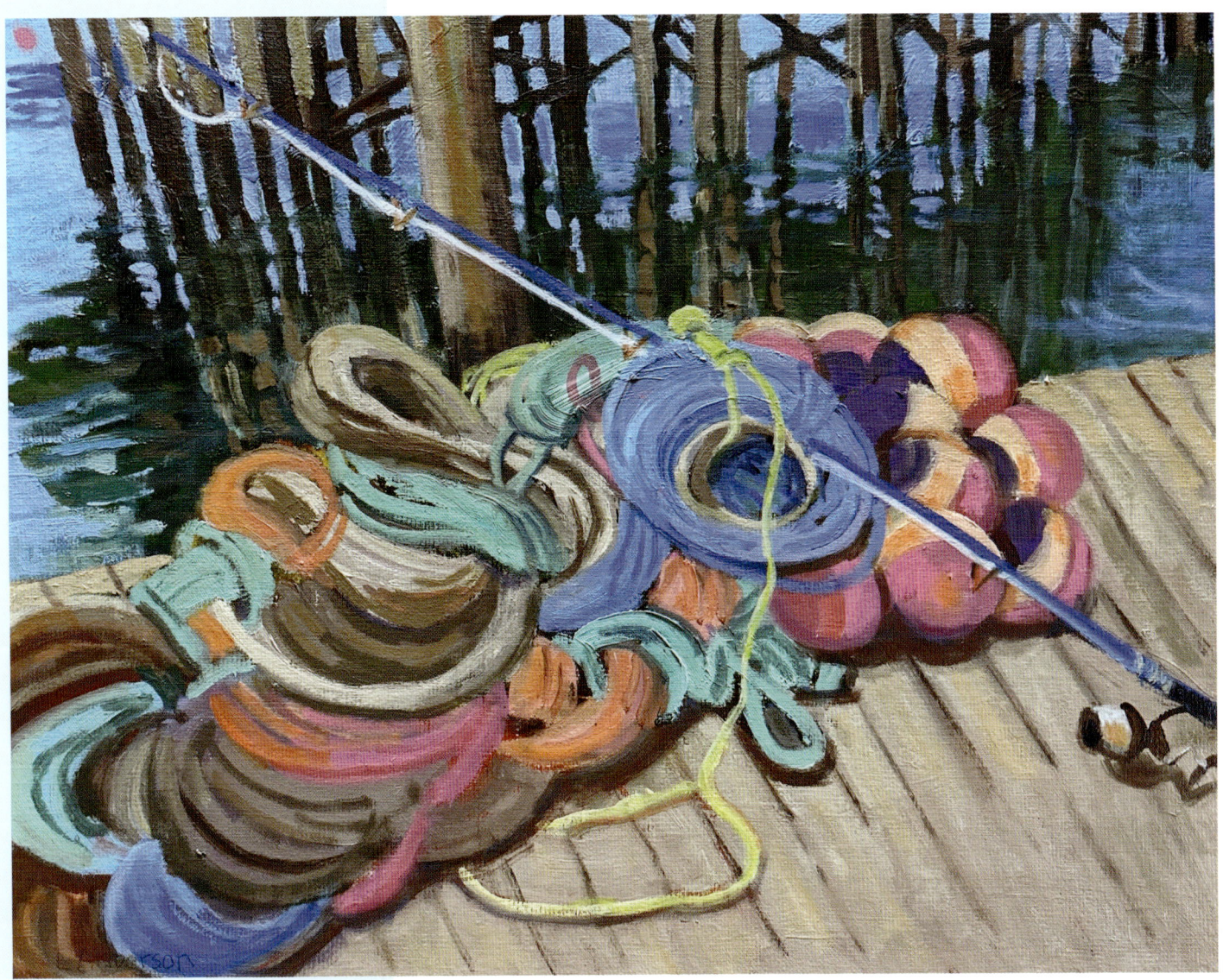

Leslie Anderson
Island Gear, 2020
Oil on canvas, 11 x 14 in.
Collection of the artist

In a similar manner **Leslie Anderson** found the subject of her oil painting *Island Gear* (2020) by chance. She had just wrapped up a day of painting in Stonington when a "fisherman's still life" caught her eye. She was drawn to the colors and patterns of the pot warp, buoys, and, especially, the blue fishing rod, which created a strong diagonal and, for Anderson, conjured the image of a lobsterman pulling in a few cod or hake for his supper.

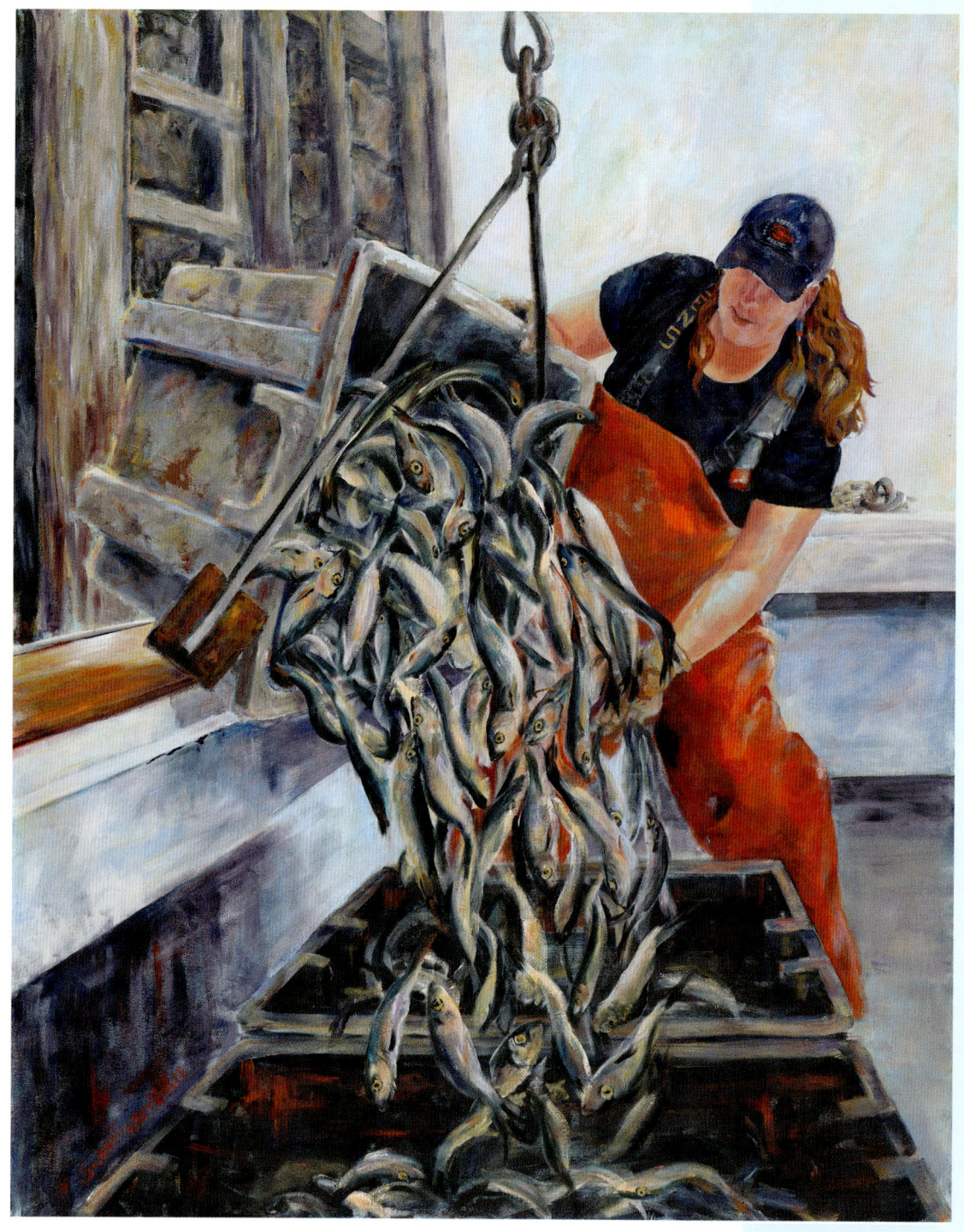

Susan Tobey White
Lobstering Woman of Maine: Genevieve, 2018
Acrylic on canvas, 60 x 48 in.
Photo by Alan LaVallee

Today

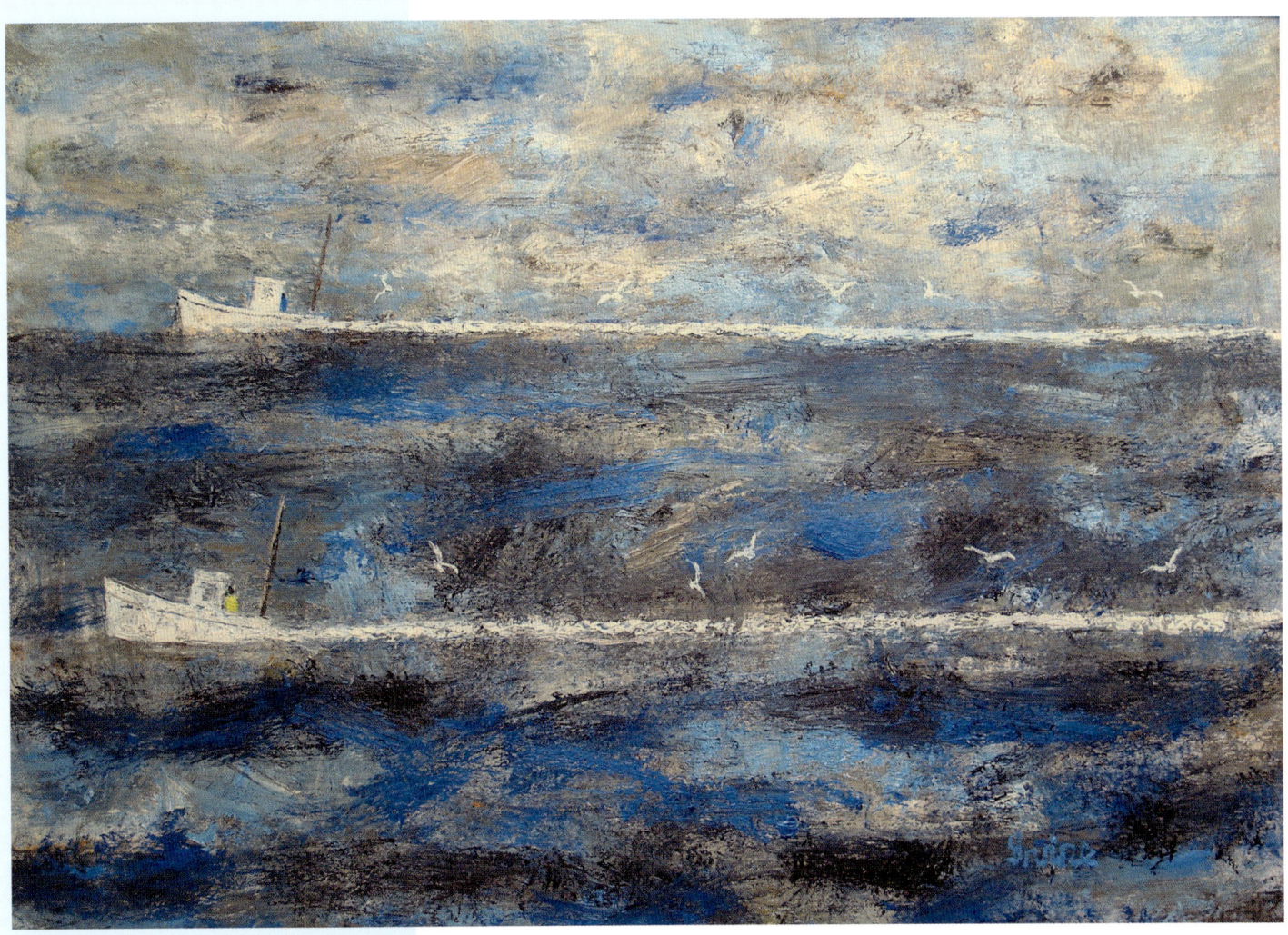

William Irvine
The Lobster Boat Race, Stonington, 2012
Oil on museum board, 26 x 36 in.
Courtesy Courthouse Gallery Fine Art, Ellsworth, Maine

Stonington is one of the busiest lobster fishing ports in New England. Belfast painter **Susan Tobey White's** series "Lobstering Women of Maine" includes a portrait of Genevieve McDonald who captains the *F/V Hello Darlings II* (2012) out of Stonington. Sporting an orange Grundéns bib she dumps a crate of herring into holding bins. McDonald was the first female commercial fisherman elected to the Maine House of Representatives, in all-island district 134 stretching from Cranberry Isles to the Marshall Island Township. White brings out the heroic in her subject.

Stonington hosts an annual lobster boat race in July. The Scottish-born painter **William Irvine**, who lives in Brooklin, depicts the contest by way of two lobster boats crossing the canvas in parallel lines leaving straight white wakes behind them. There's a looseness and energy in the impastoed surface that seem to fit the subject perfectly.

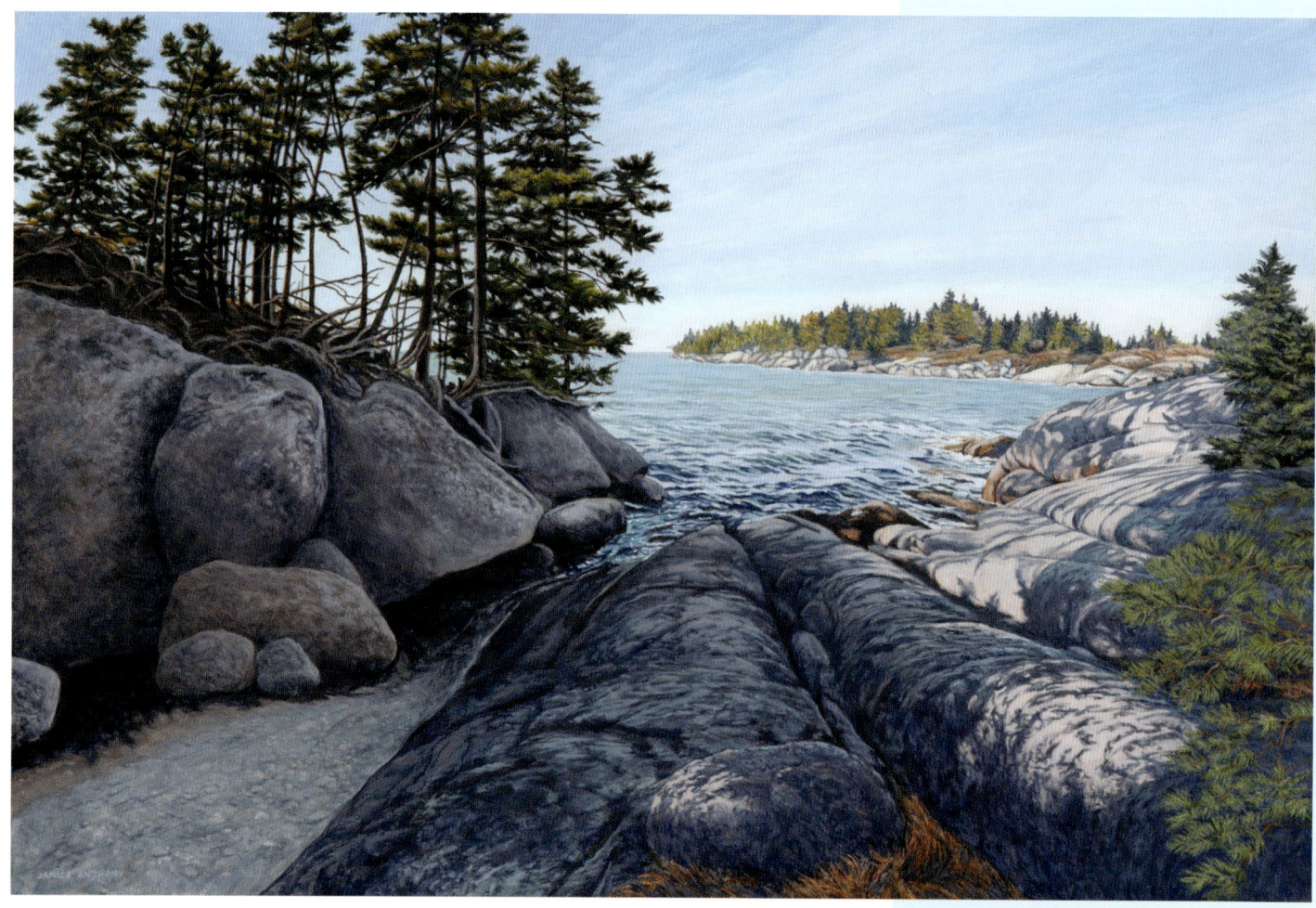

As one approaches Stonington from the west, Sand Beach provides a quiet retreat. **Janice Anthony** found the sheltered place on a trip from her home in Jackson, Maine. She admired the large granite boulders and the sweeping branches of spruce and pine protecting it. The scene is bathed in cool light and features complex shadow play.

Janice Anthony
Stonington Granite, 2021
Acrylic on linen, 20 x 30 in.
Courtesy of Courthouse Gallery Fine Art, Ellsworth, Maine

Today

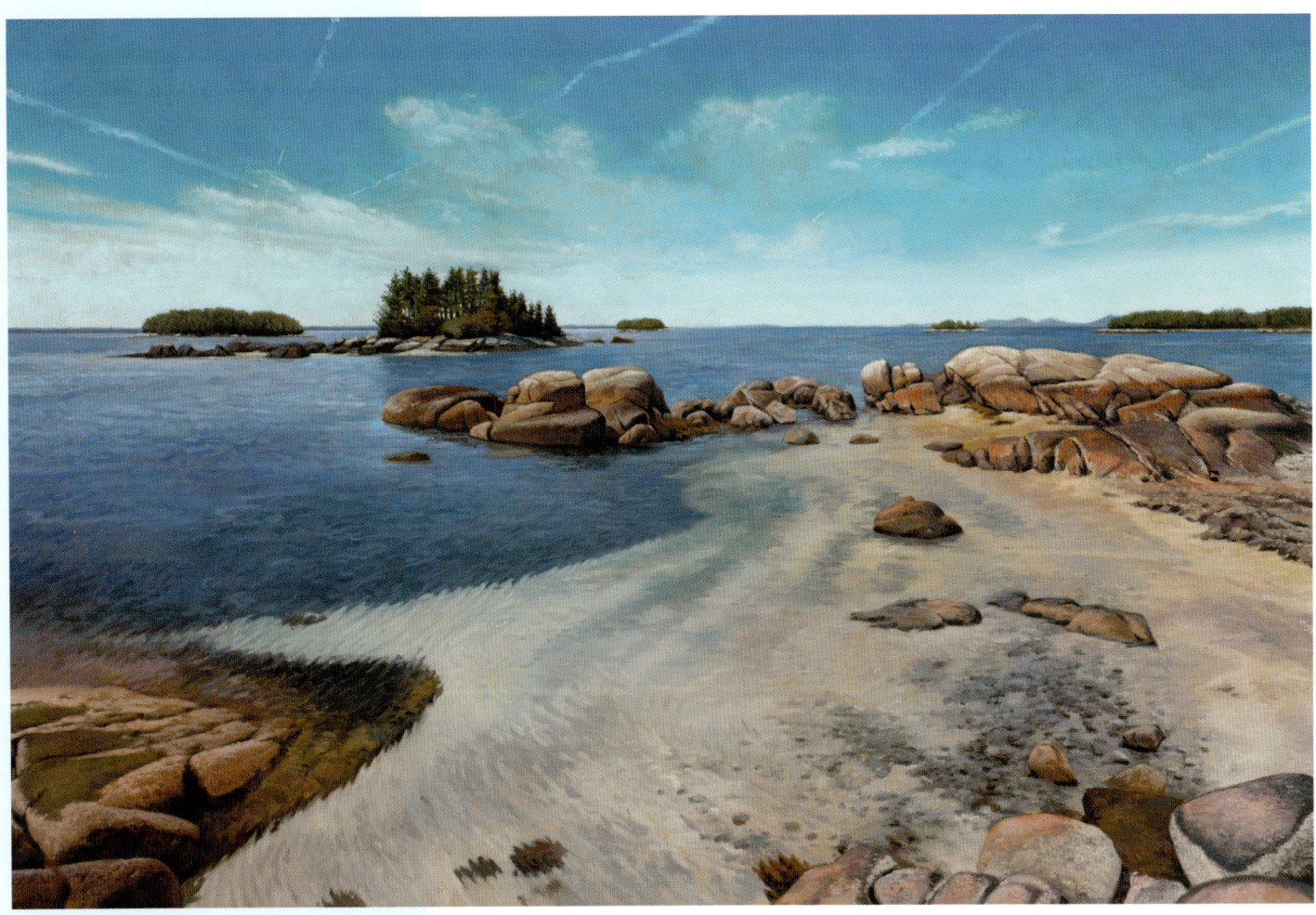

James Mullen
Sand Beach, Stonington, 2021
Oil on canvas, 40 x 60 in.
Photo by Luc Demers

In search of the sublime, the painter **James Mullen** often travels the Maine coast from his home in Brunswick where he teaches at Bowdoin College. His *Sand Beach, Stonington* (2021) offers a crystal-clear view of Penobscot Bay and the islands of Merchant Row. "Sand Beach has a dramatic scale as it wades into Penobscot Bay," wrote Mullen. "Depending on the tides, sometimes the rocks on the beach act as a parallel for the islands that punctuate the horizon and float off the shore."

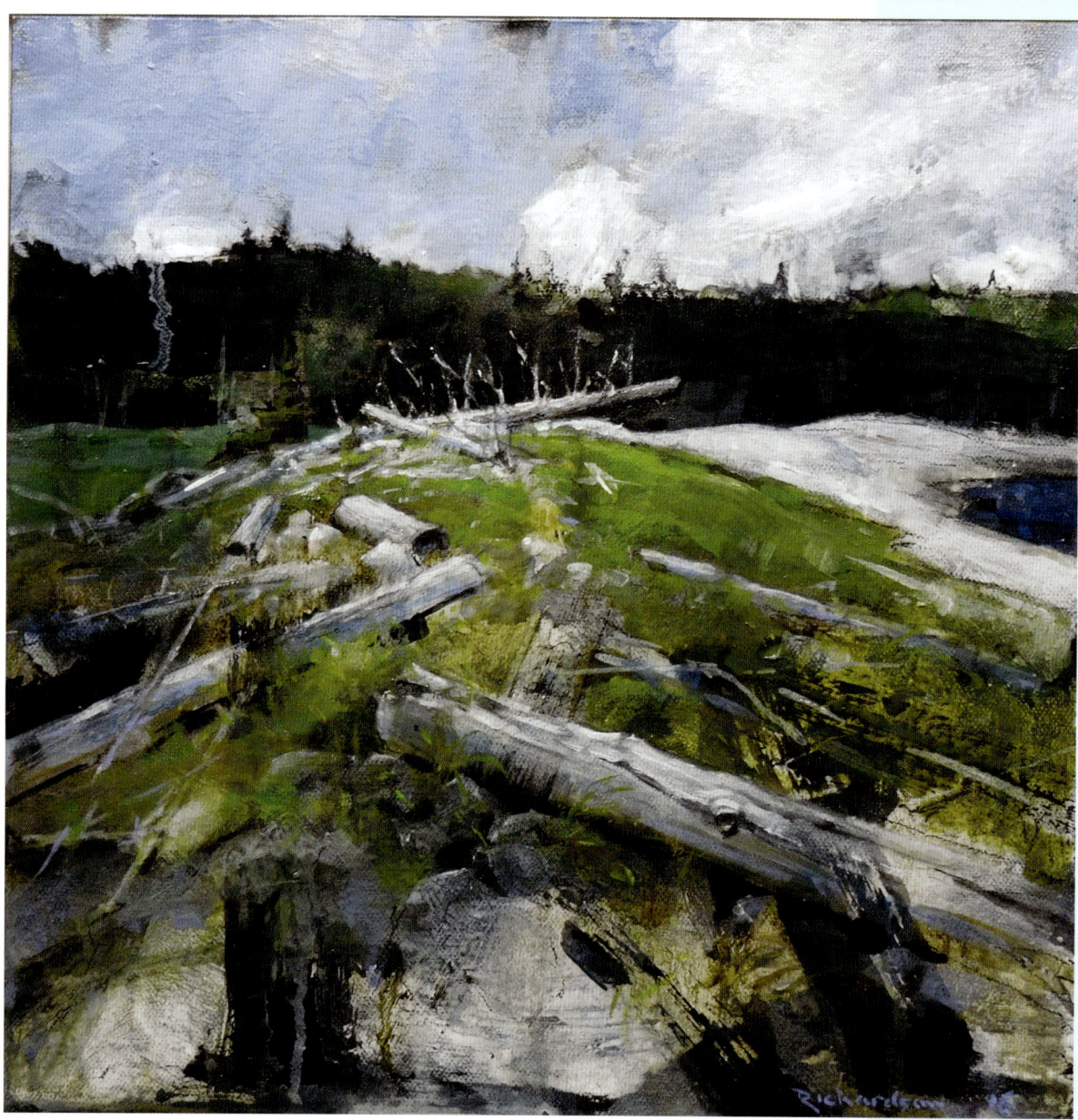

Alec Richardson
Walking the Seawall, 2016
Oil on canvas, 10 x 10 in.
Private collection
Photo by Alec Richardson

Alec Richardson grew up believing his 104-year-old grandfather's words: "Maine doesn't start until you cross over the Wiscasset bridge, and you'll find no sailing grounds in the *world* lovelier than Penobscot Bay." As a young man, he was fortunate to sail the bay waters and treasures his memories "of the endless islands, their fascinating geology, and the communities nestled among them."

Richardson noted his preference for subjects and locales that contain "much more than simply a view." Among his favorite places to paint is Marshall Island, a 985-acre unorganized territory that lies between Stonington and Isle au Haut (Maine Coast Heritage Trust established the Ed Woodsum Preserve there in 2003).

Today

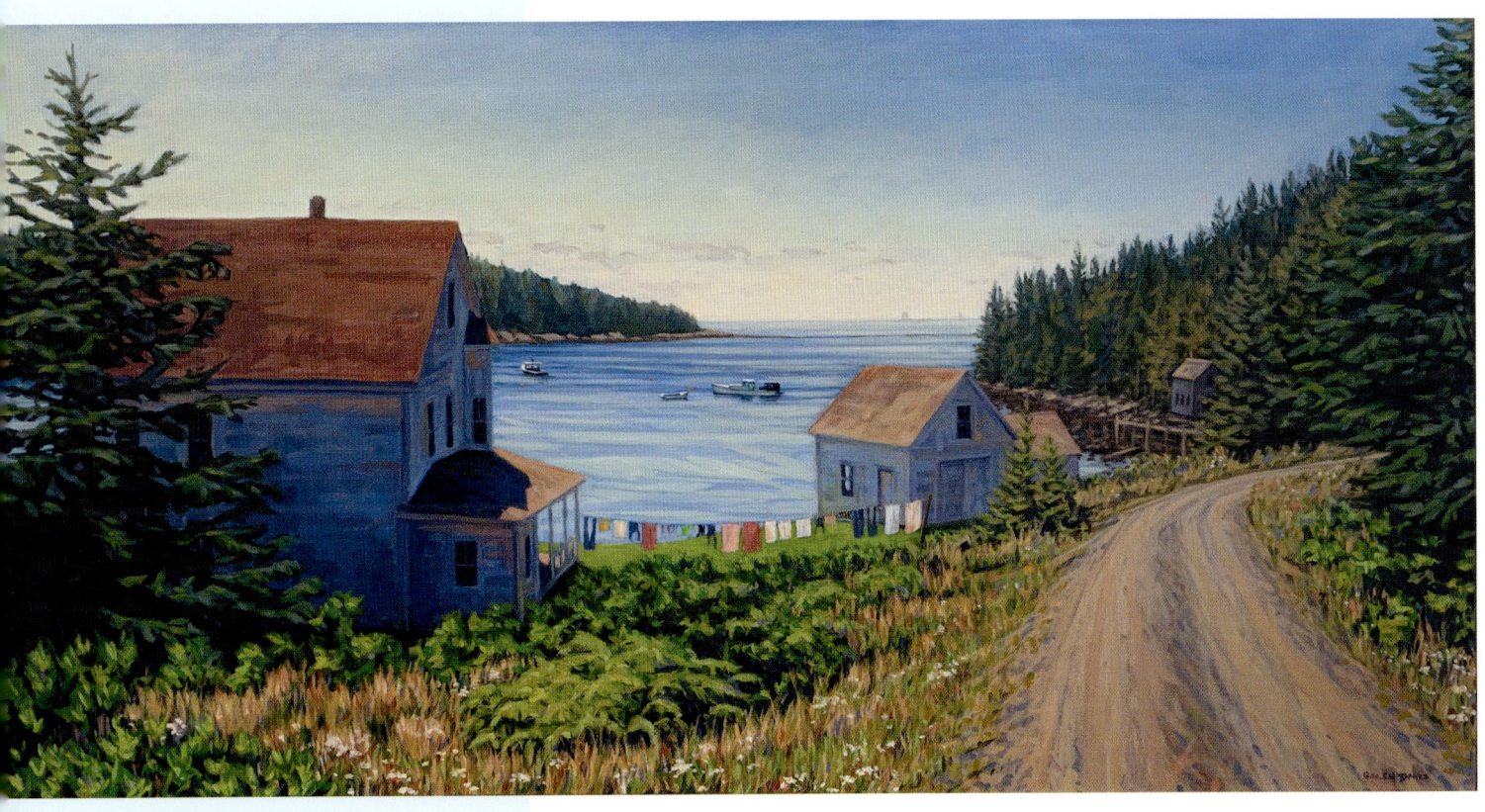

Galen Davis
Head Harbor and Gooden Grant's House with Laundry, 2021
Oil on canvas, 18 x 36 in.

His painting of the island's seawall features driftwood trees tossed up by storms, their gray lengths lying here and there on the embankment. His brushwork matches the wild energy of the place.

"But I'll haul down the sail/Where the bays come together/Bide away the days/ By the hills of Isle au Haut." So runs the chorus of Gordon Bok's beloved song, "The Hills of Isle au Haut" about the "high island" the French explorer Samuel de Champlain named on one of his voyages to America.

Over the years, painter **Galen Davis**, who lives in Brooksville and on Isle au Haut, has created a remarkable group of images of her region, focusing on coastal subjects. *Head Harbor, Gooden Grant's House with Laundry* (2021) is, according to Davis, one of the most often painted and photographed spots on Isle au Haut. Noting its "almost storybook feeling" thanks to its heightened color and "perfect-summer-day details," Davis wrote the painting reflects her "romanticization" of the place.

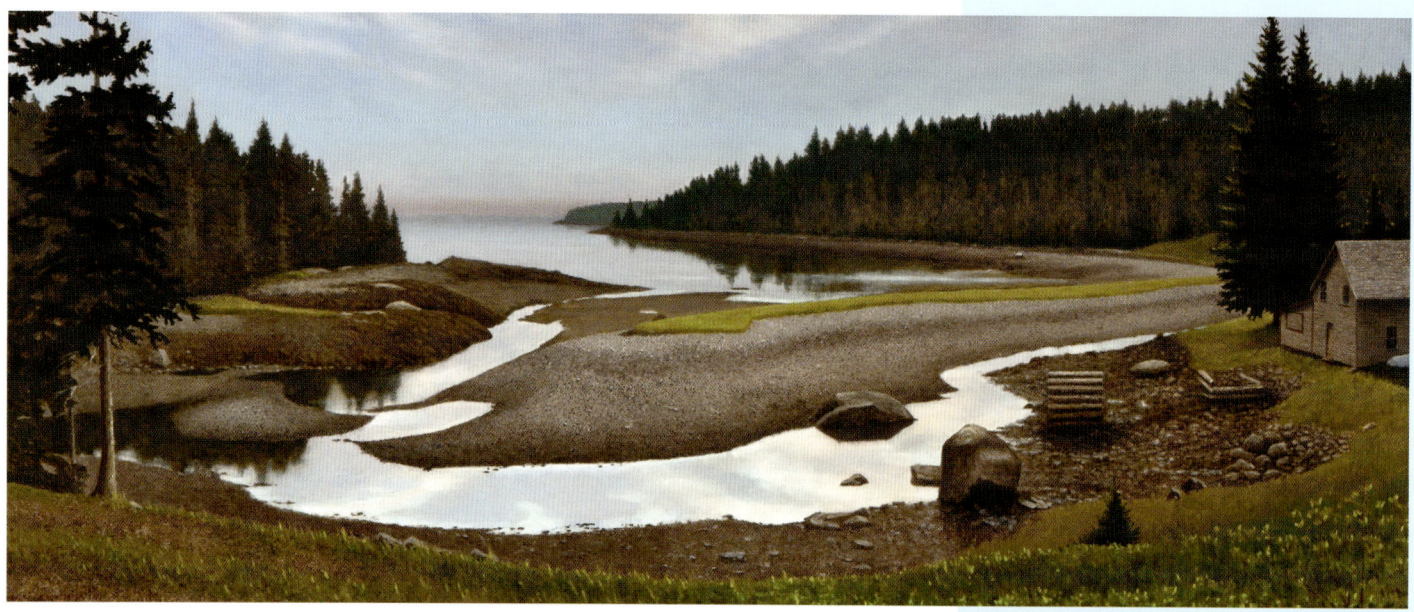

A similar passion for place marks **David Vickery's** painting of the head of Moore's Harbor on the western side of Isle au Haut. In cool tones and with a precise brush, the Cushing-based painter celebrates a still cove where the seas from the southwest have created a large gravel bar. "At lower tides," Vickery reported, "this creates elegant shapes in the water, which along with the boathouse, wharf remnants, and glacial boulders made for a painting that practically designed itself."

David Vickery
Moore's Harbor, Isle Au Haut, 2016
Oil on panel, 20 x 48 in.
Courtesy of Dowling Walsh Gallery, Rockland, Maine

Today

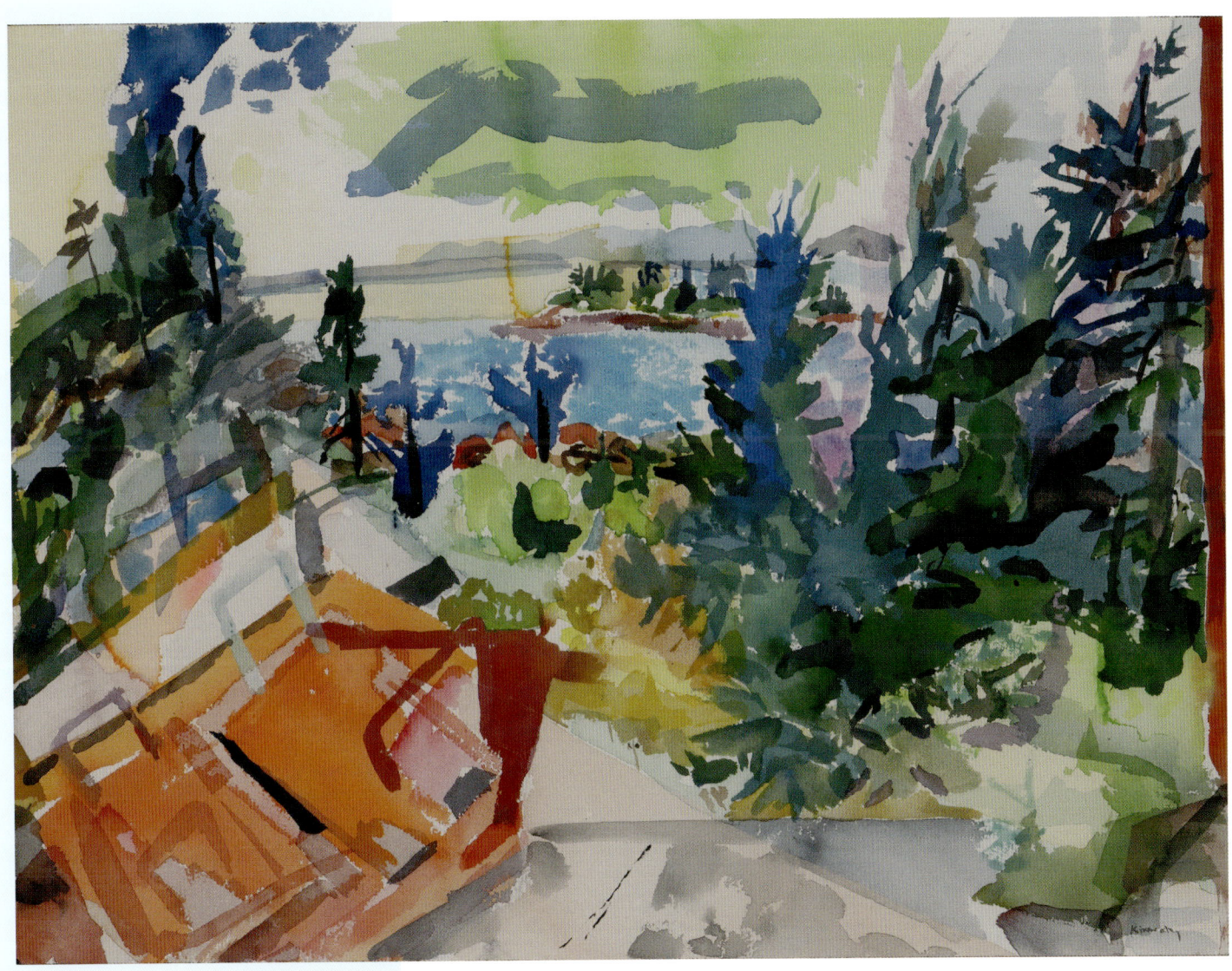

Jim Kinnealey
Point Lookout, Isle au Haut, 1994
Watercolor on paper, 18 x 24 in.
Collection of David and
Kathy Dewey
Photo by Dave Clough

Jim Kinnealey of Hope, Maine, remembers painting his watercolor *Point Lookout* on a perfect September day on Isle au Haut. Flake Island lies close by; Penobscot Bay and the sky stretch to the Camden Hills. His lively brushwork captures the vibrancy and joy of the setting. Kinnealey and his wife, artist Cynthia Hyde, have operated the Caldbeck Gallery in Rockland for more than forty years, showcasing a broad spectrum of Maine artists.

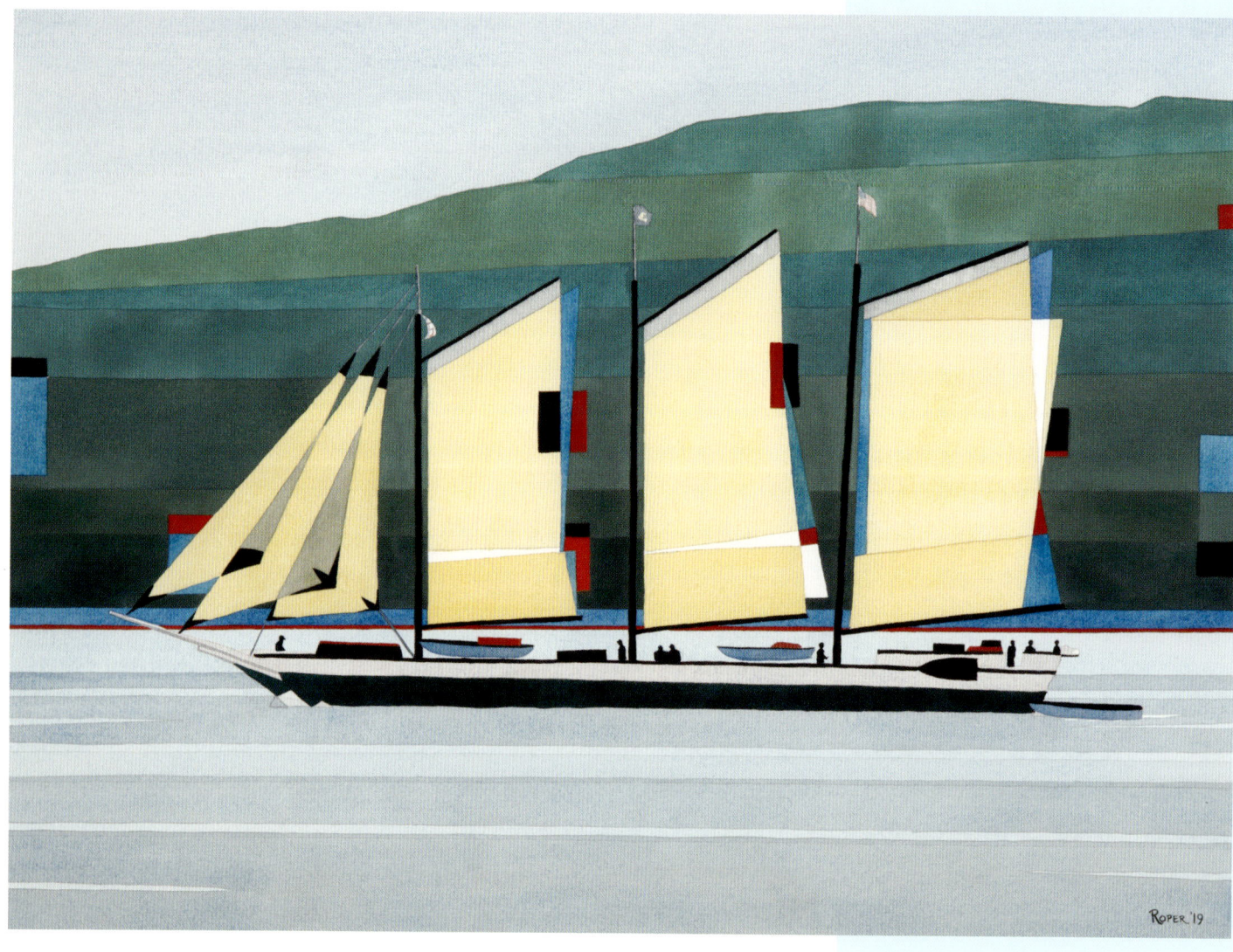

We finish our trip round the bay with **Diana Roper McDowell's** watercolor *Victory Chimes Passing Isle au Haut (2019)*. McDowell has loved the historic schooner since she saw it as a kid. Later, staying in a cabin on Saddleback Island in Merchant Row, she watched it sailing by, took a few photos, and decided to paint it. In her geometric style she transforms the three-masted, gaff-rigged ship into a dynamic image of Maine coast sailing. It's a classic form in a classic landscape.

McDowell's painting reflects the past, present, and future of Penobscot Bay. While it harks back to the glory days of tall ships and schooners, it also reflects the current catering to visitors who seek to experience Penobscot Bay from the water. As for the future, we sail on, not knowing exactly what we'll encounter around the next island.

Diana Roper McDowell
Victory Chimes Passing Isle au Haut, 2019
Watercolor on paper, 20 ½ x 28 in.
Photo by Ken Woisard

About the Authors

David Little is the author of *Art of Katahdin*, named a "Best of New England" book by the *Boston Globe* in 2013. He is co-author with his brother Carl of *Art of Acadia* (2016) and *Paintings of Portland* (2018). In 2017 he took part in a national symposium at Colby College, "Valuing the Aesthetics of Nature: The Role of the Visual Artist in the American Conservation Movement." Little holds an M.A. and M.F.A. in painting from the University of Iowa, attended Skowhegan School of Painting and Sculpture (1981 and 1982), and has had residencies on Monhegan Island and the Virginia Center for the Creative Arts. He lives with his wife Mikki in Portland.

Find more about David at www.davidlittleart.com.

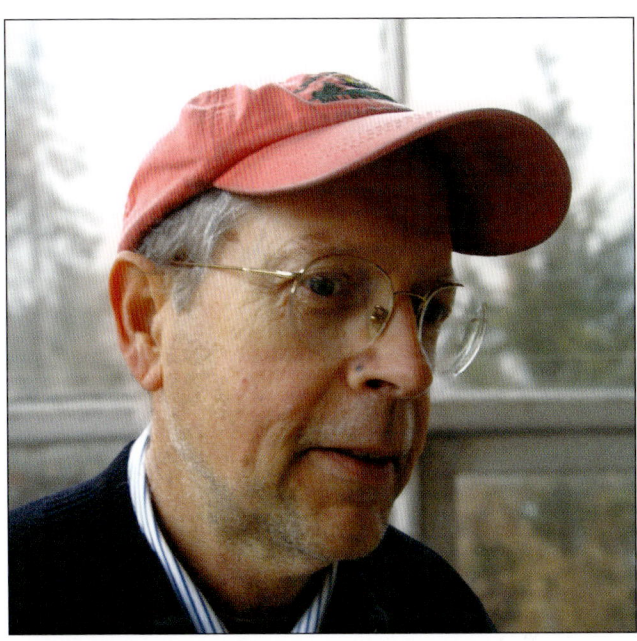

Photo by Mikki Jones-Little.

Born in New York City, Carl Little holds degrees from Dartmouth, Middlebury, and Columbia. Little is the author of more than 30 art books, including *The Watercolors of John Singer Sargent*, *Edward Hopper's New England*, and *Paintings of Maine*. His book *Eric Hopkins: Above and Beyond* won the first John Cole Prize from the Maine Writers & Publishers Alliance in 2012. Little writes for *Art New England*, *Hyperallergic*, *Maine Boats, Homes & Harbors*, *The Working Waterfront*, *Island Journal*, and *Ornament*. In 2021 the Dorothea and Leo Rabkin Foundation honored Little with a Lifetime Achievement Award for his art writing. He lives and writes on Mount Desert Island.

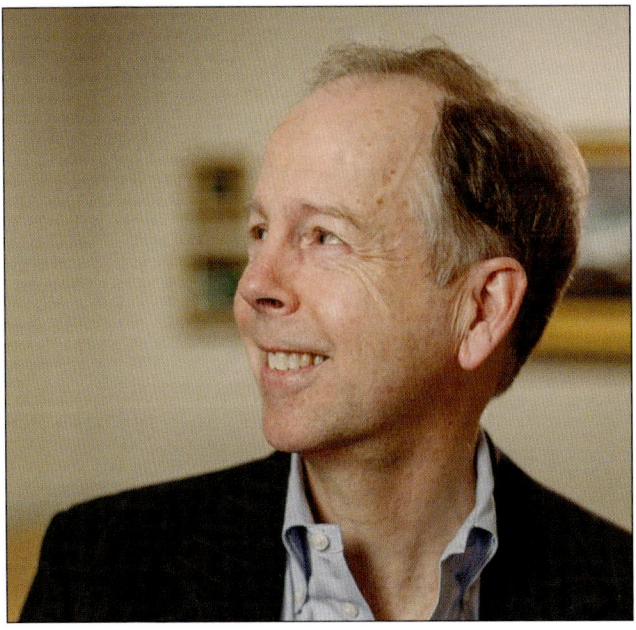

Photo by Erin Little.

Acknowledgements

Assembling the many images for this book would not have been possible without the help of generous sponsors, museums, galleries, libraries, private collectors, photographers, and, most of all, painters.

We thank the following individuals for their financial support, which helped cover the costs of permissions, licensing, digital files, tech help, and photo editing. Their backing allowed us to reproduce some of the key historical images in the book.

> Bruce Brown, Alison Hildreth, Melville and Alyssa Hodder, Kelly Lehr, James Mason, Douglas Payson, Marilyn Moss Rockefeller, and Ian McKibben White.

Once again, Svet Kirtchev lent a tech hand and William Bentley worked his magic with picture editing. We also thank the staff at the Burbank Library in Portland for processing many loan requests.

The following individuals and institutions helped with various parts of the book:

Leslie Anderson
Faith Andrews Bedford
Sharon Bocelli
Lydia Brown
Diana Edkins, Art Resources
Sarah Faragher
Joel Freedman
Anina Porter Fuller
Abe Goodale
Julia Gray, Wilson Museum
Ipcar/Zorach family
Kevin Johnson, Cipperly Goode, Penobscot Marine Museum
Heather Kahn
Zip Kellogg, University of Southern Maine
Norma and Lisa Marin
Kris Aro McLeod and Kit Aro
David McCaskill
David Neikirk, Robert Spencer, Osher Map Library
Micah Pawling, University of Maine
Bruce Bourque, Laureen LaBar, Maine State Museum
Peter Ralston
Curtis Rindlaub and Jan Taft, *Cruising Guide to the Maine Coast*
Deidre Scherer
Gail Scott
Dan Trujillo, Artists Rights Society
Katherine Wangh

Special thanks to Elizabeth Noyce (1930–1996). Part of her philanthropic legacy lies in the remarkable paintings she gave to Maine museums, including several in this book.

Thanks to rights and reproductions staff at the following museums, collections, auction houses, and internet sources:

Amon Carter Museum of American Art
Art Institute of Chicago
Bates College Museum of Art
Blue Hill Library
Chrysler Museum of Art
Colby College Museum of Art
Crystal Bridges Museum of American Art
Detroit Institute of Arts
Eskenazi Museum of Art
Farnsworth Museum of Art
The Hyde Collection
Frances Lehman Loeb Art Center, Vassar College
Morphy Auctions
National Archives of Canada
National Museum of Women in the Arts
Stephen and Palmina Pace Foundation
Peabody Museum of Ethnology and Archeology at Harvard
Penobscot Marine Museum
Philadelphia Museum of Art
Rhode Island School of Design
Lauren Rogers Museum of Art
Smithsonian American Art Museum
Sotheby's Toronto
Timken Museum of Art
United Missouri Bank
Wikimedia Commons

Today

A special thank-you to the following galleries for their help in tracking down images—and artists:

Cynthia Hyde and Melanie Essex, Caldbeck Gallery
Jake Dowling, Anna Queen, and Virginia Walck, Dowling Walsh Gallery
Kelly Lehr, Greenhut Galleries
Colin Page and Kirsten Surbey, Page Gallery
Sabeena Khosla, DC Moore Gallery
Karin and Michael Wilkes, Courthouse Gallery Fine Art
David Hopkins, Hopkins Wharf Gallery
Carey Vose, Vose Galleries
Tom O'Donovan, Harbor Square Gallery
Susan Robertson-Starr, Bayview Gallery
Bridget Moore, DC Moore
Meg Hurdman and Steve Wyman, Thos. Moser
Meg White, Gallery Naga
Elaine Crossman, New Era Gallery
Elena Kubler, Turtle Gallery

The encouragement and enthusiasm of Genevieve Morgan, Dean Lunt, Piper Wilber, Shannon Butler, and Emily Lunt at Islandport Press have been critical to the project.

Finally, great gratitude to all the artists who submitted work. We wish we could have accommodated all the painters of Penobscot Bay.

Selected Bibliography

Faith Andrews Bedford, *Frank W. Benson, American Impressionist*, Rizzoli, 1994.

Pamela Belanger, *Maine in America: American Art at the Farnsworth Art Museum*, Farnsworth Art Museum, Rockland, ME, 2000.

Jane Bianco, Michael Komanecky, Angela Waldron, *Maine and American Art*, Farnsworth Art Museum, Rizzoli Electa, 2020.

Bruce J. Bourque and Laureen A. LaBar, *Uncommon Threads, Wabanaki Textiles, Clothing, and Costume*, Maine State Museum, Maine & University of Washington Press, Seattle and London, 2009.

Philip W. Conkling, *Islands in Time: A Natural and Human History of the Islands of Maine*, Down East Books, Camden, ME, 1981.

Samuel Adams Drake, *Nooks and Corners of the New England Coast,* Harper & Brothers, New York, 1875.

William A. Haviland, *Canoe Indians of Down East Maine*, The History Press, 2012.

Christopher Huntington, *Maine: 100 Artists of the 20th Century*, Friends of Art at Colby College, 1964.

Nina Fletcher Little, editor, *Maine and Its Role in American Art, 1740–1963,* Viking Press, Inc., New York, 1963.

Charles B. McLane, *Islands of the Mid-Maine Coast: Blue Hill and Penobscot Bays*, The Kennebec River Press, 1982.

Gorham Munson, *Penobscot: Down East Paradise*, J. B. Lippincott Company, Philadelphia and New York, 1959.

David Platt, editor, *Penobscot: The Forest, River and Bay*. Island Institute, 1996.

Eliot Porter, *Summer Island*, Sierra Club and Ballantine Books, 1968.

Harald E.L. Prins and Bunny McBride, *Asticou's Island Domain: Wabanaki Peoples at Mount Desert Island 1500–2000*, Volume I, Abbe Museum and Northeast Region Ethnography Program, National Park Service, Boston, MA, 2007.

Louise Dickinson Rich, *The Coast of Maine: An Informal History and Guide,* Thomas Y. Crowell Company, New York, 1970.

Henry W. Taft and Jan B. Taft, *A Cruising Guide to the Maine Coast,* International Marine Publishing, Camden, ME, 1991.

George S. Wasson, *Sailing Days on the Penobscot,* British edition reprint, Macdonald and Jane's, London, 1974.

The Champions of Penobscot Bay

Penobscot Bay boasts a wide range of protectors and preservers. We salute the efforts of the many organizations dedicated to the welfare of the bay and beyond, including the following:

Coastal Mountains Land Trust
Colby College Environmental Studies Department
Friends of Harriet L. Hartley Conservation Area
Friends of Penobscot Bay
Friends of Sears Island
Island Heritage Trust
Island Institute
Islesboro Islands Trust
Maine Center for Coastal Fisheries
Maine Coast Heritage Trust
Maine Department of Inland Fisheries and Wildlife's National Estuary Program
Maine Sea Grant College Program, University of Maine
National Audubon Society
North Haven Conservation Partners
Penobscot Bay Watch
Upstream Watch

We also recognize the Penobscot River Restoration Trust. Each of these partner organizations plays a key role in protecting the vast watershed that flows into the bay:

Penobscot Indian Nation
American Rivers
Atlantic Salmon Federation
Maine Audubon
Natural Resources Council of Maine
The Nature Conservancy
Trout Unlimited